198

120

stati rapidissimo cursu uener duxit illos. ad litus eiusdem īsule usg dūm nauis reseditur. nō longe a ora. erat
namqz ripa illa Arnense alatudinis ita ut sicmua
tem illa iux potuissent uidere z erat color illius sicut
carbonū z mare bectiudis sicut nutu. Arnus quīdo
qui remansit ex tribz frilb q surerūt st scm. b. de
suo monasterio exiluit foras de naui z cepte dam
bulare usg ad fundamentū ripe z cepit clamare
dicens. Ve in pter predce a uob z nō hco pretece ut
possim uenire ad uos. frres cōsesti naui ad ora
reducebant z clamabat ad dūm duces. miserere
nobi dūe miserere nobis. Se nō uerialrlus pter cū
plus stcays assrnaebat. quoni ducebat ille tbetu
a mltaudine demonū ad tornita. z quoni incende
bat ino illos. Atqz dicebat. Ve tibi fili qa z una cū
a meruisti tale fine. Item errqit illos prosper ue
tus ad australē plagam. Cu asperustent aloge
retro illa insulā uiderūt montē discopuit a fumo
z a se stumantem flamas usg ad echera. z cū ad
se casse flamas respirate. ita totus mōs usg
quasi un rogus apperuisset. Ecat scd. b. cu nauitas
set contra meridiem ut septem dies appauit illis
z mare qeda formula. quasi hōis sedentis sup
petra z uelū an illa a longe qi mesura unus
sagi pendes mt duas forcellas fereas z sic a
strabat flurculbz sicut nauita solet. qi audirtce
a turbine. alii ex frilbz dicebar qd aims est. Alii

To Jim,
I love you, forever
'N' ever?
Pam

The Brendan Voyage

The Brendan Voyage

TIM SEVERIN

Drawings by Trondur Patursson

McGRAW-HILL BOOK COMPANY

NEW YORK • ST. LOUIS • SAN FRANCISCO

DUSSELDORF • MEXICO

Book design by Stanley Drate.

1234567890DODO78321098

Library of Congress Cataloging in Publication Data

Severin, Timothy.
The Brendan voyage.
1. Brendan (Coracle).   2. Voyages and travels—1951-   I. Title.
G470.S48   910′.41   78-867
ISBN 0-07-056335-7

Contents

The author wishes to thank the National Geographic
Society for material aid and assistance, and for help in
making the photographs that appear in this book.

PHOTO CREDITS

NAME	PLATE NUMBERS
Nathan Benn	20, 46, 48
Cotton Coulson	13, 17, 19, 26, 27, 28, 31, 32, 33, 34, 36, 37, 43, 44, 45, 47
Arthur Magan	15, 18, 22, 23, 24, 29, 30, 35, 38, 39, 40, 41, 42
Peter Mullett	14
Tim Severin	21
Ian Yeomans	1, 2, 3, 4, 5, 6, 7, 8, 9, 10, 11, 12, 16, 25

Maps by Eugene Fleury.
Schematic diagram of *Brendan* by Peter Cook.

Foreword

When *Brendan* set sail from Ireland, the enthusiasm and kindness of many people had already turned an idea into reality. By the time *Brendan* reached the New World, that circle of friends and supporters had grown even larger. So one of the most gratifying results of *Brendan*'s Atlantic achievement is that her success can be offered as a partial repayment to those people who did so much for her and the project as a whole. Several of the leading personalities will be met in the text of this book and the appendices. Others deserve special mention: In particular there were my literary agents Julian Bach, Anthony Sheil, and Gill Coleridge, who appreciated at the very start the importance and potential of the project and labored on its behalf. They in turn introduced me to the two leading editors, Bruce Lee in New York and Harold Harris in London, whose steady encouragement was the motive power to keep the project moving in the right direction through troughs as well as peaks. In Iceland Hjalmar Bardarson was always working behind the scenes and always seemed to be able to smooth our path; while the very efficient Arnor Valgeirsson made sure that *Brendan* received her supplies. Johann Sigurdsson and Icelandic Airlines held open one avenue of transport, while the Icelandic Steamship Company was equally generous with another. Finally in Iceland the British Ambassador there, Sir Kenneth East, was a most generous and thoughtful host.

Anyone looking at the photographs in this book will readily appreciate how very hard the photographers must have worked, and under what adverse conditions. Individual photographic credits are listed separately, and the photographs themselves display the talents of their makers better than my words. But here I would like to say how enjoyable were the visits of Ian Yeomans and Cotton Coulson, who joined us on shore and aboard while they were taking pictures for the *National Geographic* Magazine, whose unstinting collaboration made the photo coverage possible. On photographic coverage of a different sort, but equally important if the experience of the Brendan Voyage was to be widely shared, I should like to express special thanks to Dick Odey of Barrow Hepburn. But for him, and his associates in Barrow Hepburn Films, there would have been no motion picture record of the project. He took up the challenge and turned an imminent disappointment into an exciting success.

It is also interesting that before *Brendan* had covered a single yard of her Atlantic crossing, the project itself was half over. Her departure from Brandon Creek was the halfway point in the time span of the venture. Thus many of the firms whose names follow had helped *Brendan* long before she came to any public notice, and even longer before there was any chance to recognize their involvement. Often the help was the result of personal decisions made by individuals within the firms concerned, and although these individuals have not been listed person by person they themselves will know who they are. To all of them I should like to say—thank you:

B & I Line and Blue Peter Shipping (St. Johns) for transport; Brookes & Gatehouse, Lucas Marine, Flint & Brown, Incastec, Royada, John Gannon, Wiggins Teape, Earnshaw Ltd., Rolex, Ronson, Taylors Para-Fin, Morelands and Mallory Batteries for chandlery and equipment; Dr. David Ryder and Bandon Medical Hall for medical advice and equipment; Irish Distillers, Jordan Mills, Glynn Christian, Guinness, Rieber & Son, and Tiedemanns Tobaksfabrik for stores; Henri-Lloyd, Helly Hanson and Underwater Instrumentation for clothing; Bord Failte, Lloyds Intelligence Unit, Meteorological Office at Bracknell, U.S. Parks Service at Charleston Navy Yard, M. J. Higgins, Gomshall Tanneries, Emerald Star Lines, and Tanners Council of America for a great variety of vital services.

A glance at this roster of the Friends of *Brendan* shows just how complex and diverse a project like the Brendan Voyage can become. While in one sense it may be exhilarating to tackle new and bizarre problems day after day (where, for example, does one find a horse-collar-maker's palm on twenty-four hours' notice?), the office work can be a nightmare. Throughout, there was just one desk for the whole unlikely system; and there, keeping track of the enterprise, was the poised figure of Brigid Aglen who, working only part time, was utterly indispensable. To her and all the others I hope that this account of the Brendan Voyage is a worthwhile record.

Tim Severin

1
Storm

The seventh wave is said to be the worst, the one that does the damage in the turmoil of an ocean gale. Modern oceanographers know this is just a superstition of the sea; they have complex wave-train theories and the laws of wave mechanics to prove it. But still the notion of the seventh wave lingers on; and, clinging to the helm of a small open boat in the heaving waters of a bad Atlantic storm, one's temptation to count the waves is irresistible. The mind longs for anything which might impose a pattern on the jumble of destruction unfolding each time the boat rises to the crest of a roller. A frightening grey vista stretches endlessly to the horizon, rank upon rank of massive breaking waves, each one capable of swamping, destroying, or capsizing. So always, at that brief moment before the boat drops into the next trough, the eye seeks to pick out the seventh waves, real or imaginary, the monsters lifting their heads in menace above their companions, altering the whole line—even the level of the horizon itself—before they too then sink down to hide in ambush.

On that wind-torn evening in late May 1976, it seemed to my tired mind that the wave pattern was changing. Instead of the seventh waves, the sea appeared to be collecting its strength in random groups of three. The leading wave of each group would come rolling down on us, steeper and steeper by the moment, until it could no longer support its own mass. Its crest toppled forward, and then came sliding down the wave front in a self-generated avalanche of foam and released energy. When it struck, the boat shuddered and faltered. The helm twisted savagely in my hand, then went slack, and we were picked up bodily and rushed forward in the grip of the white water. In that dangerous instant the gale clawed at us, striving to slew the boat sideways so that she would be parallel to the advancing wave crests. Should that happen, we were lost. Then the second or the third great wave would sweep over the vulnerable length of the hull, and each time I feared it would be the last wave my crew and I would ever face.

No one could tell us how to steer our boat through the gale. No boat quite like her had been afloat for the past thousand years or so. To a casual observer our craft looked like a floating banana: long and slim, with her tapering bow and stern curved gently upward in an odd fashion. Yet her most extraordinary feature was only apparent if one examined her closely: the boat was made of leather. Her hull was nothing more than forty-nine oxhides stitched together to form a patchwork quilt and stretched over a wooden frame. It was this thin skin, only a quarter of an inch thick, flexing and shifting as the boat moved—just like the skin over a man's ribcage—that now stood between us and the fury of the Atlantic. Watching the waves, I recalled the bleak warning of one of the world's leading authorities on leather science before we started our voyage:

"Oxhide," he had explained in his precise, university tone, "is very high in protein. It resembles a piece of steak, if you like. It will decompose in the same way, either quickly or slowly, depending on various factors such as the temperature, how well it has been tanned to turn it into leather, and the amount of stress imposed upon it."

"What happens when the leather is soaking wet in sea water?" I had asked.

"Ah, well. That I'm not sure," he replied. "We've never been asked to test it. But leather will usually break down more quickly if it is wet, though perhaps the salt in sea water may have a pickling effect. I really don't know. . . ."

"And what happens in the end?"

"Just the same as if you left a piece of steak out in the air on a saucer. In time it will turn into a nasty, evil-smelling blob of jelly. Just like a rotting piece of oxhide."

The hull's turning to jelly was now the least of my problems. The gale was showing signs of getting worse; the waves were increasing in size. They were smashing into us more violently; and if the leather hull was not strong enough, the first result would be when the thread holding the oxhides together simply ripped through the weakened hides like tearing the perforations on a cardboard packet. Then the oxhides would peel away like petals, and the wooden frame underneath would spring open like a flower in a brief moment of disintegration. Privately, I doubted it would ever come to that. Much more likely was the possibility of a capsize. Our boat had no keel beneath her to hold her steady. If one of the tumbling wave crests caught her wrong-footed, she would be sent spinning upside down, and her crew tipped into the water, where there was no hope of rescue.

Why on earth, then, were my crew and I sailing such an improbable vessel in the face of a rising gale? The answer lay in the name of our strange craft: she was called *Brendan* in honor of the great Irish missionary, Saint Brendan, who had lived in the sixth century. Tradition said that Saint Brendan had made a voyage to America, and this astonishing claim was not just a wild fairy tale, but a recurrent theme based on authentic and well-researched Latin texts dating back at least to A.D. 800. These texts told how Saint Brendan and a party of monks had sailed to a land far across the ocean in a boat made of oxhides. Of course, if the claim was true, then Saint Brendan would have reached America almost a thousand years before Columbus and four hundred years before the Vikings. Such a notion, declared the skeptics, was harebrained. To suggest that anyone could have crossed the Atlantic in a boat made of animal skin was unthinkable, impossible, a mere fantasy, and the idea of a leather boat proved it. But the Latin texts were absolutely positive about the boat being made of leather, and they even explained how Saint Brendan and his party of monks had built this vessel. The obvious way of checking the truth of this remarkable story was to build a boat in similar fashion and then see if it would sail the Atlantic. So there we were, my crew and I, out in the ocean to test whether Saint Brendan and the Irish monks could have made an ocean voyage in a boat of leather.

The gale could not have caught us at a worse time. Our adventure had only just begun. *Brendan* was still untested; and only thirty miles to starboard lay Saint Brendan's own country— the jagged Atlantic coast of Ireland. Thirty miles was much too close for comfort. To a navigator this was a coast to be treated with the utmost respect. The southwest winds beat upon it all year round. Sailing ship upon sailing ship had been lost upon it, their hulls so fouled with weeds after an Atlantic crossing that, like *Brendan,* they could not tack out to sea against the wind and were driven helplessly ashore. This same coast had destroyed at least twenty galleons in the Spanish Armada, and, compared to a Spanish galleon, our *Brendan* was a seafaring nightmare. We could not sail upwind, and if the gale swung into the west, we would be driven as helplessly as a leaf down onto the iron-bound cliffs and half-submerged reefs which now broke the steady onslaught of the great Atlantic rollers hissing past us after their immense journey from the far side of the Atlantic. In such a gale and seaway even a modern yacht would have been hard pressed to hold up against the weather. For us in a medieval boat there was no choice but to turn tail and run helter-skelter before the gale, driven along by a single square sail slung as low as we dared, while *Brendan* tobogganed down the waves.

I looked at my crew and wondered if they appreciated the situation. George, I knew, was well aware of the danger. He was one of the best sailors I knew, and we had sailed many miles together on small boats. For that reason he now held the job of sailing master on *Brendan,* the man responsible for getting the very best performance from the boat under sail. Rolf, too, knew the risks. He was from Norway and normally spent his summers exploring his country's coastline in a massive sailing boat built at the end of the last century. But Peter, the cameraman of our team, worried me. Not so long ago, Peter had sailed single-handed from England to Greece in his own boat, and so he was no stranger to the sea. But now he was looking very glum. Partly, I suspected, he was concerned about our situation; but even more he was feeling the pain from damaged muscles that he had strained two days previously as we were rowing *Brendan.* Now his face had a grey look, and clearly he was very uncomfortable as he tossed about with the constant motion of the boat.

Arthur, the youngest member of the crew, was totally oblivious to any danger, for the very good reason that he was laid low by seasickness. Rarely had I seen anyone so miserable. *Brendan* had a most peculiar sea motion, more like a life raft than a conventional vessel. She heaved and swayed, then bobbed, swayed, and heaved while Arthur curled up in misery. His eyes screwed tight shut, his body slumped under the gunwale, every now and again a burst of spray swept over him, running down his face and dripping off his oilskins. Only when his turn came to go on watch did Arthur take an interest in his surroundings. With a visible effort of self-discipline he hauled himself into a sitting position, clipped on his lifeline, and dragged himself to the helm. Secretly I applauded the effort of will power, but it was obvious that only three men from a total crew of five were in a fit state to handle *Brendan* if the gale picked up.

One difficulty was that it was almost impossible to get any rest between watches. *Brendan* was essentially an open boat, swept by the spray and the wind. Just behind the stubby mainmast was a low tentlike structure with room for three men to lie down, head to tail like sardines. But here we also had to find space for our spare clothes, our cameras, and sleeping bags, and all the navigation equipment. Besides, whenever a wave broke over the stern, it had the nasty habit of sweeping forward and dropping a thick dollop of water right into the shelter. Farther forward by the short foremast there was another small tent, not much larger than a good-sized kennel. Here the two other crew members were expected to sleep, but there the leaks were even worse. Each time a wave broke against *Brendan*'s bow, it sent a fountain of cold water squirting up under the tent flap and thoroughly doused the occupants.

When my turn at the helm was over, I crawled into my berth in the main shelter, wedged myself into position, and lay there worrying: Our voyage had started barely a week ago and already we were taking a hammering, which I was not sure the boat could stand. Where I lay in my sleeping bag with my feet and head touching the bulkheads under the thwarts, I could feel them shifting as the boat rose and fell with the waves. What disturbed me was that the bulkheads were shifting *in opposite directions.* It was uncanny. The boat was like an animal, perhaps a whale, and I was lying inside its ribs like Jonah and feeling the boat change her shape to meet the enormous pressures of the sea. All around I could hear creaks and groans from the wood and the leather. The stresses and strains were colossal. The sides of the boat pumped gently in and out as though the *Brendan* were breathing. I tried to think rationally, remembering the theory that the boats of the Vikings had been built on exactly the same principle. It was said that they had flexed with the sea and so had sailed faster. But the

Vikings built their boats of timber, and no one knew if leather could stand up to the same sort of treatment. How long could *Brendan*'s structure hold together? There was no way of telling. And it was little comfort to remember that this was precisely why we were out in *Brendan,* hoping to discover the truth by practical experiment.

I closed my eyes, and immediately my sense of balance told me that the sea had become worse. I could feel *Brendan* being overtaken by a wave group of three. The first wave swelled up, and it seemed ages as *Brendan* climbed its face, lifting up and up in apparent slow motion as if she would never clear the top. Then came the agonizing pause as she teetered on the brink, half the length of her hull poking out over the face of the wave, suspended in the air as if she would snap in half. Finally there came the slithering surf ride, caught helplessly in the tumbling crest, with the helmsman fighting to maintain control and *Brendan* heading down-wind, and the log went spinning madly up to its maximum reading of twelve knots. After what seemed an age, the main body of the wave swept on, released *Brendan,* and casually dropped her into the trough behind it, only to be picked up and hurled like a tormented plaything through the whole process again and again by the second and third outsize waves.

Once, when George was at the helm, a wave crest caught *Brendan* and without warning spun her back to front. "Help! Help! We are sailing backwards!" George roared. Peter and I bolted out of the cabin. Lightly dressed, we were quickly soaked to the skin, but we had to bring the headsail under control. We swarmed forward to where the sail was pinned against the mast by the force of the gale, and with brute strength wrestled it around again. With a soggy thud the sail bellied out, and began to pull *Brendan* out of trouble. Slowly, very slowly, the boat wheeled away downwind, and for two aching wave-lengths we watched and waited as the vulnerable side of our leather craft was exposed to the rollers. But they swept under us without doing any harm, and we went careening onward.

Night came. A foul, black night complete with driving rain that reduced visibility to a few yards, broken only by the flashing white manes of the breakers and distant flares of lightning. As I returned to my sleeping place, my tired mind failed to register when Peter, who had taken over the helm, remarked that he thought he glimpsed ship's lights, no more than tiny pinpricks a long way off to port. I mumbled to him to keep an eye on them and to call me if they came any closer. Then I crawled into my sleeping bag and closed my eyes, feeling utterly limp.

"Jesus Christ! Where the hell did that come from!" Peter's gasp woke me instantly. Something was wrong. In a mad scramble I tumbled out of the shelter, and found Peter heaving desperately on the tiller. Rolf, the rain trickling down his glasses, was gaping into the night. There, less than a hundred yards away, and with all her lights blazing, was a large factory trawler bearing straight down on us. Her bows were sending up huge bursts of spray as she slammed down on the waves, and she was pitching and rolling wickedly. It was impossible that she could have seen us in the murk. Later I was to find out that *Brendan*'s leather hull was nearly invisible to radar scanners, while our metal radar reflector was blotted out by heavy seas. In effect, *Brendan* was invisible to the other vessel.

"Light a white flare!" I yelled at Peter. "Light a flare!"

"What about shining a torch on the sails?" asked Rolf.

"No good," I bellowed above the shriek of the wind. "Our sail isn't big enough to work as a light reflector. Besides, it's made of leather and won't reflect the light efficiently."

But it was already too late. Someone found a white flare from the emergency kit, but fingers were too cold and stiff to unwrap the tape and strike it before the ship was heaving down on us. Peter struggled with the helm, trying to turn *Brendan* away, but the wind had locked us on what seemed to be a collision course. Then the factory trawler's streaming black hull slid past us so close that we could make out the welding on the steel hull plates that towered over us. The lights from her portholes, though they penetrated only a few yards in that blackness, swept over us as we stood aghast looking up at the high side rolling over us. Then we were level with the trawler's stern, and so close that as she swung her stern toward us it felt as if the *Brendan* would be sucked up the great stern ramp where they hauled their fishing nets. *Brendan* was dwarfed.

"Hang on! We'll be in the propeller wash in a moment." The water boiled white around us from the trawler's screws, and then she was gone, swallowed up in the raging gale, and totally unaware that she had nearly run us down. How ironic, I thought to myself, that our greatest danger should be from Man, not from Nature, a risk that Saint Brendan never had to face. I doubted that anyone aboard the trawler had even seen us. If they had, what would the lookout say to the trawler's skipper? That he had seen a boat from another century running wildly before the gale with a square sail bearing the Celtic cross in crimson and steered by five desperate-looking men in sodden clothing? Any watch-keeper who reported that sight to his captain on a night in the Atlantic was liable to be dismissed for drunkenness or sent to a psychiatrist.

By dawn the wind rose to its worst, just short of storm force, tearing the tops off the waves. Rain and spray driven almost horizontally kept us pumping the *Brendan* every watch, five hundred strokes of the bilge pump to keep her from getting sluggish. The ropes holding the sail were in shreds. They were made of flax, as they could have been in Saint Brendan's day, and there was something wrong with them. Every time two ropes touched, they cut into one another, frayed in a few seconds, and snapped. Again and again someone—usually Rolf—had to go forward, clinging precariously to the heaving bows, and rerig new ropes to keep the sail and the boat under control. My chart case was ripped open by the wind, and a few seconds later a breaking wave reduced the chart to mush. The only consolation was that the gale had long since blown us off the limits of the chart, and it was of little use to us anyway. *Brendan* was rushing madly farther and farther out to sea. To slow her down we streamed a heavy rope in a loop from the stern and let it trail in the water behind us to act as a brake, and, hopefully, to smooth the worst of the wave crests. From the stern also dangled a metal bucket; only twenty-four hours earlier we had been using it to cook an excellent meal of Irish crabs. Now it clanked mournfully every time a wave broke against it. Arthur, poor fellow, looked like a dead sheep clad in garish foul-weather trousers. His hood had blown off, and his hair was plastered down on his scalp. The inside of the main shelter was a shambles of camera lenses, pilot books, sodden clothing, and wet paraphernalia. There Peter had finally taken refuge. He had strained his arm even more during the near mishap with the trawler, and he was obviously shaken. Only George and Rolf still looked in control. George had been through heavier gales than this; and Rolf had taken off his glasses so that he could no longer see the worst of the waves.

Then, as so often happens, the new day brought an improvement in the weather. The gale began to ease, and by degrees our spirits rose. Our matches had been ruined by the sea water, but after rummaging around in the emergency kit a box of waterproof matches was discovered, and the Primus stove was lit. Hot coffee followed an anonymous stew of macaroni and vegetables, and *Brendan*'s crew began to take a more intelligent interest in their surroundings. George made the happy discovery that it was much easier to steer the boat if the helmsman stood back to front, facing out over the stern and watching the waves. It was an odd sight, but then we were beginning to appreciate that most things aboard the *Brendan* were going to be highly unorthodox. The only audience to appreciate our small triumph was the seabirds, who promptly reappeared after the worst of the gale. Mostly they were common and herring gulls with an occasional puffin who scurried busily past, his stubby wings jerking frantically up and down and his clown's face with the great colored beak making him look for all the world like a child's wind-up toy. A number of yellow-headed gannets, the largest seabirds of this part of the world, patrolled majestically for food, cruising steadily on their six-foot wingspan before plummeting down on their prey, or swooped lower to indulge in slick aerobatics in the up-currents that lifted briefly from the face of the big waves left by the gale. Their nonchalance made the rough water seem less threatening, as did the seagulls who, landing on the water, bobbed among the waves with an air of unconcern.

So too, it occurred to me, *Brendan* might defeat the sea. Perhaps this was one of the secrets Saint Brendan had known when he started out on his voyage to the land in the West. We still had more than 3000 miles of sailing through some of the trickiest waters in the world to find out, but I felt a quiet satisfaction that we had survived our first gale of the voyage and could at least claim to be a few more steps toward our goal.

Shearwater

2
The Idea

"There's something odd about the Saint Brendan text," remarked
my wife Dorothy one evening. Her casual comment immediately
caught my attention.

"What do you mean by 'odd'?" I asked her.

"The text doesn't match up with much of the other literature
written at about the same time. The best way to explain it is that it
doesn't have the same feel. It's a curiosity. For instance, it is the
story of a voyage by a saint, so one would normally expect to find a
long list of miracles performed by him. But Saint Brendan doesn't
perform any miracles. His only special skill is that he possesses
extraordinary wisdom, almost clairvoyance. He knows exactly
what is happening and going to happen at any stage of the voyage,
when his crew are simply puzzled or frightened. And of course he
has complete faith that God will look after them in the end."

I pressed her further. "What else seems unusual about the
text?"

"Well, the story has a remarkable amount of practical detail, far
more than most early medieval texts. It tells you about the
geography of the places Brendan visits. It carefully describes the
progress of the voyage, the times and distances, and so forth. It
seems to me that the text is not so much a legend as a tale that is
embroidering a first-hand experience."

My wife's critical judgement was worth listening to. As a
specialist in medieval Spanish literature, she had a wide knowledge
of medieval texts. In fact, we had first met in the library at Harvard

University where we were both doing research: she for her doctoral thesis, and I into the history of exploration. In our own ways we had both known about the tale of Saint Brendan since undergraduate days. "Saint Brendan has certainly puzzled the historians of exploration," I commented. "No one seems to be able to make up his mind whether the saint's voyage was fantasy or fact. Some scholars have tried to show that he actually reached America; others dismiss the idea as highly conjectural."

"Well, I don't see why Saint Brendan couldn't have got there," said my wife firmly.

"No, neither do I. You and I know that it's possible to cover enormous distances in small vessels. We've done it ourselves. Perhaps it's time someone tried to find out whether Saint Brendan's voyage was feasible or not. But it would mean using the boats and materials of that time to make it a fair test."

So the idea of the *Brendan* Voyage was born. It happened during an after-dinner conversation across the kitchen table in the house in Courtmacsherry where we spend our holidays in the southwest of Ireland. As I look back on that conversation, it was uncanny how our separate views of Saint Brendan's text had overlapped. To my wife the text was "odd" as a work of literature; to me the whole Saint Brendan story was equally unusual in terms of the history of exploration. And, by a very important coincidence, both of us shared the experience of sailing our small sloop *Prester John,* usually with our three-year-old daughter Ida aboard, as far afield as Turkey. Thus we knew there was nothing theoretically impossible about Saint Brendan's voyage in a small boat from one side of the Atlantic to the other, and back again. In our personal backgrounds in literature, history, and sailing were three polarized lenses that had swung onto the same axis. Suddenly we found ourselves looking through at the possible solution. There we were, sitting in the west of Ireland, not so far from the area where Saint Brendan had been born and lived, preached, and been laid to rest. In that evocative atmosphere it seemed entirely logical to research and to build a replica of Saint Brendan's vessel, and see if his famous story could have been true.

Of course there would be an immense amount of work to do before the idea could be advanced. First, I had to satisfy myself that the scholarship behind the project was sound. I was determined at all costs not to let the Brendan Voyage, as I had already chosen to call it, become a mere survival test. I was under no illusion that it would require many months of painstaking preparations to prepare the voyage, followed by a fair amount of physical risk during the Atlantic passage itself. To warrant such risk and effort the endeavor had to produce worthwhile results. It had to strive toward a precise and serious purpose; at no time must that serious purpose be shaken.

The obvious place to begin was in the British Museum Library, and there I worked for several months, carefully dredging up all the data I could find about Saint Brendan, about early voyages across the Atlantic, and about the key text itself, the *Navigatio Sancti Brendani Abbatis, The Voyage of St. Brendan the Abbot.* The background of Saint Brendan gave me useful clues. He was one of Ireland's most important saints, classed as a saint of the second order. He was a man who had a profound influence on the Celtic Church. The date and place of his birth are both uncertain, but most probably he was born near the lakes of Killarney in County Kerry in the west of Ireland about A.D. 489. He was baptized and educated by Bishop Erc of Kerry, later studied under the famous teacher Saint Enda, and in due course rose to become an abbot. At that time the Irish church was organized almost exclusively into monasteries scattered around the country, and Brendan was responsible for the foundation of several of these monasteries: at Ardfert in County Kerry, Inishdadroum in County Clare, Annadown in County Galway, and Clonfert—also in County Galway. Indeed, it was at Clonfert that he was buried sometime between A.D. 570 and 583. But what struck me most about Saint Brendan's career was his proven reputation as a traveler. Again and again I found references to journeys made by him. He sailed on several voyages along the west coast of Ireland. He also voyaged to the Western Islands off Scotland to hold an important conference with Saint Columba, who founded the great monastery at Iona. Then, too, it was said that Saint Brendan had traveled to Wales, where he became the Abbot of Llancarvon and tutored Saint Malo, the Breton saint. Other less well-documented reports spoke of Brendan going to Brittany, to the Orkney and Shetland islands, and even as far afield as the Faroes. These were all boat journeys, and the real Saint Brendan had obviously been a man who spent a great deal of his time traveling around the northwestern perimeter of Europe in small vessels. In short, Saint Brendan was a sailor's saint, so it was hardly surprising that he had come to be known as Brendan the Navigator.

But it was the *Navigatio Sancti Brendani Abbatis,* more usually known as the *Navigatio* or *Voyage of Brendan,* that sealed his reputation. This was the text which my wife and I had both read as students and remembered as something remarkable. It had been written in Latin, and it described how Saint Brendan, living in the west of Ireland, had been visited by another Irish priest who described to him a beautiful land far in the West over the ocean where the word of God ruled supreme. The priest advised Brendan to see this place for himself, and so Brendan built a boat specially for the voyage, making a framework of wood on which he stretched oxhides for the hull. Then he loaded ample stores, spare oxhides and fat to dress the hides, and set sail with seventeen monks to find this Promised Land. They had a long, hard journey. They wandered from one island to another and had many adventures until they finally won through to their destination, and managed to explore the fringe of the Promised Land before setting sail once again for Ireland. Some of their adventures were obviously fabulous. For instance, they were said to have landed on the back of a whale, mistaking it for an island. The monks lit a fire to cook themselves a meal, and the heat of the fire woke the whale, so that the monks only just managed to scrambled back into their boat before the whale swam off with the fire still burning on his back like a beacon. Other episodes seemed equally unlikely: the *Navigatio* described how Brendan and his crew came upon a huge pillar of

An early Irish boat, carved in the 8th century on the stone pillar of a cross overlooking Bantry Bay in southwest Ireland.

crystal floating in the sea. Later they were chased by a sea monster breathing fire from his nostrils. At one island they were pelted with hot rocks; at another they discovered Irish monks living under the rule of silence in a monastery. So it went. The *Navigatio,* some scholars said, was a splendid collection of seafaring yarns, a farrago of wild fantasy, one tale more colorful than the last.

But several eminent authorities disagreed. They pointed out that, seen in another light, the episodes in Brendan's voyage bore a striking resemblance to geographical facts. The floating pillar of crystal could have been an iceberg which the travelers had met at sea. Perhaps the sea monster was a pugnacious whale or a walrus. The burning rocks hurled at them might have been molten slag thrown up by an eruption in Iceland or in the Azores, which are both seats of volcanic activity. As for the monks of the silent community, it has long been known that groups of Irish holy men formed religious colonies on outlying islands around Britain. But there was one great stumbling block: how could Saint Brendan and his monks have made such a huge journey, which lasted, the text said, for seven years, in a boat made of perishable ox skins? Everyone knew that leather disintegrates in sea water, and one would no more contemplate going to sea for several months in a leather boat than standing in the sea in a pair of good leather shoes. The results would be catastrophic.

I pulled out modern atlases and sea charts, and tried to match up these theories with the practical realities of the North Atlantic. The way Saint Brendan's itinerary fitted the various Atlantic islands was certainly startling. A single similarity like, say, the volcanos of Iceland as the basis for the story of the hot rock could have been explained as a coincidence. But it would have required a whole string of coincidences to explain the complete run of other similarities—from the Islands of Sheep, which Brendan visited early on in his journey and which sounded very like the Faroe Islands, right through to the thick white cloud he encountered just off the Promised Land and might have been the notorious fog zone off the Grand Banks of Newfoundland. As a practical sailor, I knew that it was awkward to sail by a direct route from Ireland to North America. This track is contrary to the prevailing southwesterly and westerly winds that blow across the Atlantic. It would have been easy enough to sail from the Promised Land straight home to Ireland with the wind behind the oxhide boat. But outward bound, Saint Brendan would have had a more difficult time. Unless he was very lucky with the wind, he would have been forced to go around the westerly wind belt, either to north or south. And on the way out he would experience great difficulty, battling his way from island to island and working his way west by stages.

Excitedly I consulted the navigation charts that marked the winds and currents of the North Atlantic. The logical route leaped off the page. Using the prevailing southwest winds, one could sail north from Ireland and up to the Hebrides. Then north again, slanting across the westerly winds to the Faroes. From there lay a tricky passage to Iceland, but after that the currents were all favorable, helping the boat across from Iceland to South Greenland, and then sweeping down to the coast of Labrador, Newfoundland, or beyond. On the map this route looked very roundabout, but that was an illusion of map projection. It was very nearly the shortest way between North Europe and North America and, above all, it was the Stepping Stone Route, the same route taken by early aviators in short-range aircraft, also by the Vikings, and earlier still . . . perhaps by the Irish.

It dawned on me that the Brendan Voyage was going to be a detective story. I had the clues before me in the text of the *Navigatio.* One by one they might lead toward a solution, providing I could find out how to follow them. But how? Again, the obvious answer was with a boat exactly like the one Saint Brendan had used. Such a boat would take me to inspect the places along the Stepping Stone Route that might conform to the places recorded in the *Navigatio.* At the same time it would also show whether such a boat could survive an Atlantic voyage. But what exactly did the *Navigatio* mean by a boat made of oxhides stretched on a wooden frame? Could such a vessel make an Atlantic crossing? The Stepping Stone Route is comparatively short, but it is notoriously stormy. Few modern yachts would attempt this northern passage, and to try it in an open boat seemed suicidal. It would take a strong sea boat to complete this route. A boat of leather certainly did not sound very promising.

So it was one March day that I found myself walking down a steep track leading to the spot from where Saint Brendan was said to have set out for the Promised Land. I was deeply affected by my

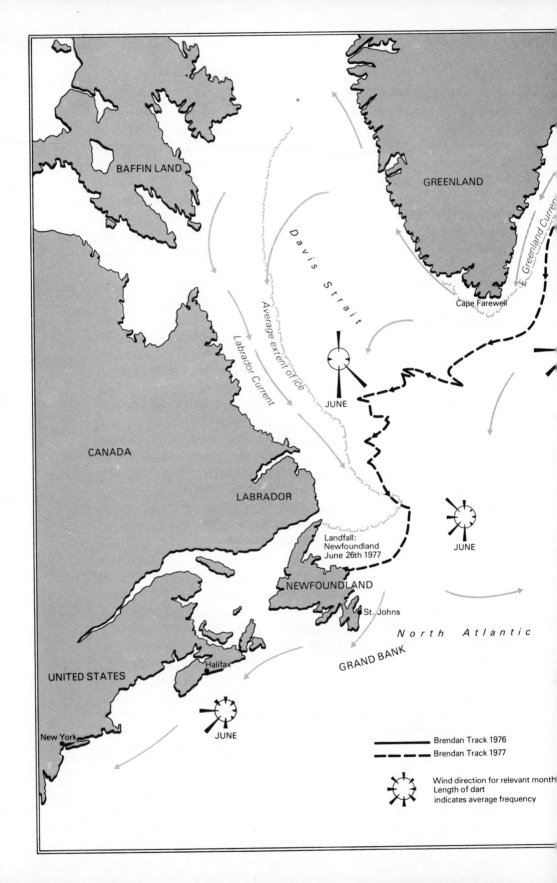

BAFFIN LAND

GREENLAND

Davis Strait

Average extent of ice

Labrador Current

E. Greenland Current

Cape Farewell

JUNE

CANADA

LABRADOR

Landfall:
Newfoundland
June 26th 1977

JUNE

NEWFOUNDLAND

St. Johns

North Atlantic

GRAND BANK

UNITED STATES

Halifax

New York

JUNE

Brendan Track 1976
Brendan Track 1977

Wind direction for relevant month
Length of dart
indicates average frequency

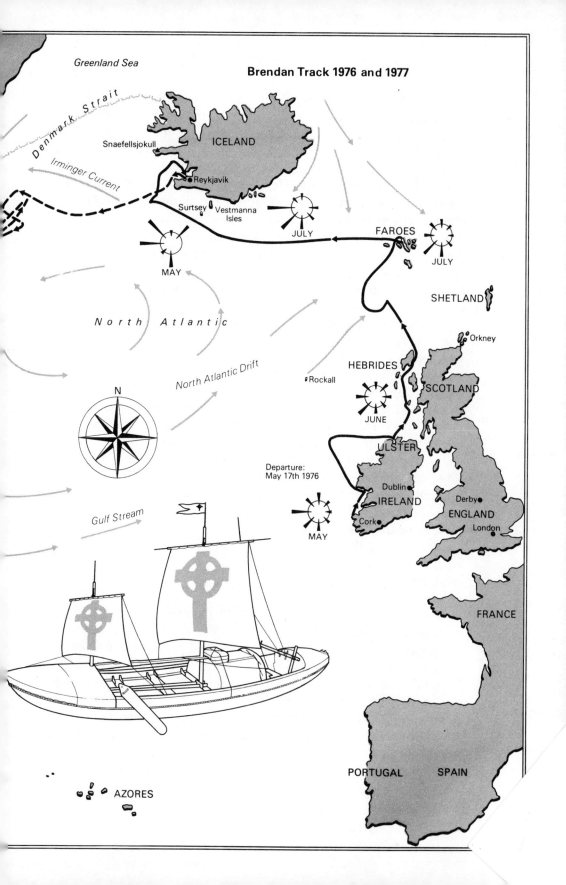

Brendan Track 1976 and 1977

surroundings. This was Saint Brendan's own country, the Dingle Peninsula of County Kerry and the farthest point of Ireland reaching out into the Atlantic, a place where the sweep of green hills and moorlands ends in the blue-grey ocean, and the air is so clear that one almost has a sense of vertigo as the land seems to tilt toward the distant horizon. Here Saint Brendan is still commemorated in almost every natural feature. His name is spelled by the older version of Brandon, and one has Brandon Head, Brandon Bay, Brandon Point, the little village Brandon, and Mount Brandon itself, to whose summit on Saint Brendan's Day a pilgrimage is made in honor of the Saint, and in past years strong young men carried on their shoulders the altar table to the peak as an act of worship.

Brandon Creek lies on the north side of the Dingle, a cleft in the line of massive cliffs that guards the coast. To reach it one crosses bog country, marked by clumps of brown peat stacked for drying and occasional tiny fields rimmed with walls of loose rock. It is a place of few inhabitants, though where the road finally runs out on the lip of the creek I found two houses, one on each side of the narrow road. The second house could have been cut from a picture postcard. Its rough stone walls were beautifully whitewashed. A water pump stood by the half-open door. There were flowers in tubs, and the neat thatched roof was held down against the ferocious blast of the winter gales by a lacework of cords, their ends weighted with smooth oval rocks gathered from the sea, every rock as neatly whited as a pearl in a necklace.

Just beyond the cottage was Brandon Creek itself, a sheer drop where the Atlantic heaved and swirled in the constriction of the cleft, even on a calm day booming among the sea caves near the mouth of the creek.

It was an unforgettable day, with brilliant sunshine alternating with stinging showers so typical of west Irish weather, and the aquamarine waters of Brandon Creek would not have looked out of place in a tropical island, so clear was the color. As I gazed away from the mouth of the creek to the northwest, my feeling of vertigo was even more pronounced. Out there, I thought, lay North America. Tradition dies hard, and if this is where tradition says Saint Brendan started on his voyage, this is where my boat will start too.

I began walking down the track leading past the thatched

cottage, curving down to the base of the creek where a stream emptied out the water it had collected from the slopes of Mount Brandon above us. At that instant, with a thrill of excitement, I saw them. Drawn up on the side of the road were four strange black shapes. They were boats, turned upside down so that their hulls were pointing to the sky. They were the traditional canvas-covered boats of the west of Ireland called curraghs, a type found nowhere else in the world. They are relics of the Stone Age, and believed to be among the last surviving descendants of one of the oldest types of boat in the world—the skin boat. Here, in Brandon Creek, I first laid eyes on the heirs to the craft Saint Brendan was said to have sailed.

Crouching down, I peered underneath a curragh to see how it was made. Inside was an elegantly beautiful cagework of thin laths, frail-looking but in fact capable of withstanding great compression. Stretched over this frame was a tight skin of canvas, tarred on both sides to make it waterproof. Later I learned that this canvas, which has replaced the original leather skins, is still called the "hide" in some localities. Tucked under the curraghs were sets of oars of a pattern I had never seen before. About nine feet long, they were so slender that they had no blade whatever, and they were fitted with curious triangular blocks of wood, pierced with a hole that matched a pivot pin when rowing. I judged the curraghs too small for anything more than inshore skiffs, yet to my eye they were perfect. They seemed so delicately engineered and so gracefully curved. After I had climbed out of Brandon Creek, I turned back to look down on the four curraghs once again. A rain shower had slicked their hulls so that the four black shapes glistened and glinted in the sun. They looked as sleek as porpoises rolling through the sea.

I yearned to go for a ride in a curragh, not just for my research but because I was captivated by them. A cheerful woman at the thatched cottage directed me on to the village of Dunquin, where, she said, I was likely to find a number of curragh men in the bar, as the weather was too rough to take the curraghs out fishing. I drove there, and asked the barman for advice. He pointed out a group of three elderly men sitting in a corner. "Any of them could take you," he said, "but the sea's no good today. Too rough."

I went over to the men. Not one of them could have been under fifty-five years old. They were uniformly dressed in baggy tweed jackets and battered trousers. They all had gaunt knobby hands, large and reddened raw faces, with strong noses and heavyset bones.

"I am interested in going for a spin in a curragh," I said. "I wonder if any of you could take me out in one."

I was met with blank looks.

"In a curragh, your canvas boats," I repeated.

"Oh, you mean in a canoe," said one man. He turned to the others and muttered something incomprehensible. He was speaking Irish, which is still the common language in the Dingle. "We have canoes all right. But the weather's not right for it. And you need to know what you're doing before you go out in a canoe. It would be dangerous for a stranger."

"Of course I will pay you for your trouble, and I'm prepared to take the risk," I coaxed.

"No," said the spokesman, "it's too dangerous today. We'd all be killed. Maybe tomorrow."

"What if I paid you three pounds each just for a quick spin?"

"Ah now! That would be different!"

So off we went to find their "canoes," a strange little procession that kept stopping and starting and changing its composition. One old man dropped out. Another was hallooed from a field to take his place. And the fourth—a younger man with a bright yellow flower stuck jauntily in his hatband—was recruited at the cliff edge just before we started down a steep path to the landing place where a dozen curraghs lay upside down on their stages or props beside the water's edge. The crew talked in Irish all the while, so I needed an interpreter. As luck would have it, on the road we passed a young man who was evidently a trainee schoolmaster, one of many sent to spend a few months in the Dingle to improve their knowledge of Irish before taking up their jobs.

"Would you care to come for a boat ride?" I called out to him. "You could help me with some translation as well."

"Why of course," came the cheerful reply, and ten minutes later the poor fellow was sitting nervously beside me on the rear thwart of a curragh as it bounced up and down in the spray.

"Have you ever been in a small boat before?" I asked him.

"No," he replied, looking startled and clutching the gunwale. "Will we be away long?"

The trip was fascinating. To carry the boat to the water's edge, the crew crawled beneath one of the upturned curraghs, crouched so their shoulders pressed up on the thwarts, and then straightened their backs so that the curragh shot smartly into the air like a strange black beetle heaving itself up onto four pairs of legs which then marched off to the edge of the slipway. With a swift movement the boat was lowered to the ground, tipped right side up, and when the next wave washed up, she was swirled afloat as casually as a toy. One by one we jumped in, taking care not to put a foot through the thin canvas. The oarsmen settled in their places; one good strong heave, and the curragh shot forward into the waves faster than any oared sea boat I have ever ridden in. In a moment we were out in the sound and curvetting like a horse over the waves. Balance was critical. If the boat stayed level, she flew over the waves and scarcely a drop of water came aboard. Through

Dingle curragh

my interpreter I bombarded the crew with questions. How many curraghs were still used in the Dingle? About a hundred. What were they used for? Lobster pots and setting salmon nets. Would they stand a really rough sea? If they were handled right, came the response. What happens in a capsize? The boat stays wrong side up, and you drown.

"Can you carry heavy loads all right?" I asked.

"Why, yes. In spring we take cattle out in the canoes to leave them to graze on the islands," came one answer, and someone else added a comment which made the other laugh.

"What did he say?" I asked my schoolteacher-interpreter.

"He said the cows are less trouble. They don't ask so many questions."

When we were ready to return to the slipway, I asked the curragh crew to perform a small but important experiment. I asked them to row the boat on a figure-eight course, because I wanted to learn how the curragh rode the seas at different angles. Up to that moment, I had noticed, the oarsmen had been keeping the boat heading directly into the waves or directly away from them. My request caused some anxiety. The crew muttered and shook their heads. But I insisted. Eventually they agreed, and off we went rather gingerly. Everything turned out splendidly. The curragh skimmed away through the troughs and crests, then turned handsomely as the waves curled under her. My crew beamed with pleasure, and so did I. Now I knew for certain that the curraghs of Brendan's homeland were not just inshore skiffs. They handled like true sea boats. The voyage was one step closer.

Back ashore I paid off my curragh men, who were evidently delighted with such apparently easy money, and asked them who could tell me more about their "canoes." They were unanimous in telling me that John Goodwin of Maharees was my man. No one else, they said, knew as much about canoes or built them so well. Yes, I had to see John Goodwin.

So it was that I met the curragh-builder of Maharees, whose advice was to underpin a major part of my boat-building. Seventy-eight-year-old John Goodwin was the last man in the Dingle Peninsula who made curraghs for his living. He was the only survivor of an industry that had once seen a curragh-builder in every coastal village. A number of the Dingle farmers still knew how to build themselves a curragh in a back shed during the winter months, but John Goodwin was a professional. More than that, he had spent his lifetime accumulating information about curraghs because he loved them. As a young man he had emigrated briefly to America, only to return to the Dingle to take up his father's trade and his grandfather's trade before him. He even used the tools he had inherited, a few hand drills and wood chisels, a knife and a hammer, and a small selection of wooden battens marked like yardsticks that were all John needed to measure out his work and produce the sophisticated and elegant curraghs for which he was famous.

Just as important for me, John loved talking about curraghs. For hour after hour he plied me with stories about curraghs and their crews, about building curraghs, about the days when every creek and cleft in the coast had its population of these small boats, hundreds upon hundreds of them, when the mackerel fishing was so rich that Dingle men living in America would come home just for a few weeks in the summer to reap the sea's harvest. Proudly John showed me a photograph of himself and his three brothers sitting bolt upright in a racing curragh in which they had been champions of Kerry. Walking past a row of upturned curraghs, he would stop and point out minute differences between each boat; indeed, he had built most of them with his own hands. Once I showed him a faded photograph taken in the 1930s of a curragh frame, and without a second's hesitation he identified the man who had made it. Another time I asked him about the days when curraghs were sailed as well as rowed. After a moment's thought he began rummaging around in the rafters of the tarred shack where he built his boats and pulled down an old sail. It was a museum piece, and he let me measure and copy it, while he spent another half hour telling me how to rig and sail a curragh to best advantage. It was advice that was to prove vital.

One story in particular stayed in my mind. On a wintry day earlier this century, John said, a steamer had been driven into a local bay by a terrible storm. The vessel was in real danger, but she managed to get down an anchor to hold her temporarily. Her master sent up distress rockets to call out the lifeboat from Fenit before the anchor broke. But the storm was so fierce that the Fenit lifeboat was unable to get out of the harbor, and had to turn back after suffering damage. Then two local curragh men decided to help. They carried their frail craft to the rocks, launched her into the raging sea, and with great daring rowed out to the steamer. One man leapt aboard and persuaded the steamer's master to hoist anchor. Then he piloted the vessel through the shoals and reefs to safety. "A canoe will go through any weather," John summed up. "Just so long as her crew know how to handle her, and there's a man aboard who still has the strength to keep on rowing."

I asked John if he would build a curragh for me, and show me how it was done. With him I spent a hot afternoon tarring and stretching the canvas hide into position, and in the end I had a small two-man curragh of my own, built to the traditional pattern right down to the place to step the obsolete mast. When I collected the boat from him, I asked John, "Do you think a big canoe could get all the way to America?" He looked at me with his old man's grin.

"Well, now. The boat will do, just as long as the crew's good enough."

I decided to call my little curragh *Finnbarr*, in honor of Saint Finnbarr, the patron saint of Munster, said to have been the priest who showed Saint Brendan the way to the Promised Land. I hoped the little curragh would do the same for me, and to my wife's chagrin, I stole the linings from the dining-room curtains to make a sail for *Finnbarr,* and spent all of Christmas Day stitching it by hand. Then I sailed up and down the little estuary outside our house to see how the boat behaved. It was bitterly uncomfortable, but the effort was worth it. By the end of the Christmas holidays I knew that although *Finnbarr* wobbled alarmingly and refused to sail upwind, she and her ancestors had been designed to carry a mast and sails.

It was about this time that I became aware of a curious phenomenon which I could only call Brendan Luck. This was the strange way in which I began to have stroke after stroke of good fortune in my preparations for the voyage. The entire Brendan project seemed lucky. My encounter with John Goodwin was one example of Brendan Luck; the unusual circumstances of the original idea was another; and a third was when I discovered that a definitive study of Irish curraghs had been written by the man who virtually started the study of traditional craft: James Hornell, the naval historian. At one stroke I was presented with a complete record of curragh history, tracing the boats back to Saint Brendan's day and beyond into the writings of Julius Caesar and other classical authors who had recorded the skin-covered vessels of the natives of Britain. Caesar's army engineers had even copied the boats, building skin-covered landing craft for amphibious river crossings. But perhaps the most bizarre stroke of good fortune occurred when I was trying to work out how Saint Brendan might have rigged his ocean curragh.

It seemed to me that such a long, slim boat must have carried two masts, but in all my research I had never seen a picture of an early medieval boat equipped with more than one. They all had a single mast, even the Viking ships. Then one day I was in the cellar stacks of the London library. I was not working on the Brendan project at all, but on quite another subject, and by chance I happened to walk through a section of the library that was little used. As I passed the stacks, a book caught my eye. It was misshelved, having been put in back to front. Casually I pulled it out to turn it the right way around, and my eye fell upon the title. It was in German, long and scholarly, and roughly translated as *A Record of Ship Illustrations from the Earliest Times to the Middle Ages.* My curiosity was aroused, and I flipped the book open. From the page where it fell open, one illustration jumped up at me. I caught my breath. It was a drawing of a two-masted ship! And it was undoubtedly medieval. Hastily I turned to the index to see where the original illustration was to be found. To my astonishment I read that the picture was copied from a privately owned medieval bestiary, an illustrated collection of animal descriptions. What was incredible was that the twin-masted boat came from the letter B under the Latin word *Balena* for whale. The picture was of Saint Brendan's ship stranded on the whale's back! I had not thought of myself as superstitious, but I took the trouble to count the number of illustrations reproduced in the textbook. There were some 5000 of them, and only one showed a twin-masted boat. It was on that single page that the book which I found accidentally had fallen open.

An important name kept cropping up in the libraries: John Waterer. He had written the majority of books and articles on the historic uses of leather. It was a subject vital to my project, so I got in touch with him and found myself invited to a most suitable rendezvous in the vaults of Saddlers' Hall, the headquarters of one of the ancient guilds in the heart of London. John Waterer turned out to be as deep-dyed an enthusiast as John Goodwin. An energetic gnome of a man, his activity belied his eighty-three years. His twinkling eyes and huge ears, as he darted about his vault full of leather saddles and bridles, leather tapestries and book bindings, even leather mugs and jugs, reminded me irresistibly of an industrious dwarf in *Snow White.* John Waterer could not have been more helpful. Patiently he introduced me to the subject of leather science and leather history. He told me about the different ways of turning animal skin into leather by tanning and by other treatments. He explained how and when the various methods had first been used, why one leather differed from another according to the treatment or whether it came from the skin of ox or calf, goat or sheep, or such exotic animals as moose and buffalo. The depth of his knowledge was profound. He was not a university-trained academic, but had begun work in the leather trade as a luggage-maker. Like John Goodwin the curragh-maker, he too had been gripped by the fascination of his work and had probed deeper and deeper into its history. Now he was the acknowledged authority in the field, consulted for his opinions by archaeologists and museum curators. To me there could not have been a better guide into the esoteric subject of leather.

A fortnight later I attended a meeting at the headquarters of the British Leather Institute. John Waterer had written to John Beeby, who handled public relations for the institute, and explained I needed help.

"I want to build a leather boat to sail across the Atlantic," I told John Beeby.

"Does John Waterer think it can be done?" he asked.

"Yes."

"Then I think we'd better help you. I will get in some experts."

I was elated. Brendan Luck was still with me, and forty-eight hours later I found myself at the Institute explaining my ideas about Saint Brendan to three men whose expertise could help to turn my dream into reality. Dr. Robert Sykes was head of the Research Association of the British Leather Manufacturers and had an international reputation in leather science. He was precise, sensible, and at first a bit skeptical. Next to him sat Carl Postles, tanyard manager from the firm of W. & J. Richardson in Derby, a family business making saddlery and other fine leathers since the seventeenth century. Finally there was the burly figure of Harold Birkin, whom I was to get to know and admire very much over the next few months. Harold was the direct opposite of the scientific Dr. Sykes. Harold lived, talked, and doubtless breathed the business of making leather for special purposes. From a small tannery in the delightful town of Chesterfield, overlooked by the crooked wooden spire of St. Mary's Church, he sent a variety of exotic leathers to customers all over the world. His leather was used deep in the coal mines for air pumps or out on the snowfields for dog-team harnesses in the Antarctic. Harold was a one-man thesaurus on the best sort of leather for any job. He could tell you the right leather for a naval fire hose, a sewing-machine drive belt, or an industrial safety glove. One of his prize possessions was a two-inch-thick chunk of walrus hide that sat on his desk like a petrified slab of wasps' nest. Yet he could also make you leather for a tiny airseal, 0.8 mm thick, on a pocket tyre pressure gauge.

"Saint Brendan is said to have built his boat from leather tanned in oak bark," I told these experts. "Do you think this was right, and would it have survived an ocean crossing?"

"Oak-bark-tanned leather is certainly authentic," said Dr. Sykes. "The normal way of tanning leather in western Europe right up to this century was some form of vegetable tannage, usually oak bark if it was available, and taking as long as twelve months to tan fully."

"At Richardson's we still do a vegetable tannage," added Carl Postles, "but not in oak bark any longer. It's too difficult to get and it takes too long."

"What about dressing the leather?" asked Harold. "It sounds to me as if the currying or dressing of the leather hull is going to be just as important as the leather itself."

"The *Navigatio* merely says that the monks rubbed the skins with a grease or fat before they launched their leather boat," I told him. "The Latin word that's employed for grease doesn't define what sort of fat it was. But the text does add that Saint Brendan took along a spare supply of this fat to dress the leather during the voyage."

"Sounds very sensible," commented Harold. Turning to Dr. Sykes he asked, "What sort of fats would they have had, Bob?"

"Tallow, or sheep's fat, beeswax, perhaps cod oil, and for waterproofing . . . ," and here Dr. Sykes paused, "possibly the grease from sheep's wool. It's virtually raw lanolin, and has been known since Pliny's time; people have used it for waterproofing shoes right up to recent times."

For about an hour we talked the problem over, and finally agreed that Carl and Harold would send to Dr. Sykes samples of all the suitable sorts of leather they had in their tanneries. Dr. Sykes would then test these samples at his laboratories. There they would be soaked in sea water, rolled and dried, flexed and stretched, measured and weighed, to see what happened.

"What about oak-bark leather?" I demanded. "We must have some of that."

"Of course," agreed Dr. Sykes, "but it's very rare nowadays. In fact, I only know two, perhaps three tanneries who make oak-bark leather. There's one in particular down in Cornwall in the West Country, a very, very old-fashioned place, almost a farm really. They supplied genuine oak-bark leather to the British Museum when the museum was restoring a leather shield from the Sutton Hoo burial ship. I'll ask them to send up some of their leather, and we'll test it in with the other samples."

So began a delightful period of work. The British leather industry took the Brendan project to heart, and what splendid people the leathermakers turned out to be. It was a close-knit industry in which everyone seemed to know everyone else in friendly rivalry, but with a shared appreciation of leather. While Dr. Sykes and his technicians exposed various leather samples to every test they could devise, I visited tanneries, saddlemakers, and luggagemakers who still worked with leather. At the Richardson's tannery in Derby I found that they even made drinking tankards out of leather, and I noticed small scraps of leather floating in jam jars and saucers of water on several windowsills. "What on earth are those?" I asked Carl.

"Oh, the tannery workmen have heard about your crazy Saint Brendan idea, and everyone has been testing pieces of leather to see whether they float."

"And do they?" I asked.

"Not for longer than four days," he grinned. "You are going to need a life raft."

Then one afternoon, after ten weeks of tests at the laboratories, I had a momentous telephone call from Dr. Sykes.

"I think we've identified your hull leather," he said. "You were right. Oak-bark leather is the best."

"How do you know?"

"We've done every test we can manage in the time available, including putting the samples on a machine designed to test leather-shoe soles. This machine rolls the sample back and forth on a mesh kept flooded with water, like a foot walking on a wet road, and we can test how much water penetrates the leather."

"What happened?" I asked.

"As supplied, the oak-bark leather wasn't as good as the others. In fact several of the other leathers were much better. But after dressing with grease and extensive testing, all the other leathers began to fail; many became waterlogged, rather like wet dishcloths. But the oak-bark samples scarcely changed at all. In the end the oak-bark leather was actually two to three times more resistant to water than any other sample. If you still want to make that leather boat, then you should use oak-bark leather."

With a glow of triumph I put down the telephone. Once again the simple factual accuracy of the *Navigatio* had been demonstrated, this time in the opinion of a skilled scientist.

There remained the problem of where to get the oak-bark leather, and here I had another stroke of luck. John Beeby arranged for me to meet Bill Croggon of Josiah Croggon and Son Ltd., the oak-bark tanners from Cornwall, at a leather fair in London. I was warned that the Croggons were a very conservative firm. "They've been making oak-bark leather in the same manner and in the same place for nearly three centuries," John said. "People have been advising them to change to some more modern methods. But they won't. I don't know what they'll say to your idea of a leather boat, and it's up to you to persuade them to let you have the leather."

When I explained to Bill Croggon that I wanted enough oxhides tanned in oak bark to cover a medieval boat, he looked thoughtful. "I'll have to talk it over with my brother," he said. "And you must realize that it takes a very long time to make oak-bark leather. Every single piece is nearly a year in preparation and we might not have it ready in time. When would you want your leather?"

"Well, I'd planned to set sail on Saint Brendan's Day," I said.

"When's that?"

"May sixteenth."

"What a coincidence! That's my wife's birthday!" he replied, and somehow I knew then that the Croggons would be helping the Brendan project.

So it turned out. I went down to the Croggons' tannery in the little Cornish town of Grampound and met the Croggon family themselves, grandmother, sons and grandsons, a whole clutch of Croggons, helpful, hospitable, and soon as excited about the Brendan Voyage as I was. They took me around the tannery, starting with the lime-soaking pits where the animal hides were stripped of their hair. There I was astonished to see one workman actually scraping the surface hair from an oxhide by hand. He was using a double-handed scraper, and as he leaned over the "beam" or block he looked exactly like a woodcut illustration of a leather-worker printed four hundred years ago. We walked across a field, past a string of ducks, and went up to the tanning pits, row upon row of tanks dug into the ground and filled with a rich liquid made of ground-up oak bark and water, which looked like thick beer with a creamy froth and smelled sickly sweet. In this "oak-bark liquor" lay the oxhides, slowly absorbing the tannin in the mixture, which entered the skins and formed a tight bond with the skin fibers, turning a perishable oxhide into some of the finest leather known. "It's a technique that can't have changed much since Saint Brendan's day," commented John Croggon. "It takes good oxhides, the right oak-bark mixture, and lots and lots of time. Of course, many people say that today it's very old-fashioned. But some of the very best handmade shoes are soled with our leather, and orthopedic hospitals specify oak-bark leather for certain uses because it is so pure that it is less likely to cause skin irritations."

"Do you think you could find enough medieval-sized oxhides for me? The cattle in Saint Brendan's day were smaller than now. I need small-sized hides about a quarter of an inch thick to be authentic, maybe as many as fifty of them."

"You are in luck. We've got some hides just like that in the tanning pits now. Of course you'll have to have the best. You're trusting your life to them."

Much later I discovered just how unstintingly the Croggon brothers worked on my behalf. They and their men personally sorted through oxhide after oxhide, hauling them out, wet and dripping, from the tanning pits. They examined each hide minutely for flaws, for barbed-wire scratches, for the holes left by warble flies, for cuts made by a careless skinning knife. It must have taken days of back-breaking work, and without ever a word to me. In the end, the Croggons provided fifty-seven of the finest oak-bark-tanned oxhides I could have wanted. When a professional saddle-maker saw them stacked together, he gave a low whistle of appreciation. "I've never seen leather like it," he said. "I've been told about it, but never expected to see so much of it in one place. We seldom see it in our workshops."

"That's because it's all been earmarked for a leather boat," I teased him.

From the Croggons' tannery the hides went up to Harold Birkin to be greased. Tests at the research laboratories had revealed that wool grease was in fact the best dressing for the leather, and through a friend in the wool business I had been given the name of a wool mill in Yorkshire that might help. I telephoned one of the directors. "I wonder if you could supply me with some wool grease."

"Yes, of course. How much do you want?"

"About three-quarters of a ton, please."

There was a stunned silence.

The only trouble with the combination of wool grease and leather was the appalling smell. My wife complained that the leather smelled like blocked drains, and this smell now competed with the odor of rancid fat. Even the workers in Harold Birkin's tannery—and tanneries are notoriously pungent places—complained about the stench of the grease. They claimed that they could smell the stuff half a mile away from the factory gates.

Under Harold's close attention, each evil-smelling oxhide was folded down the backbone and suspended in a tub of hot wool grease. Then it was withdrawn from the tub, allowed to drain, and put flat on the ground. Now molten wool grease was literally poured onto it, another hide placed on top, and the process of pouring hot grease repeated for all fifty-seven oxhides until there was a huge, sticky, multilayer sandwich of leather gently absorbing the vital wool grease.

The project was now moving ahead rapidly, but I still lacked a vital expert. I needed someone who could produce a proper design study of my medieval curragh, complete with a set of technical drawings from which to build the boat. It would have to be someone who was a historian as well as a fully qualified naval architect, and one afternoon I sat down in the library of the Royal Geographic Society and wrote to all of the maritime museums I could think of, asking if they could recommend such a man. The replies were polite, but nobody could help. However, one museum told me that I should ask the secretary of the Royal Institute of Navigation, who personally knew most of the experts in this field. I looked up the address of the institute. It was in the same building as the Royal Geographic Society. All the time I had been writing my requests, I was sitting directly under the man who could help me! I went upstairs, and was promptly given one name: Colin Mudie.

The name seemed distantly familiar, and then I remembered. Colin Mudie had sailed with Patrick Ellam across the Atlantic in the tiny yacht *Sopranino* in the 1950s. He also had designed an extraordinary balloon to cover the same route, using a gondola that doubled as a boat when, after a record time aloft, the ballooning ended in a storm. Colin Mudie had a reputation as one of the most unorthodox designers to be found. Nothing daunted him. Arctic explorers took their sledges to him to have them made into convertible boats; he designed power craft for high-speed racing, kites to fly radio aerials, even a submersible yacht with the mast sticking out of the water. Yet he had also been selected to design a sail training brig for the Sail Cadet Corps, designed production boats built in thousands, and was chairman of the prestigious Small Craft Group of the Royal Institute of Naval Architects.

Yet when I went to Colin Mudie's home, a very unexpected figure opened the door. I had anticipated a bluff, bearded seadog. Instead I was greeted by a small, fragile-looking man with a darting manner, a huge mane of long hair, and the most piercing blue-gray eyes I have ever seen. For all the world he looked like a hungry and alert owl, blinking as he invited me into his study.

In two hours I found out exactly why Colin Mudie was so highly regarded. He sat at his desk listening intently to my thesis, and absentmindedly sketched on a pad. From the point of his pen flowed little ships and shapes, details of oars and masts, water lines and carpentry details. He was a gifted draughtsman, and a man whose thoughts literally turned themselves into pictures. When I finished, he merely looked up at me and said, "There's nothing impossible either about a leather boat or the voyage you want to make. I can do a design study for you, and then, if you want to go ahead, follow it with drawings for a boatyard to work from. But what neither I nor anyone else can give you is the knowledge of how to handle this boat at sea. That knowledge has been long lost. It is up to you to rediscover it. Always remember you are trying to follow men who went to sea with generations of experience behind them. That may turn out to be the unknown factor in your venture."

In eight weeks Colin put together all the data about Irish leather boats I had gleaned in the libraries and in the Dingle. Twice he telephoned me. Once to tell me that he thought he'd found a reason for the characteristic double gunwale of the Dingle curragh, one above the other. It was, he suggested, a throwback to the days when the leather hull skin was pulled over the gunwale like a drum skin. This would require a basic frame of great strength, especially in compression, and the double gunwale is an ideal construction. On the second occasion he confirmed my hunch that the original leather curraghs had carried two masts. His calculations showed that the traditional mast position, which John Goodwin had put into my small curragh, was exactly the right place for a foremast. If so, it was reasonable to suppose that in the old days there had been a central mainmast to balance it. But Colin was also practical. He wanted to hang pieces of oak-bark leather in the sea to learn what happened. So once a fortnight the staff of the Lymington ferry pier was treated to the bizarre spectacle of a renowned naval architect solemnly standing on their jetty and hauling up slabs of very smelly leather on the end of long strings. Some of the station's staff must have thought it mad, but soon there was also a rumor that Colin was designing a waterproof shoe. No one would have believed the truth: that he was working on a leather boat.

In the end the drawings were ready, four large sheets covered with lines and figures in Colin's neat hand. They were the end product of all my labor so far, and with them under my arm and fifty-seven slippery, greasy oxhides pungent with wool grease, I set out for Ireland.

It was time to start building the boat.

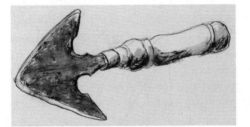

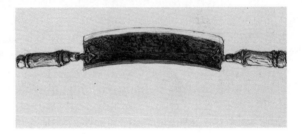

Half-moon knife and hide scraper

3
Building

"What have you got there?" asked the Irish customs officer as he slid back the van door with a rumble, poked in his head, and withdrew it again very sharply, wrinkling his nose at the eye-watering smell.

"Oxhides," I replied. "They're for a boat I'm building and hope to sail to America."

"Oh, they are for re-export then. Thank heavens for that. We won't want that sort of smell around too long." He laughed as he banged the door shut. I was on my way to the boatyard in County Cork where the boat would be built, and an important new stage in the Brendan project was about to begin.

Not so long ago I had been worrying whether I could find a boatyard to do the job. After all, it's not often that a modern boatyard is asked to construct a medieval boat. But as it turned out, I need not have fretted. Only in Ireland was it possible to stroll into the local boatyard, spread out a drawing, and casually ask, "I wonder if you could help build this for me? It's a sixth-century design, and I'll be covering the hull with oxhides myself, but I want an expert to build the wooden frame." The boatyard manager's eyebrows rose a quarter of an inch. He took two slow puffs on his pipe, and then he murmured, "That shouldn't be any trouble. I'll check with our head shipwright if he's got space."

This was no run-of-the-mill boatyard. The Crosshaven Boat-yard was where the Irish lifeboats were sent for overhaul; where

Sir Francis Chichester built his record-breaking *Gypsy Moth V;* and where I heard it stated that they preferred never to build two boats to the same design because this was "too dull." Crosshaven was a boatyard in the old style: no fiberglass, scarcely any steel, but masses of timber and a cheerful confidence in their ability to build anything that was meant to float. Above all, it was a boatyard that didn't mind my bringing smelly oxhides onto the premises, to be followed shortly afterward by a medley of saddlers, leather-workers, students, amateur helpers, and a mascot dog.

Pat Lake was the head shipwright. With his spectacles and rubicund face he looked more like a country doctor than a boat-builder. He was what County Cork called a "flier." When he got started into a job, it simply flew along. To my delight Pat himself elected to build the frame for the boat, working in the evenings in his spare time and helped by a pair of picked assistants. "Pat," I told him, "what I would like you to do is to build me the wooden frame according to Colin Mudie's drawings. Can you do it in such a way that the frame is held together temporarily? Once you have shaped the main structure, I will then replace your fastenings with authentic medieval fastenings of the type Saint Brendan would have used to hold the wooden frame together."

"What were those fastenings made of?" he asked.

"Strips of leather thong were most probably used to lash the frame together. In those days metals was too valuable to be used where other materials would do the same job. Besides, I think if we lash the frame together like a wicker basket, this ought to make the hull more flexible."

"What sort of timber do you want me to use?"

"Oak for the double gunwales, and ash for the frames and the longitudinal stringers. We know from the analysis of hearth ash that these types of wood were growing in Ireland in Saint Brendan's day."

"Oak sounds fine to me," commented Pat. "We've got some oak here in the yard that has been seasoned for eight or ten years and is as hard as iron. But I wouldn't be happy about using ash. It's not a timber that goes well in a boat. If ash keeps getting wet in sea water and then drying out, it begins to rot. Before long you'd be able to poke your finger through it."

"I'm sure that ash is the right timber," I repeated. "No other

[36]

wood available in medieval Ireland was supple enough to follow the sharp curves of the hull frames."

"Right then. But it's going to be difficult to find ash in the long straight lengths we'll be wanting."

Here was an unexpected snag. I found that very little ash is now used in the timber industry. And when ash trees are felled, they are cut up into short lengths to make it easier to haul the logs from the forest. But for my boat I had to have trunks of ash thirty feet long and straight in the grain. These were rarities in the timber trade. It looked very much as if I was going to have to begin yet another hunt for my medieval materials, and I feared that I had no time for such a quest.

But I had forgotten Brendan Luck. I was given the name of a consultant expert in the timber trade, and I went to see him at his office. By now I was thoroughly accustomed to opening such meetings with a long introductory explanation about my project for a leather boat. So I took a deep breath and began. "This may sound strange to you, but I want to build a medieval boat made of . . ."

The timber expert held up his hand to stop me. "Some years ago a man called Heyerdahl came in to us for advice about balsa wood," he said. "I believe we found some for him. Just tell me what timber you want, and we'll see if we can help."

Through his contacts I found myself in County Longford in the very heart of Ireland, at a timber yard run by a family called Glennon. Had it not been for the flat Irish countryside and the strong Irish accents, I could have imagined myself with the leather-making Croggons in Cornwall. The two situations were strikingly similar. In each case there was a small family business specializing in a traditional material. In Ireland it was Paddy Glennon who ran the business, supported by Glennon brothers, Glennon children, and Glennon cousins. And once again it was a family that gave to the Brendan project a huge enthusiasm that no money could ever have bought. The Glennons took me on a tour of their timber yard, providing a running commentary much like that of an art connoisseur showing a visitor around his picture gallery. Here was the trunk of an oak tree that had been hand-picked to make a keel for a new wooden trawler. It was a massive giant that had flourished for about four hundred years. "Aren't you sorry to cut down such splendid trees?" I inquired. "Oh, no. You see this black mark here near the root? That's rot. The tree has entered its old age. It was sick, and in time it would have rotted right through and been destroyed."

"Do you think you could possibly find me some really large fine ash trees to provide the timber for my boat?"

"Just as it happens," said Paddy, "we are felling timber on one of the great estates near here, and there's some beautiful ash to be cleared. It should be just what you want."

So I found the ash I needed, and once again the experts guided me into the fascinating subject of fine timber. "Heart of oak, bark of ash" was one of Paddy Glennon's mottoes. He advised me to use the heartwood from the oak tree for the gunwales, but it was the fine white wood from the outer trunk of the ash tree that was the strongest. Best of all the ash, Paddy advised, was the wood from a mountain ash "which had to scrabble for its living" and grew light and strong. And when it came to selecting a suitable ash tree for the mast and oars, Paddy himself took me on a squelching tour across the countryside, hunting from tree to tree until we found just the one he sought—tall and straight, about eighty years old, an ash tree in its prime. "We'll fell this one," he said, "and I'll see to it personally that the mast timber is taken from the north-facing side of the tree where the white wood is best. You'll find no ash that is stronger for your purpose."

Quite by chance, I mentioned to him Pat Lake's worries about using ash in a boat. "Wait a minute," said Paddy Glennon, "I think there's someone at the timber yard who might be able to help you. In the old days the mill was powered by water from a pond, and the tools the men used were always getting soaked and then dry; perhaps they had some way of preserving the wood." We returned to the mill and Paddy made some inquiries. "It seems that the old fellows used to soak their wooden tools in oil or grease, and this kept them in good condition. How does that sound to you?" It sounded just right and another piece of the jigsaw puzzle clicked into place. The *Navigatio* had said that grease was used for preserving the leather. Logically the same grease would have been available to protect the timber frame if it had been built of ash. Indeed, the grease from the leather would unavoidably rub off onto the wood as the boat flexed in the sea. The logic was inescapable: here were two materials, leather and ash, which were normally vulnerable to sea water. But the same treatment with the same basic material—grease—rendered them suitable for a medieval boat.

The first of my visits to the Glennons' timber yard ended with a conversation that was to stay in my mind. When we had toured the yard, Paddy Glennon invited me to meet his wife and have supper with him in their home. During the meal he asked all about the Brendan project, and cross-examined me about the reasons behind it. And when I was about to leave the table, he suddenly said, "There's something else I want to tell you. I'll find the timber for your boat, and I'll see that it's cut exactly right, even if I have to run the saws myself. What is more, you are not to expect to receive a bill from Glennons. I want to make you a present of the timber."

I was overwhelmed. This was a most generous gift indeed. I started to thank him, but he went on:

"You ought to know why I'm doing this," he said. "It's because I feel I'm repaying a debt. My family has made a good living out of Irish-grown timber. We've always dealt with native-grown hardwoods when most other firms were importing their timber, and we've done well. If you're going to build an Irish boat out of Irish timber, I want it to be made of Glennons' timber. It'll help to pay back some of what the native timber has given to us. But . . ." and here he grinned, "there's always a 'but.' If your early Christian boat gets across the Atlantic, I want you to bring back just a small piece of our timber so that we can keep it in the office."

Paddy Glennon was as good as his word. A week later a lorry delivered a load of superb ash to the Crosshaven Boatyard, and later another shipment arrived of the long straight ash baulks, cut on the north-facing side of the great tree, that we shaped into the masts and oars on which our lives would depend.

With this material Pat Lake and his shipwrights set to work. They used exactly the same methods that John Goodwin followed when he built his canvas "canoes" up in the Dingle. The two gunwales were made from flint-hard oak joined with wooden pins. Then the two gunwales were placed one above another in a sandwich, and shaped to the characteristic banana curve of the Dingle curragh. Next, the double gunwales were turned upside down so the boat could be built bottom upward. Only an Irish boat, I thought to myself, would be built in reverse, beginning with the gunwale and finishing with the keel.

Yet there was good sense to it. One by one the light, curved frames of bone-white ash were carefully put into position until they looked like a line of hoops that carry nets over strawberry beds. By pulling and pushing on these hoops, Pat Lake got exactly the right profile he wanted. Then he began to attach the stringers, the long slim strips of ash running fore and aft which completed the latticework of the boat frame. He lightly tapped in a single wire nail at each intersection of frame and stringer, until the entire basketwork was the correct shape of Colin Mudie's drawings.

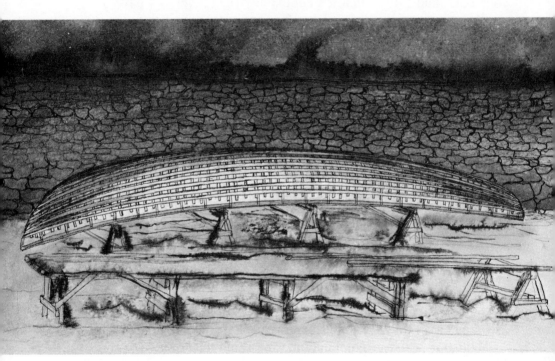

Now it was up to me. While Pat was making up the frame, I had been busily experimenting with the leather thongs to lash the frame together. Doctor Sykes at the Leather Research Laboratories had advised that the best leather for this job was made by "tawing," a process using alum, known since Roman days. Carl Postles at the Derby tannery had sent over two big bales of these thongs, and I began a few practical tests with them by tying together wood laths and hanging them in the tide water of the estuary. I quickly found that it was vital to soak the thongs in sea water beforehand, stretch them, and then tie the lashings while the leather was still wet. Otherwise the thongs did not grip. Unfortunately, tying knots in slippery wet thongs was like joining two snakes. The thongs simply slid apart. One hilarious Sunday morning I was testing a new type of knot in the garage, and had tied the thong to a ring bolt in the floor. I was heaving away with all my might, when suddenly the thong slipped, and I went hurtling backward out of the garage door onto the pavement. There I tripped and fell flat on my back waving a wet thong in the air, right in the path of the village congregation on its way back from church. "That's what education does for you," someone muttered.

In the end I found a knot that seemed to hold effectively, though it required much interlacing and twisting, and in a curious way it looked very like the braided patterns found in Irish manuscript illustrations; and to help with the long job of lashing the frame together, George came out from England to join me.

George had always been my first choice for crew. Twenty-six years old, he had served in the army and later gone to the Middle East to train soldiers for an oil-rich sheik. With the money saved from this venture, he had decided to take a couple of years looking around the world and pleasing himself. He answered an advertisement in a yachting magazine looking for someone to help sail a small yacht in the Mediterranean, and in this way he had come cruising with my wife and me aboard our *Prester John.* Six foot tall and rangy, George was a consummate sailor. He could get more out of a boat by tirelessly resetting sails and adjusting the helm than anyone I had ever sailed with. Above all he was reliable. When George said he would get something done, it was done. One weekend he had promised to help transport some of the oxhides to Harold. On the Friday evening he loaded them; and on the Sunday he delivered them. On the Saturday in between he had got married!

Now, leaving his wife Judith to keep her job as a schoolteacher in London, George came out to Ireland to join me, and together we started the laborious task of lashing the boat frame. Day after day we crouched inside the upturned frame of the vessel. Each wire nail had to be pulled out and discarded. In its place a leather thong was wrapped around the wood and tightened, knotted, and then the free end led on to the next thong, and so on and so on. It was backbreakingly slow work, poking fingers through the gaps in the frame, groping for a slippery strip of leather, and heaving the knots

tight until our muscles ached. Some days we were joined by friends from the village, and their help made the work move a bit faster. By the time we finished, we had hand-lashed 1600 joints in the latticework frame, and used nearly two miles of leather thong to do so. But it was worth it. The wooden skeleton of the boat was now gripped in a fine net of leather. This net was so strong that a dozen men could jump up and down on the upturned hull, and not a lath groaned or moved out of place. Finally, to protect thong and timber, we boiled up buckets of wool grease and painted it over the hull in a spattering mess. It looked and smelled abominable but, as George pointed out, the wool grease had one benefit: though we had been hauling and clawing at the work for almost a month, not one of us had raised a single blister on our hands. The lanolin in the wool grease was a first-class handcream.

On the afternoon we finished, we went down to the local pub to celebrate, and were promptly pursued by the landlord's dog, who smelled the wool grease on our clothes. So that evening we ceremoniously burned our workclothes as the first, though not the last, sacrifice to medieval working conditions.

Now came the most crucial step in the whole reconstruction. How were we to cover the wooden hull with oxhides? What should we use for thread? How did we join the hides together? What method of stitching was best? How far apart should we make each stitch hole? There was a host of questions, and if we made one error, the consequences would be disastrous. For example, if we stitched too closely, the leather might rip between stitches. On the other hand, if we stitched too widely, the leather would buckle between them and water would pour in through the joints.

The Irish National Museum in Dublin had a superb collection of early Christian artifacts, and I spent hours examining the skills of the craftsmen from Saint Brendan's day. What exquisite skills they had displayed! These were men who had worked metal and wood and leather so cunningly that their craftsmanship stood comparison with the very best modern examples, and their decorative metal-work and jewelry was still unsurpassed. Naturally, I was more interested in their everyday objects. These items, too, were sometimes so well made that I realized we would not be limiting our own techniques to conform with medieval practices, but rather we would be hard put to it to rise to their level of skill. In metalwork, for example, the early Christian craftsmen had cast fish-hooks in bronze as robust and sharp and well-designed as anything we could obtain today. They had hammered rivets so delicately and accurately that it was virtually impossible to dupli-cate the effect. And as for their leather work, the museum displayed a rare example of early leather—an early Christian book satchel made to carry a Bible. To stitch this satchel, the medievel craftsman, who may well have been a monk himself, had worked with his hand inside the satchel, running his needle down the length of the leather so that the stitches actually stayed within the thickness of the skin and were totally invisible. No less an authority than John Waterer had declared that few modern leather-workers would have cared to try to duplicate this meticu-lous craftsmanship.

A master saddler also came across from England with his best apprentice to advise George and me on possible leather-working techniques for the boat. We numbered every oxhide and heaped them under piles of weights to flatten out the wrinkles as much as possible. We trimmed the hides with sharp knives, and hung them on the wooden boat frame, turning them this way and that to try to make them fit the compound curves of the hull. We warmed oxhides to try to mold them; we soaked them in water; and we beat them with great hammers to try to shape them. We tried every technique I had seen in the museum, and we tested the traditional methods of the master saddlemaker, methods with splendid-sounding names like back-stitching, two-hand stitching, blind stitching, and the furriers' stitch.

Occasionally the results were disastrous. For example, when we tried lacing the hides together with finely cut leather thong, the lacing popped apart like rotten string. "If only we could get fine thong made from horsehide; it's so much stronger," bemoaned the master saddler. Another hide we tried dipping in water that was too warm, and the leather turned brittle and lifeless. It cracked and split like a neglected shoe, and George and I looked at one another, wondering what would happen if we made a similar mistake but failed to spot it before we put to sea in the Atlantic. At last we worked out a technique that seemed simple and effective. We overlapped the oxhides by a margin of one to two inches, and then stitched a strong double line of thread along the joint. It took care and patience, but the workmanship was at least within our capabilities, and the joints showed a crude strength. Just before he left to go back to the firm who had kindly loaned him to us, the master saddler looked at the long, gleaming, naked frame of the boat, then at the stack of hides lying waiting, and then at George and me. "That's probably the biggest single leather-working job of the century," he said. "If you get it done, you'll be able to teach others something about stitching."

The task was truly daunting. I was under no illusion that without constant advice and supervision, George and I and any amateur helpers were likely to make a shambles of the work. It was immensely frustrating. Here we were with the materials and the enthusiasm, but we lacked the expert to guide us through the job. But where could I possibly find him? The men trained in heavy leather work were a vanishing breed. Fifty years ago most villages in Ireland had a man who repaired bridles and made harnesses; most country towns might have had a saddler. But these craftsmen had all but vanished, gone into limbo with the farm animals. Only a handful remained; there were probably less than a hundred trained saddlers still at work in the entire British Isles. Such men were eagerly sought after. They made saddles for the export market and were kept permanently busy. Even if I could find one with free time, I could not see how I could possibly afford to pay him.

From the very beginning of the project, I had been visiting saddlemakers in London and Birmingham. I had driven the length and breadth of Ireland to every saddlery firm on my list. Everywhere I had asked if they could spare a man or tell me where I might find one. Everywhere I was told politely but firmly that it was impossible. Every good saddler, and there were desperately few, was needed at the saddler's bench. My only compensation was that I earned a first-hand impression of fine leather work. I met the deft craftsmen who still handled tools that had not changed for centuries: the awls and punches, the pincers and scribers, the half-moon knives, crimpers, and edge-shavers. The saddlers' benches smelled richly of leather and beeswax polish; and the saddlers sat in their leather aprons, bent over their work endlessly stitching away with their huge strong hands and powerful shoulder muscles, developed by years of pulling taut the double-handed thread with a snap that still made good hand-sewn leather far stronger than any machine stitch. I learned why English saddles were considered to be the finest in the world; why Australian racing stables would wait four years for a light saddle from a top maker; and how the Shah of Iran had placed a legendary order for six sets of harness for his state coach at his coronation, every piece of harness to be made in blue leather. I learned too that the premier firm of English saddlemakers had closed down when its owner died, and its team of saddlers and harnessmakers—perhaps a dozen men—had scattered to other firms, while the Royal Warrant as Saddlers to the Queen had passed to a rival firm. Saddlemaking was such a tightly knit world that the top men could recognize their own handiwork across the width of a room and tell you the names of most of the other craftsmen in the same line.

I never failed to ask a saddler if he could recommend a colleague to me, but the bench workers themselves could not help, except once. At the saddlemakers who now held the Royal Warrant, one of the saddlers told me of an Irish harnessmaker who

[45]

had vanished from the world of leather-working. His name was John O'Connell, and my informant told me that no one knew where he had gone. John O'Connell had worked on harness for the royal stables, and he had been one of the quickest, surest harnessmakers in the trade. "Always laughing was John O'Connell," the saddler told me, "and if you find him you can't miss him. He's about the same around the middle as he is tall. Built like a barrel. And a great one for the girls. He married a girl from Ireland, and I believe he decided to go back home, and I've never heard from him again. Find John O'Connell," he added, "and you'll have found one of the best harnessmakers in Ireland."

Of course I mentioned John O'Connell's name at all the Irish saddlery firms I visited. But they had never heard of him. Then one day after we had begun boat-building at Crosshaven, I went to Cork to interview a retired saddlemaker. Unfortunately he had long since lost his skills, but I stayed to chat with him about the saddlery business and, as we talked, he happened to mention the famous blue harness sets made for the Shah's coronation. At once I came alert.

"Did you work on that job?" I asked him.

"Yes, it was worth thousands and thousands of pounds, and I remember we had to make it in a special way. The organizers of the Shah's coronation ceremony didn't know until the last moment whether they would use a six-horse team or a four-horse team to draw the imperial coach, so we had to make the harness set to fit either six horses or to be divided down into a four-horse team and harness for two more horses drawing a separate coach."

"Did you by any chance know of someone by the name of John O'Connell?"

There was a pause, while he thought back. "Yes, I knew John. He was very good."

"I'm told that he came back to Ireland after he got married. You don't know by any chance where I might be able to get in touch with him?"

Then, incredibly, came my answer.

"I heard some time ago from John O'Connell. I was looking for someone to help me in the business, and I wrote to him but he wasn't interested."

I was agog with excitement, but calmed myself with the thought that John O'Connell might be living at the other end of Ireland. "Do you remember his address?"

"Let me think." Another agonizing pause. "It was in Summerstown, a place in Summerstown. In Summerstown Road itself, I believe."

"Where's Summerstown?" I asked. He looked at me in surprise.

"It's here on the edge of Cork City."

Scarcely believing the luck, I stayed a few minutes longer and then hurried out to my car and drove straight to Summerstown estate. Summerstown Road was easy to find, and I banged on the door of the first house in the street, trusting to the fact that in Ireland everyone is liable to know everyone living in the same street.

"Excuse me. Can you please tell me if there's someone called O'Connell living near here?" I inquired.

"There are three O'Connells in this street," she said. "Which one are you wanting?"

"The man I'm looking for is short and very strong, and he's got big hands and thick strong forearms." I was describing the classic physique of a harnessmaker.

Without a second's hesitation the woman replied, "That's John O'Connell. He's at number seventeen."

I dashed across the road, and rang the bell of number 17. The door was opened by a small keg of a man. He had the weatherbeaten complexion of an outdoor worker, and also massive hands and shoulders. He looked at me inquiringly.

"You're John O'Connell . . . the harnessmaker?" I asked.

He looked stunned. "That's right. How did you find me?"

John O'Connell, one of the most skilled harnessmakers in the craft, had come back to Ireland, failed to find harness work in Cork, and had taken a job as a construction worker. He lived not fifteen miles from the boatyard where we were working, and he had kept his skills in trim, occasionally mending leather shoes for friends, or school satchels for local children. I asked him if he had still kept his leather-working tools.

"My wife complains that I never throw anything away," he said with a chuckle. "Just wait a minute while I go upstairs and fetch them down."

He came back with a battered leather Gladstone bag and pulled open the top, and I found myself looking at as varied a collection of harnessmaker's tool as I had ever seen in my life.

"I inherited most of them from my father," John O'Connell explained. "He was a horse-collar maker. Of course you don't find that trade now. I was apprenticed to him, and served my full term before I went to England."

So John O'Connell was found and agreed to join us at Crossha-ven Boatyard. At first he visited us in the evenings after he had finished his regular job on the building site. But later I was able to make arrangements so that he could join us full time, and our good fortune was difficult to believe. John was experienced in making horse collars, the branch of traditional leather work closest to our heavy leather work for the boat. Step by step, he began to train George and me and all the volunteers I recruited. He taught us to roll flax thread, turning a single strand into a thick fourteen-strand cord. We were started at the deep end. Clad in leather aprons we looped and twisted the flax, rubbing it with lumps of black wax mixed with wool grease and beeswax, and rolling it on our thighs like cigarmakers. At first we got into terrible tangles, finishing up with cats' cradles of flax that had to be thrown into the dustbin. John O'Connell merely grinned at us over the inevitable cigarette stuck in his mouth, and started each man over again. Gradually we picked up the knack of spinning the thread and how to break it against the twist with a casual flick of the wrist, but we never equaled John himself. His hands moved in a blur, and he never even needed to watch the threads spinning and twisting as if by magic they rolled as neatly and regularly as from a machine. To the finish John could roll two cords for every single one that George or I turned out.

Next, John turned to the stitching of the leather. He started us on the plain back-stitch, and showed us how it was made. He taught us to thread the needles properly. He demonstrated how to pierce half-an-inch thickness of leather straight and true with a quick stab of the deadly saddlemaker's awl and, before the hole closed up, to run through the blunt needle, its tip touching the point of the awl as it was withdrawn. Hand and eye had to match the movement exactly. A second's delay and the advantage was lost as the leather closed around the hole. At the start we almost abandoned hope at ever being able to copy his methods. In four days of work we averaged a paltry six inches of stitching per day, and we knew that we had at least two miles to go. We broke needles by the score, split and tore the threads, snapped awl blades, and pricked our fingers till they bled profusely. Our hands were soon a mass of cuts, and we kept a large box of sticking plaster by the workbench. Even John's hands were bleeding, but for quite a different reason. After ten years away from the saddler's bench, his hands, despite carrying bricks, had grown soft for harness work. When John pulled the thread tight into each stitch, he did so with a massive jerk that brought into play the enormous muscles in arm and shoulder, and the thread wrapped around his fists sliced into the soft flesh like a knife. But John merely laughed. "It'll soon mend," he grunted as drops of blood spattered out. "Inside a week my hands will be back in trim, and then we'll really get going."

"Won't the cuts get infected?" I asked him.

"No, not at all. A waxed thread never leaves a dirty cut. In the old days if we cut ourselves with a knife on the bench, we always treated the cut with a dab of black wax. Nobody ever had any trouble."

We began with the easier work, piecing together the oxhides that covered the central segment of the hull, joining each hide as if stitching together a quilt. Neighbors and friends came from my village to help us, and we learned that it was knack rather than brute strength that mattered in driving a good stitch. Some people had a true feeling for the work, others hadn't. Our best recruit was a mere slip of a girl with less muscular strength than anyone else, but she left a neat, firm line of stitches that joined the hides as if they had been welded together.

Once we had mastered the back-stitch, John O'Connell took us on to the faster but more complicated two-hand stitch. Two needles were used to carry two separate threads down the line of awl holes, working from both sides of the leather. Normally a harnessmaker would have done the two-hand stitch by himself, holding the leather clamped between his knees. But our oxhides were too big, averaging four feet by three and a half feet, and so it was impossible for one man to reach both sides simultaneously.

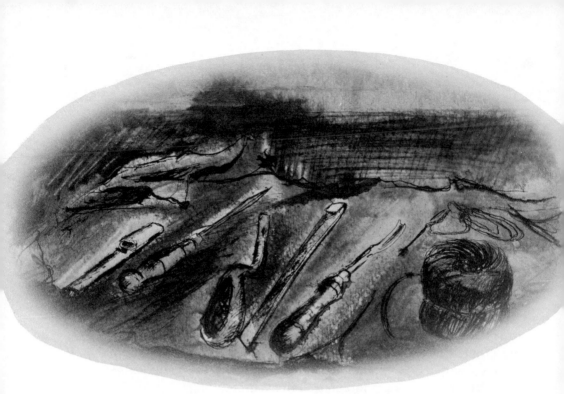

Harnessmaker's Tools

We had to have the stitchers working in pairs, poking the needles back and forth to one another through the leather. One stitcher stood on the outside and opened a hole with a stab of the awl. His partner, curled up inside the upturned boat, poked the needle out to the pinprick of light. Back came a second needle; then the partners gathered up the slack of the two threads in their fists; a grunt, and both tugged the stitch home simultaneously. The technique took patience, dexterity, and a sense of rhythm if it was to be done right. And if it was done wrong, John O'Connell was merciless. "Rip it, rip it!" he would say, and out would come his razor-sharp saddler's knife and one slash would sever an entire day's painstaking labor.

Gradually the work crept forward . . . two oxhides in place, four . . . six, and then suddenly we were working on the second tier of hides. John was satisfied with the quality of the work, but I was growing worried that we were falling behind schedule. If the boat was to be launched on time, I had to find more stitchers. I had already scoured the village and the neighborhood, and recruited every available housewife and friend. Then I had a brainwave. There was a technical college in London that gave a course in saddlery. Perhaps I could get a class of students to come over to help. I had never met the saddlery instructor, but I knew he had once been foreman at the Royal Warrant saddlers. I wrote him a letter and then telephoned him.

"Hello. This is Tim Severin. I wrote to you about a medieval leather boat I'm building. Do you think there's any chance that some of your students would like to come over to help? It would be good experience for them, and I'll pay their fares to come to Ireland."

The instructor sounded doubtful. "I've talked to my students, and they're very keen. But what would they learn? I don't want them picking up any shoddy techniques, and somebody will have to keep an eye on them."

"I've got John O'Connell looking after the work at the boatyard," I pleaded.

"What! John O'Connell the harnessmaker?" He sounded impressed. "Well then, you've got the best man. I'll give the students permission to join you for a week."

So nine students came across to Ireland, tumbling one morning from a battered van at the Crosshaven Boatyard to the amazement of the shipwrights. The students brought with them their transistor radios, sleeping bags, and a strange assortment of old clothes ranging from moleskin overcoats to long woollen scarves and striped sports shirts. They chattered and joked . . . and they worked superbly. At its peak the boat had no less than nine students, eight volunteers, George's sister Ellen, George, myself, and John working on it; and if you peered underneath, there was our mascot: George's dog, Biscuit, who sat all day under the upturned hull, licking the faces of the "inside" stitchers and begging lunchtime sandwiches. In the evenings we drove back, completely worn out, to the village, where kindly neighbors had cooked up vast pots of stew and left them on my doorstep.

"Good Lord, where did that lot come from?" asked a student as Ellen Molony staggered in with a four-gallon tub of Irish stew.

"Leprechauns!" was the instant reply.

The students set the timetable right, and on the day they were due to go back to college, their spokesman took me to one side.

"We are enjoying ourselves so much," he said, "that we would like to stay on two extra days. Would you mind?"

"Of course not," I answered. "I would be delighted. But the agreement with your college was that you would only be here for a week."

"Oh, that's all right," he said gaily. "We'll just arrange to miss the ferry boat, and the next boat doesn't sail for two days."

So the students blithely missed the boat, and by the time they roared off cheerily in their dented van, we had only to make and fit the bow and stern sections of the leather. We anticipated extra wear and tear in these areas, and so we doubled the thickness of the leather, and on the bow where it might run on a rock or onto sharp flotsam, we made it four layers thick, more than an inch of solid leather. Only John O'Connell had the strength for this work. From his Gladstone bag he produced a pair of great heavy half-moon needles and an antiquated collarmaker's palm that was almost a museum piece. As I watched him drive the needles through the leather with his prodigious strength, I thanked our luck that we had found such a man.

Finally, the leathering was done. We had used forty-nine hides to cover the frame. Several hides had been damaged in our first attempt to sew them, but we still had an ample supply of extra material if the boat needed repairs during the forthcoming trials or the voyage itself. George and I crawled for the last time under the upturned boat. With rope cut from oxhide, we pulled down the hanging edge of the skin and fastened it upward to the lower gunwale. Pat Lake the shipwright and Murph, his second-in-command, climbed onto the upturned hull to fit on a shallow skid of oak to protect the leather when we should run the boat up on to a beach; and our medieval boat was manhandled the right way up. From the finest Glennon ash we fashioned masts and oars to the same pattern as the Dingle curraghs, and at last she was ready.

To bless our new boat there was no better person than Eammon Casey, Bishop of Kerry and the spiritual descendant of Saint Brendan himself. On January 24 the Bishop arrived in full regalia at the beach where the boat lay ready. The weather was cuttingly cold, with a sharp wind that sent the flags on the boat's rigging snapping and crackling. On the peak of the mainmast flew the flag of Ireland, and on the foremast our own pennant, the twin-tailed Brendan banner of a ringed Irish cross in red, "the cross of glory" on a white background. I had chosen the ringed cross, not only for its Irish association, but also because this cross was found in one form or another at many of the monastic sites which the medieval seafaring monks had visited, leaving the Celtic cross scratched on native rocks or as a magnificent free-standing monument.

A bottle of Irish whiskey had seemed more appropriate than French champagne for the first ocean-going leather boat to be launched in Ireland for perhaps forty generations, but there was a last-minute hitch. How did one break a stout glass bottle against a leather hull? The bottle would just bounce off. Crosshaven's shipwrights came to the rescue. They hung an anchor on the bow and fixed the whiskey bottle into a wooden arm that would swing down on the target. Just to make sure, one of the shipwrights hid inside the bow throughout the service, ready to tug on a cord that made the bottle descend at full speed. A sizeable crowd had gathered to witness the ceremony. Movie cameras were focused; and the inevitable Doubting Thomas bustled among the spectators, offering to take bets. "Five to one she doesn't float; five to one she sinks within the hour," he offered. "You're on for fifty pounds," called one of my friends, but by the time he got out his money, the little bookmaker had discreetly vanished. Bishop Casey was magnificent. Isolated from the gale inside his purple and lace, he spoke the traditional prayers over the new boat. He blessed her mission, her crew, and the watching audience, and he read a poem in Irish he had specially composed for the occasion:

> Bless this boat, O True Christ,
> Convey her free and safe across the sea.
> You are like a blessing of Brendan's time,
> Bless this boat now.
>
> Guide our journey in it to sheltered land,
> To go to the land of promise is your right,
> You are like a guide of Brendan's time,
> Guide our boat now.

Then came the moment. My daughter Ida stepped forward with the scissors, and in a small clear voice she announced, "I name this boat *Brendan*," and cut the ribbon. The whiskey bottle, propelled by its hidden shipwright, whipped down with a tremendous crash. Shards of glass showered everyone within range, and the cloud of atomized Irish whiskey swept over the crowd. "That's the real stuff!" shouted a hoarse voice, and *Brendan* began to slide down toward the water. With scarcely a ripple, she floated lightly off her cradle; her crew of shipwrights heaved at their oars; and *Brendan* pulled away, floating high with her bunting rippling and the crowd applauding. The boat of leather was afloat.

It was much too stormy and cold to risk *Brendan* at sea, so one of Paddy Glennon's giant timber lorries trundled her up to the shallow lakes of the River Shannon for trials. We stepped the masts, hung the steering paddle over the starboard quarter, and pushed off to see what happened under sail. It was an idyllic morning. A gentle breeze filled *Brendan*'s two square sails; the hull canted slightly in response, and the long slim boat glided over the peaty brown Shannon water. We were deep in the countryside, with not a house in sight. The broad river curved past deep green meadows. Swans took off before our bows, paddling with their feet and undulating their long necks to gain speed and height as they left behind the powerful rushing sound of their wings. Clouds of ducks rose from the winter-brown reeds on each side of the river, and a cart horse that had been grazing in the water-meadow came galloping down to stop and stare in amazement at the strange, silent gliding craft before it suddenly wheeled and galloped away with soft sucking splashes in the mud, halting again at a safe distance and turning to watch the boat once more. The whole scene—the square white sails moving silently over the brown reeds—had an unreal air.

We glided into Lough Corry, scarcely more than an embayment in the river's course. A puff of wind struck us, and suddenly everything became alive. The boat heeled more steeply; the water began to surge against the steering oar; a rope jerked adrift from its cleat; suddenly there was chaos. Each sail needed four ropes to control it, and each rope developed a life of its own. When one rope escaped, the others began to wriggle and slat. The heavy crossyard swung over; the sail slapped against the mast; and without warning we found ourselves grabbing at unidentified ropes and hauling in hopefully, trying to discover which rope would quell the riot. But the wind had got stronger, a good solid puff, and

1.

1. Fine white wood of native Irish ash made *Brendan*'s lattice frame. Timber for masts and oars was hand-picked from the tough north-facing sides of the ash trees. Heartwood of oak was turned into gunwales.

2. By the time we finished building, we had hand-lashed 1600 joints into *Brendan*'s framework and used nearly two miles of leather thong to do so.

2.

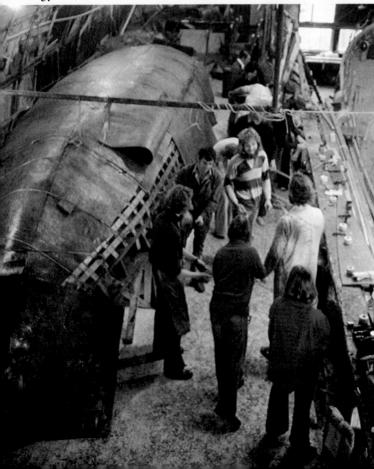

3.

3. John O'Connell watches me stitch together two of the 49 oxhides used to cover *Brendan*'s frame. George Molony, sailing master, is to the right. If a stitch was done wrong, O'Connell was merciless. "Rip it, rip it!" he would say. One slash would sever an entire day's labor.

4. Students of saddlery volunteered to come from London to Ireland to work on *Brendan* under O'Connell's supervision. Here they are getting their instructions. They chattered and joked; they worked superbly. And *Brendan* was built on schedule.

4.

5.　**6.**

5. A good-luck talisman, a bicentennial silver dollar, was set under the mainmast. Inside *Brendan*'s double gunwale, too, *Brendan* carried a phial of holy water as does every Dingle curragh, however small. **6.** The oxhides were too big (averaging 4 feet by 3½ feet) for one man to reach both sides. Looking as though he has been swallowed up by *Brendan*, John O'Connell stitches from the inside while George works from the outside. **7.** To protect thong, timber, and oxhide, we boiled up buckets of wool grease and painted it over the hull in a spattering mess. It looked and smelled abominable. On the afternoon we finished we went to the local pub to celebrate, and were promptly pursued by the landlord's dog.

7.

8. ▲9. ▼10.

8. A blustery January wind whips *Brendan*'s flags and pennants on launch day at the Crosshaven Boatyard.
9. First attempts at sail-handling on a medieval square-rigger prove exciting and difficult. **10.** Rowing home in the sunset after sailing trials on the River Shannon.
11. Skeptical Kerrymen look down on *Brendan* as she rests on the slipway the day before she sailed from Brandon Creek—by tradition the departure point of the saint. Most of the local people thought we were insane. Kerrymen are famous for mixing optimism and caution. One onlooker remarked, "Sure they'll make it—but they'll need a miracle." **12.** "Give way together!" I called and *Brendan* turned and began to roll out of Brandon Creek. To starboard skittered a curragh, and I noticed that it boasted a tiny Irish tricolor tied to its prow. **13** (*next page*). *Brendan* on her 4500-mile odyssey to the New World.

12.

Brendan shot forward. The crew clung on, ropes burning their hands. *Brendan* whizzed forward and the far bank of the little lake loomed up. I leaned hard on the steering oar, and *Brendan* began to turn. But it was too late. With a splintering of dry stalks, we went hurtling spectacularly into the reed beds and found ourselves condemned to half an hour of prodding oars into the peat bottom to punt *Brendan* free.

A dozen times a day we crashed into the reeds, which served as handy buffers, and gradually we got to know the boat. *Brendan*, we discovered, had her limitations. With only four oarsmen on board she was too unwieldly to row against the wind, because her bows were blown downwind and we hadn't the strength to get her back on course. More ominous was the fact that when left to her own devices, *Brendan* lay broadside to the wind at a dangerously exposed angle. We dropped marker buoys in the lough, and by sailing between them learned that *Brendan* refused to go against the wind like an ordinary yacht. She pointed her bows bravely enough to the wind, but lacking a keel she slid sideways across the water like a tea tray. On the other hand she was far more stable than we had anticipated, and running with the wind astern she went famously. She twisted and turned at a touch of the great steering paddle so that I was reminded of surf boats.

This was how *Brendan* would be at sea, a one-way exhilarating ride with the wind on the stern. A pair of ash shovel handles extended the breadth of our main crossyard so we could carry more sail; and after a day on which it snowed, we rigged the two tent structures that would give us shelter on the voyage. We practiced hauling *Brendan* up onto the bank, and we covered her with a thick layer of wool grease like a long-distance swimmer. And always we watched the leather hull for signs of leaks. We knew that 30,000 stitches pierced the hull, most of them made by amateur leather-workers. Any of them could leak with dire results. At first the water did trickle in, perhaps ten gallons a day, but then the trickles gradually slowed to half the rate and we found it scarcely necessary to bail *Brendan* unless it had rained.

When we were sufficiently confident, we took *Brendan* back down to the coast and tried sailing her in the estuary where I had first tested *Finnbarr*. Sometimes we were dispirited; sometimes we were greatly heartened. Once again we found it was impossible to row against the wind, and spent one dreary and uncomfortable night bottled up in a bay, anchored just out of reach of the surf that creamed and roared past us onto the beach. On another day we tried capsizing the *Brendan,* and found that she floated like an upturned whale, virtually impossible to turn the right way up. So we placed inside her some blocks of buoyancy so that we could spin the boat the right way up. In this state, when totally swamped, we learned that five of us using buckets could bail her dry inside ten minutes.

In Saint Brendan's *Navigatio* it had been written that the monks "got iron tools and constructed a light boat ribbed with wood and with a wooden frame, as is usual in those parts. They covered it with oxhides tanned with the bark of oak and smeared all the joints of the hides on the outside with fat. Into the boat they carried hides for making two other boats, supplies for forty days, fat for preparing hides to cover the boat, and other things needed for human life. They also placed a mast in the middle of the boat and requirements for steering a boat. Then Saint Brendan ordered his brothers in the name of the Father, Son, and Holy Spirit to enter the boat."

In the twentieth century it had taken nearly three years of work and research to reach the same point. Now, like the original monks, it was time to put to sea to look for our way to the Promised Land.

4

Departure

Yellow and brown, *Brendan* lay at the head of Brandon Creek on
Saint Brendan's feast day. Bright yellow tarpaulins had been
stretched over bow and stern to make her easier to locate if a
search-and-rescue mission had to be mounted to save her, as some
Cassandras prophesied. "They'll need a miracle if they hope to
cross the Atlantic in that—more than Saint Brendan ever did!" was
how one spectator put it.

But we weren't going anywhere that particular day. Although it
was May 16 and the day I had scheduled for our departure, a
full-blown gale was raging. The rain was sheeting down, and the
wind buffeted against the damp cliffs of the creek. In the open
Atlantic, outside, the surface of the sea was torn to smoke as the
squalls rushed across it. The crew and I stood dejected and
dripping around *Brendan* where she lay dragged up on the landing
slip. The boat was in chaos. It had been a hectic, last-minute flurry
to get her into position. In theory, at least, we had a stowage plan
for *Brendan* to help us find room for enough stores, water, and
equipment for five men. But there had been no time to stow
anything properly. Everything lay higgledy-piggledy, tossed in the
bottom of the boat—kit bags, torches, food, first-aid kit, the
hurricane lamp, even the ship's bell, which looked like a large
Swiss cowbell but was in fact a copy of the chapel bells that in
Saint Brendan's day had hung outside the monks' oratories and
called their congregations to prayer. How much easier it had been,
I thought to myself, for Saint Brendan and his monks all those

years ago. They would have simply put to sea with spare leather and currying fat; the woollen clothes they used for everyday wear, especially the hooded gowns of heavy wool; a supply of water in leather flasks; wooden dippers for bailers; dried meat, cereals, and roots for their food; and—most important—a sublime faith that God would take care of them.

They were men accustomed to extraordinary hardship. From the other side of the Dingle Peninsula one could see the twin pinnacles of the Skellig Islands, thrusting out of the Atlantic. Out there it was so exposed that spray from the waves broke the lighthouse windows four hundred feet above the surface of the water. Yet, in Saint Brendan's day, a community of monks chose to live on those bleak rocks. With devoted labor they had cleared a ledge and built six beehive huts and two oratories of rough stone. Here they had lived huddled together in Christianity's most lonely outpost. Flailed by the great winds of winter and early spring, they were cut off from contact with the mainland when no skin boat, however skillfully handled, could have reached them. Yet somehow they survived, and clung as stubbornly to their faith as their hemispherical homes clung like housemartins' nests to the rock. They were so constant and so isolated that long after the Church calendar was amended, the monks of the Skelligs still celebrated Easter on its original date.

To try to emulate such hardy men would prove little. They had shown their fortitude for all history to see; and now for *Brendan*'s crew to set out wearing medieval clothing or eating a medieval diet would teach us nothing new. It would only make our modern task more difficult and uncomfortable. We were embarking on the Brendan Voyage not to prove ourselves, but to prove the boat. *Brendan* was what mattered. No wonder I envied the monks their simplicity. They had not worried where to stow camera equipment so that it kept dry, nor how to find space for the pair of twelve-volt car batteries that powered our small radio telephone. As for the radio itself, it was still in its carton. The radio had arrived so recently that there was no time to unpack it, let alone install or test it properly. Like many other items of our equipment, our radio was an unknown quantity. Radio manufacturer after manufacturer had been approached for help in supplying a suitable set, but most of them were appalled at the thought of exposing their radios to conditions in an open boat. Even the makers of military radio sets designed to be dropped by parachute had doubted if their equipment would survive aboard *Brendan.* Only at the very last minute was a set offered.

The rest of our equipment was relatively basic. We had a life raft and a box of distress flares, jerry cans of water and paraffin, a small radio direction finder, a sextant and tables, and a bundle of charts. Most of our drinking water was stored in soft rubber tubes—the modern equivalent of the leather flasks of the monks— tucked under the slatted floor of the boat where it would also serve as ballast. Our food was packed in plastic bags, one bag to be opened each day and, if my calculations were correct, containing sufficient food for five men for twenty-four hours. The food itself was a gourmet's nightmare. There were the usual tins of meat and fish and baked beans; packets of dried soups and vegetables; dried fruit and bars of chocolate; and an apparently endless supply of Scots oatmeal cake, which I hoped would prove a substitute for bread. On our past record, George and I doubted if we would catch many fish to supplement our diet, and looking at all those dehydrated packet foods, I had a premonition that all would not be well. Everything seemed to be plastic. More than half the items were wrapped in plastic or came in plastic tubs, and we had spent a hectic day wrapping every item in a second plastic bag before sealing the full day's rations in an even larger plastic bag. Our food looked and smelled of plastic and—as it turned out—soon began to taste of plastic, too.

Brendan's monks had probably cooked on a peat or wood fire kept burning in a fire tray or in a cauldron, which could also be carried ashore. And, of course, they were accustomed to eating cold food. On the other hand, I had placed great value on the morale-boosting effect of regular hot meals, and so had arranged for a traditional paraffin stove to be built into a cook box about the size of a footlocker. Its lid hinged back to serve as a windshield; two side flaps pulled up to give additional protection; and, best of all, the entire stove hung on gimbals. It was an ingenious device because the cook box could be lashed into position wherever we wanted it, and used in almost any weather.

There was one other item on the slipway in Brandon Creek that would have surprised a yachtsman but not a medieval monk. Alongside the boat lay a soggy heap of sheepskins, looking grubby and smelling strongly. I had read that polar explorers had found sheepskins excellent insulation when sleeping on the ice; and as they were a typical material from Saint Brendan's day I thought it worth trying them as sleeping mats inside the boat. As it turned out, the smell of sheepskin was to become the third member of our triumvirate of grease and leather and wool which was to pervade our lives for the entire voyage.

Galley

For our clothing I had selected modern sailing suits. Each member of the crew was color-coded so that our garments did not get muddled. George wore orange; I had yellow; and as befitted our most Irish crew member, Arthur Magan had chosen green. Arthur already had a nickname for the voyage—Boots—because on the day he first joined the project, he showed up wearing a pair of size 12 boots that would have done credit to an oversized cowboy. In fact, nearly everything about Arthur came in the larger sizes. He was burly and stood over six feet, with a shock of yellow hair that stuck out at all angles. He exuded a genial air of crumpled untidiness that somehow gave him the impression of a friendly young bear just emerged from hibernation. At twenty-three he was the youngest member of the crew—but also the strongest. When anything was jammed, a mast needed lifting, or a mooring warp had to be hauled right, it was Boots who was called on for the job. When he heard about *Brendan,* he had written me a letter which was a model of brevity:

Dear Tim,

I am writing to offer myself as a possible crew member. Mrs. Molony gave me your address. I was at school with George's brother.

I have been sailing since I was large enough to go near a boat. I have also spent several winter months recently fishing in trawlers in Icelandic waters.

I realise nothing can be gained by writing letters to each other. I am available at any time to come down and see you if you are interested.

Yours gratefully,
Arthur Magan

So I had invited him to come to Cork, and two days later he clumped into the boatyard in his size 12s, glanced briefly around the boat, mumbled his name, took off a battered tweed jacket that was a kaleidoscope of patches and mends, and began working alongside us.

Like his letter, Boots's sentences were brief. Bit by bit, I learned that his family lived near Dublin, that he had spent much of his childhood in Valentia near the Dingle, and could "sail a boat a bit." Later I would also discover that he was a magnet for the girls. Young ladies could not resist the challenge of trying to feed him, tidy him up, and generally take care of him. Boots, it seemed, was an ideal feminine project, but a hopeless one too. At landfall after landfall on the voyage he would be returned to *Brendan* by his latest girlfriend, despair mingling with sadness in her expression, as

[61]

before her very eyes he began to dissolve into his usual chaotic state the moment he stepped aboard. And as likely as not, we later discovered that he had left some of his clothing behind, and these would be sent ahead to be at our next port of call. Arthur himself took such matters in his stride. He never offered any information unasked; and he hadn't even told his family that he had been selected for the *Brendan* crew until one morning his father read in the newspaper that a certain "Boots" Magan was going on the voyage. "Do you know anyone called Boots?" he asked over the breakfast table. "Yes, me," was his son's brief reply.

That rainy morning in Brandon Creek Arthur's crumpled green sailing suit was topped off with—of all things—a battered Sherlock Holmes stalking cap, its ear flaps lustily blowing in the wind. "Hello, wearing your Deputy Dawg outfit today?" the inevitable wisecrack came from Peter Mullett, *Brendan*'s photographer, dressed in a bright red sailing suit that made him look more like a cardinal than the London sparrow he was. Born and reared in London, Peter had been a successful magazine photographer before he had become exasperated with city life, thrown up his job, and moved with Jill, his glamorous ex-model wife, and his son Joey to the west of Ireland. There he had bought a plot of land, built a small cottage with his own hands and to his own design, and settled down to live as simply as possible. Then he too had heard about *Brendan,* and impressed me by arriving at the boatyard with a large suitcase. "Have you brought your cameras with you?" I asked him. "Yes," he replied, and opened the case. It was divided down the middle by a partition. On one side a complete professional's array of camera bodies, lenses, and sundry equipment lay neatly cradled in foam padding. But what caught my eye was the opposite half of the case. There was a comprehensive and well-used carpentry kit— complete with saws, draw knives, spoke shaves, drills, planers, and all the tools of a professional woodworker. *Brendan,* I thought to myself, was not just getting a photographer but, equally valuable, a man who could mend her wooden frame en route.

Rolf Hansen in his Norwegian blue sailing suit was the fifth and last member of the crew to join. He had come from Norway to volunteer, and was an old-boat fanatic. His hobby was interviewing retired fishermen in remote Norwegian coastal villages to collect their reminiscences about the days of sail. Short, barrel-chested, and bespectacled, Rolf was second only to Boots in physical strength; and like the Irishman, he was a man of few words, partly because he spoke only a smattering of English, but also because Rolf regarded seafaring as a serious business. When someone ventured to ask him if he was married, Rolf answered very seriously, "I am married to the sea."

So an Irishman, a Cockney, a Norwegian, and an Englishman had joined *Brendan,* and I wondered how well we would get along together during the days that undoubtedly lay ahead. We were attempting a voyage which differed in two important respects from many previous voyages in reconstructed historic vessels. First, we were embarking in a true boat, not a raft. *Brendan* was not simply a platform on which the winds and currents might carry us to our destination if we were lucky. She would have to be sailed properly if she were to survive, and there was little margin for error. A single mistake—a rope jammed around a cleat in a squall, or a sail suddenly blown hard against the mast—could capsize her with disastrous results. Second, and more important, we were about to venture into cold waters where few modern yachts cared to go. This was not to be a sun-drenched cruise in bathing suits. We were about to take a very small, open boat into sub-Arctic conditions, where we would have to be muffled in heavy clothing for weeks on end, frequently soaked by rain and spray, and according to the Royal Navy survival experts who had drilled us in safety procedures, if anyone fell overboard incorrectly dressed, he would be dead within five minutes.

Fortunately, the bad weather on Saint Brendan's day had not discouraged our friends. Many of those who had helped us came to the Dingle Peninsula to see us off, and held a farewell party at the nearby hotel with a conviviality that only the Irish could manage. Whiskey and stout were consumed in vast amounts; lively conversation culminated with an Irish public relations man, sent to calm proceedings, offering to fight all our critics; and at the right moment the roof of the bar sprung a massive leak under the weight of collected rainwater and deluged the guests.

"Why do you want to go on this voyage?" a reporter asked each crew member in turn.

"Because I enjoy sailing and want to learn how to handle this type of boat," answered George.

[63]

"It's a challenge," said Peter.

"Because I love the sea," was Rolf's answer.

"For the crack. For the fun of it," grunted Arthur, taking a long pull at his pint of stout.

"What about your wives? What do they think of your going off into the Atlantic like this?"

Jill Mullett looked at her husband. "You can't stop Peter from doing what he wants to do," she said. "Besides, it's time he had another project to occupy him."

Judith, George's wife, agreed. "I think George ought to do what he wants to do. Besides, I hope to be seeing him when *Brendan* gets to Iceland."

My wife managed to pass off the question. "Tim's always doing this sort of project," she told the journalist with a smile, "and after all, I'm a medievalist, and so I approve of anything that is good for medieval studies."

Then came the inevitable question. "Aren't you worried?" The three wives looked at one another. "No," they replied firmly.

May 17 dawned fine, with high clouds chasing across the sky and thunderheads lurking on the horizon. The swell left by the gale was heaving into the Creek as I went up to one of the two cottages at the top of the road to consult Tom Leahy who lived there and kept a curragh in the Creek. Tom was another of the breed of craggy raw-boned Dingle men, tall and soft-spoken. "You go back to the hotel and get some rest," he had told me the previous evening. "You'll be needing it. Don't worry about the boat. I and my son will keep an eye on her for you, and see that she is all right. No one can come past us without our hearing them." And he had been as good as his word. In the small hours of the morning, when I had come down to check that all was well on *Brendan,* I found the silent figure of Tom Leahy, leaning like a black shadow against the wall that rimmed the Creek, gazing out over the boat. I thanked him for his help. "There were some children scrambling down there this evening," he told me. "But they're local lads and they wouldn't take anything." Indeed, the honesty of the country children was such that although they had explored inside and out of the *Brendan,* and fingered its child's treasure-trove of torches, knives,

[64]

bars of chocolate and other delectables, not one single item had been filched.

Now, looking at the tide sucking past the mouth of the Creek, I asked Tom for his advice.

"Would you say that we could sail today?"

He looked at me steadily. "Wait till the tide turns," he advised. "You should have a few hours, two or three at the most, in which to get clear. And I wouldn't leave it any longer."

"Why not, Tom?"

"I don't like the look of the weather. We're in for some rain and wind, and if the wind swings round to the northwest it'll bring a heavy sea into the Creek. You'll be trapped there, and I wouldn't answer for the safety of your boat. The surge could break her to pieces."

"All right, Tom. Then we'll leave when the tide floats *Brendan* off the slipway. Will you be escorting us out?"

"Of course, and the prayers of my family and I will go with you," he said.

It was Tom's curragh that I had first seen at Brandon Creek so many months ago when I originally visited the area, and I remembered that Tom was the last man regularly working a curragh out of Brandon Creek. Somehow I thought it fitting that the last descendant of a tradition that stretched back for a millennium should see us on our way.

All that morning the local people began to filter down to the Creek. Farmers arrived with their families clinging to muddy tractors. Holidaymakers—for the Dingle is a favorite holiday area—came in cars. Students arrived on foot, and there were many who came on bicycles. A pair of local policemen drove up looking very self-conscious in a smart blue patrol car. Officially they were there to control the crowd, but they were far more interested in peering into *Brendan* with the other sightseers. A small group of priests settled themselves comfortably on the upper wall, and called out their blessings. Down on the quay, an old woman pushed forward from the crowd and thrust a small bottle of holy water into my hand. "God bless you all, and bring you safe to America," she said. "We'll pray for you each day," chorused some nuns. I tucked the bottle of holy water safely inside the double gunwale in exactly

[65]

the same place where every Dingle curragh, however small, still carries its phial of holy water. John O'Connell had given each of us a small religious motif to carry with us. He was looking strained with worry and tension. So too were the wives and families. "Look after our son," said Arthur's father to me. Rolf stepped ashore from Tom Leahy's curragh. He hadn't been able to resist a chance to go for a spin in this rare breed of boat. It was high time we were gone.

"Come on!" I called to the crowd. "Give us a hand to push her off the slip." There was a confused blur of faces, of hands and shoulders pushing at the brown leather hull, and with a soft slithering groan *Brendan* floated off the slipway and rode to an anchor in the middle of the narrow cleft.

"Goodybye, Daddy." I heard Ida's small voice clearly across the water. Fortunately, she and Joey Mullett were having such a good time together that they regarded the departure as a game.

"Time to put up the flags," I called to George, and he hoisted them to the mainmast. They flew in the order of the countries we intended to visit: the tricolor of Ireland, the Union flag for Northern Ireland; Saint Andrew's Cross for Scotland; the flag of Faroes; the flag of Iceland; the Danish flag for Greenland; then the Canadian Maple Leaf; and finally the Stars and Stripes. At the peak, on its own, flew the twin-tailed Brendan Banner, red cross on white.

There was so much to do at the last minute there was no time to be worried or nervous. All of us wanted to be on our way out to sea. Inevitably there was a last-minute hitch: the anchor jammed under a rock. Boots gave it a mighty heave, but it would not come free. A fishing launch maneuvered up. "Throw us the line. We'll pull it on a drum!" came a shout. Their winch took up the slack, the anchor came clear, and *Brendan* was free.

As if on cue, the wind died away almost completely. I took the helm, while George and the others settled themselves to the oars. "Give way, together!" I called, and *Brendan* turned and began to roll out of Brandon Creek into the Atlantic. Deep-laden and sluggish, we began to push against the swells heaving into the entrance. "This is like rowing a supertanker with a ball-point pen," grunted George, glancing along the slim blade of his oar. On either side of us skittered a curragh. Tom Leahy was in one of them, and I

BRENDAN

noticed that each boat boasted a tiny Irish tricolor jauntily tied to its prow.

The crowd waved and shouted good wishes; and then, as we cleared the mouth of the Creek and passed the cliffs rising on each side, I turned back and saw a sight that etched itself indelibly into my mind: two hundred or more people were scrambling and scurrying to the headland for a final view. The sight had a dreamlike quality, for the sun was in the far west and the flat light picked up the silhouettes of the people along the crest of the hill like a frieze. Their figures were very tiny and very black, cut out like a trail of disciplined insects, all clambering and hurrying in one direction and with one intent toward the farthest tip of the cliff. From there they could see us disappearing smaller and smaller into the ocean. Never before had I witnessed such an air of determination, and I felt awed that it reminded me of the pilgrims who climbed to the peak of Mount Brandon each year to celebrate mass in honor of their patron saint. So many people had helped us, so many people had shown confidence in us, I thought, that we could not let them down.

As soon as we were well clear of the entrance and there was no longer any risk of the tide setting us down on the nearest headland, I ordered our sails to be raised. The wind was from the southwest, fair for our passage along the Irish coast. The Celtic crosses on *Brendan*'s sails filled out, and soon we began to gather speed. We pulled aboard the unwieldly oars, and made fast all the loose items in the boat as *Brendan* began to settle down on her course. Tom Leahy waved goodbye; the two escorting curraghs turned back and soon were no more than specks rowing back into the mouth of Brandon Creek, dropping out of sight into each wave trough. We were finally on our way.

5
Gaeltacht

Beneath us *Brendan* rose and sank on each wave crest with a motion that managed to be both ponderous and sensitive at the same time. Very slightly, the hull bent and straightened to the changing pressures of the waves, and the masts creaked in sympathy against the thwarts. Aft, at the steering position, the massive four-inch shaft of the steering paddle nuzzled gently against the cross piece of an H-shaped frame that held the paddle in place. Every now and again the shaft dropped back into the crotch with a dull thump that could be felt as a quiver along the length of the hull. But apart from this sound, the boat was remarkably quiet. The leather skin seemed to muffle the usual slap of the wavelets against the hull, and the thong-tied frame damped out the customary tremors of a stiff-hulled sailing boat. The result was a curiously disembodied feeling, a sense of being a part of the sea's motion, moulding to the waves.

This sensation was enhanced by the way *Brendan* lay low in the water. The surface of the sea came within sixteen inches of her gunwale so that even a modest wave loomed over her. But as each wave advanced, *Brendan* canted her hull slowly and deliberately, and the wave slid underneath harmlessly. The up-and-down movement was disconcerting. First Arthur, then Peter began to turn slightly green with seasickness. It was no good advising them to breathe fresh air, for the whole boat was virtually open to the winds. The only remedy was to try to distract oneself by tackling the various tasks that had to be done. There were ropes to coil and stow; halliards and sheets had to be rearranged so that they did not tangle one another. In the waist of the boat there was such a clutter of jerry cans and food bags that it was impossible to find a place to put one's feet without the risk of twisting an ankle. We stored each item to make the best use of space, lashed down the water cans, arranged the oars neatly along the center of the boat, and made sure that the anchor was ready on top of the pile.

These chores helped to keep our minds occupied in the first, strange hours of the voyage. There was very little conversation. Each man was wrapped in his own thoughts, thinking of the days and weeks that lay ahead of us, all to be spent in the cramped conditions of our little vessel. I, for one, was acutely aware that many of the tiny decisions taken now—where, for example, to stow the binoculars, or how to fold the sheepskins—were very likely to become adopted as standard practice for the rest of the voyage. The human mind prefers order and seeks routine, and once such decisions are made they often become permanent arrangements. None of us, I fancy, cared to think too much about our main purpose in the voyage. That was a luxury reserved for the future, a mental excursion to indulge in during the long periods of tedium which characterize any small-boat trip. For the moment it was enough for us that the leather sails were filling and pulling *Brendan* along, and that the grey Atlantic lay all around.

But we had to do something about our sleeping arrangements. There was simply too much gear in both the forward and central shelters to allow anyone to lie down properly and rest. Arthur and Rolf occupied the two spaces forward, one each side of the foremast, where they lay on the duckboards under the thwarts. There it was impossible to sit up quickly and it required some wriggling to get under the thwarts, but at least our two "gorillas," as we cheerfully called the muscle squad, had room to stretch out full length, and stow their gear by lashing it with thongs to the inside of the curve of the hull. Boots and Rolf retaliated by calling the center shelter "the girls' room," and jeered as George, Peter, and I burrowed like moles into the mess, trying to sort out the equipment and find space to lie down. We soon discovered that it was an impossible task. There was simply not enough room for three men and all the equipment.

"Either we've got to find some space for this extra gear or we'll have to dump it overboard," I said, looking doubtfully at the unruly heap.

"Let's chuck out some of the aft buoyancy and use the space for our gear," suggested George.

"Okay, but don't put anything too heavy back there, otherwise the stern will be weighed down, and *Brendan* won't rise to the waves in an emergency. We want to try to keep the weight in the center of the boat, and let the banana ends lift with the seas."

"Right, give us a hand," said George briskly, and began pulling down the light bulkhead just behind the steersman's position. On the far side were blocks of buoyancy foam we had fitted in case *Brendan* was swamped. Ruthlessly George hauled out the first large block and threw it overboard, where it went bobbing off in our wake. "Still not enough," he announced. A rasping sound, and another block went floating off. "Almost enough. Pass me the saw, please," and in a few seconds he was furiously cutting out an even larger hole. Meanwhile I gathered up every item that I hoped we wouldn't be needing for some time: charts and pilot books for the Faroes and Iceland, spare parts for the cooker and lamp. They were all stuffed away in the new space. I looked at the sextant. Why bother to have a sextant when we were still near land. The Irish monks hadn't needed them. The sextant, too, was hidden away.

Next we tackled the jumble inside the cabin. The shelter measured six feet by six feet, no larger than a big double bed. Somehow we had to find enough room for three people to sleep, plus their clothing, a radio telephone, all Peter's camera gear, and my own navigation equipment. The crush was horrible. The radio was put on a makeshift shelf, and we heaped our kit bags to form a partition running down the length of the shelter. This partition divided off one third of the shelter and it was my privilege as skipper to sleep in the space behind the wall. It was no more than a trough, so that even my thin shoulders did not fit broadside, and it was easier to sleep on my side with my head under a thwart and my feet pressed against the far end of the shelter. Even so, I was luckier than George and Peter. They had to share the remaining two thirds of the space, without the benefit of a partition to keep them apart. Whenever George turned over in his sleeping bag, he could not help kicking Peter; and if Peter had to climb out of the shelter to go on watch, it was almost impossible to avoid treading on George. To make matters worse, we were so heavily dressed in sweaters and oilskins and heavy clothing that we were dreadfully clumsy. We made it a rule that sea-boots should on no account be brought into the shelter, but the penalty was that our sea-boots, even if they were left upside down in the cockpit, invariably filled up with water, so putting on a clammy boot became the first step to going on watch.

We split the watches into two-hour shifts, with two men on duty in each watch. With only five men on board this meant that each person had to do four hours on duty, followed by only six hours of rest. As *Brendan* did not steer herself, she always needed a helmsman in charge and this placed a great strain on us all. But luckily we soon discovered that the second watchman could stay on standby, out of the wind and rain, provided he was ready for an emergency. So as each helmsman finished his two hours, he would hand over to his relief man, and wake up the next watch-keeper, who would don oilskins, move to the cockpit, and curl up on the floorboards ready to help the helmsman or take over when his two hours had passed.

That first night we slept only fitfully in the strangeness of our new surroundings. Only Rolf seemed utterly oblivious to the change. He crawled into his sleeping bag and dropped off to sleep, content to be back at sea. Meanwhile *Brendan* plodded steadily northward. It was a very black night, with increasing cloud and several heavy rain showers. The rain was the worst nuisance. Even more than the spray, the rainwater seeped through the chinks in our defenses. Puddles of water collected on the stores in the waist of the boat; rain dripped down the helmsman's arm as he stood holding the cross piece on the steering paddle; and the rain saturated the sheepskins which we had left on the rowing thwarts. The sheepskins became wet and soggy, and squeezed like sponges when you sat on them. The rain had also soaked into the sails, which absorbed so much water that they doubled in weight. They

still worked properly, but in the dawn light George pointed to the main mast.

"Tim, I don't like the way the mast's bending under the weight of the sail," he said. "I think it could easily snap in a gust."

"The ash ought to be strong enough," I replied. "That timber should almost bend like a fishing rod before it goes."

"Yes, but look what it's doing to the thwart and to where it rests in the mast block," George warned. Together we inspected the area where the lower part of the mast fitted into a recess in the thwart and its foot rested on a block of oak in the bottom of the boat. "Look, as it rocks, the mast is sawing away at the thwart. It's going to chafe away the side pieces. If that happens, then the mast will come adrift. We could lose it overboard in a squall."

I agreed. We had to reduce the pressure of the wet sails before they broke the masts. So we lowered the sails a couple of feet, and fastened leather thongs to their lower edges, tying them down so that they did not swing so much to the roll of the boat. The situation improved, but the masts still swayed and bent alarmingly.

By now it was breakfast time, and we rigged up the stove to brew coffee. We had agreed that each man should cook one meal, turn and turn about, so that we would spread the burden of cooking and no one could complain of the cuisine, as we should have to suffer everyone else's cooking. But like many seemingly good ideas, this was another scheme that failed the test of time—in this case surprisingly quickly. I cooked the breakfast. Then George, who freely admitted to being the world's worst cook but is among its champion dishwashers, offered to do the dishes on my turn if I did his cooking for him. So I cooked lunch. Then Rolf cooked supper, or rather the stove nearly cooked Rolf. The paraffin stove needed careful adjustment, and Rolf's efforts became a rapid alternation of striking matches, clouds of dense smoke, and sudden bursts of flame that singed his hands and covered everything with soot. Rolf persevered until the box of matches ran out, and then as everyone else was getting hungry, I cooked supper. Peter's turn was not too bad, but his stew of vegetables was so anonymous that no one could identify the ingredients. Then came Arthur's turn. He rummaged in the day's ration bag, pulled out a packet of instant mashed potato, and looked more than ever like a seasick and crumpled young bear, inquiring: "Now, you must tell me how I cook this." From beside me, Peter let out a theatrical groan. "I'll tell you something better," he said. "Why don't we make Skipper do the cooking?" and so that was that, at least for the time being.

Unavoidably our first few meals were flavored with wool grease. We had cheerfully painted a new coat of grease on the leather hull just before we launched it, and splattered the grease heedlessly. Now we regretted it. We found ourselves sticking to stray blobs of wool grease everywhere—on the thwarts, ropes, on the stove; and of course it crept onto our knives and forks, canteens and cups. Everything we touched and tasted had the stickiness and smell of grease until the surplus finally rubbed off. Only *Brendan*'s liquor store avoided the curse. The number and variety of bottles that had been presented to us just before we sailed was legion. It seemed that our well-wishers were determined to send us off in an alcoholic stupor. Every time *Brendan* rolled, she clinked. There were bottles of whiskey and Irish stout, Norwegian aquavit for Rolf, and even a ferocious-looking brew, presented by a friendly Icelander, of a tipple called The Black Death. But pride of place went to our keg, especially made for *Brendan* by the Irish Distillers, which contained two gallons of superb malt whiskey. As soon as we had settled down and cleared the boat, we broached this keg, lifted our tin mugs, and toasted "Saint Brendan and the Voyage!"

We were making satisfactory progress. During the first full day's sailing, *Brendan* moved stolidly northward. Astern of us, between the rain showers, we could glimpse the peak of Mount Brandon steadily sinking lower and lower on the horizon. To starboard we passed the mouth of the Shannon, whose estuary was the last safe haven for about forty miles. Navigating *Brendan* along this lee shore was really only a matter of identifying each port of refuge in case a gale blew us down on the coast. In the mouth of the Shannon I had marked down Scattery Island as a possibility. In the days of the monks Scattery had been a landmark for the curraghs, a very holy place, for it was here, according to repute, that Saint Senan, the contemporary of Saint Brendan, had defeated the monster Cata and founded his monastery on the island in the first half of the sixth century. Today its most evocative relic is the

[75]

stump of a round tower, perhaps erected by the monks as a place of refuge when the Vikings came raiding the coast. And until recently the local fishermen, when they launched a new boat, sailed her "sunwise" around the island to bring the new vessel good luck and carried to sea a pebble from Scattery Island as a talisman.

I had hoped that *Brendan* on her first run could sail clear of the great finger of Slyne Head which points out into the Atlantic from the west coast and formed the first turning point of our coastal passage. But it was not to be. The wind gradually moved into the west, and blew us down on the coast. For every ten miles *Brendan* sailed forward, she lost a mile slipping sideways across the surface of the water. The darkness of our second night at sea closed in on us as *Brendan* plodded forward with so little fuss that she actually ran down a gannet sleeping on the water. The bird was not awakened until the bow actually touched, and the poor creature was tipped upside down in the water. There was a startled squawk, followed by much thrashing and flapping and an irate-looking gannet eventually surfaced in our wake, grumbling with vexation before it flew off to less disturbed waters. Dawn was slow in breaking, its light shrouded by mist that reduced visibility to less than a mile. Then rocks loomed up ahead, a group of isolated reefs with the swell breaking in a wide ring around them. A glance at the chart confirmed that they were the Skird Rocks, well inside Slyne Head, and that *Brendan* could not possibly get around the headland until we had a fair wind. So I changed course, and *Brendan* bore away to find shelter in the Aran Islands. I was not downcast. In thirty-six hours we had come over a hundred miles, and what better landfall than the Aran Islands—which, according to the *Navigatio*, had been the place where Saint Brendan came to discuss his idea for a voyage to the Promised Land with his mentor Saint Enda the great teacher-saint.

As the mist broke up before the morning sun, the Aran Islands themselves appeared. *Brendan* came sailing in past their northwest tip, and we saw first the lighthouse, then the high line of the land itself with its green patchwork of fields sloping down to limestone screes that dipped into the sea. George was steering to take best advantage of the wind, and we hugged the coast as closely as we dared. We could see only one or two farmhouses, standing by

[76]

themselves, and could just distinguish the figure of a man going to work in a field. What would he think, I wondered, if he looked out to sea and saw a sight which harked back a thousand years—an ocean-going curragh coming in from the Atlantic, a small black curve against the glittering surface of the ocean, and the distinctive black squares of medieval sails? As we drew in behind the island, we glimpsed a small black speck bobbing about in the waves. At first sight it looked like a channel marker buoy. "I think that's a curragh," I called to George, and he altered course to investigate. A few minutes later we could pick out the outlines of two men in the boat. They were hauling lobster pots, but the moment they noticed us, they left their work. They bent to their sculls, and sent their curragh racing toward us. Their teamwork was superb. The two oarsmen rowed in perfect unison. If one man took a half stroke, so did the other without even watching his companion's sculls. Their curragh was not like the Dingle boats, but of the typical Aran type with the stern cut off square. Yet the difference did not seem to affect the sea handling. The two fishermen brought their curragh to within five yards, neatly spun her, and kept pace with *Brendan,* gazing at us. One of them had a fiery red bush of curly hair and a splendid beard to match. "Are you the crowd for America?" he called out. He had a strong accent, for Irish is the language of the Aran Islands. "Welcome to the islands."

"Thank you very much."

"Would you like some crab?"

"Yes, please!"

A hail of crabs flew in an arc from the curragh to *Brendan,* and Rolf scrambled about the boat trying to seize them before they scuttled into the bilges.

"Thank you. Thank you very much," I called. "Where's the best place to land?"

"Go into the bay. You'll be safe enough there. Just follow the line of our lobster pots, and turn in when you no longer see the lighthouse behind you. But don't turn before then, or you'll be on the bank." He meant the Brocklinbeg Bank, a hump of sand and rock lurking just below the surface. "Sea breaks heavily," said my navigation notes, and as we cautiously dropped sail and rowed into the bay we saw why: for five minutes the sea was calm, and

[77]

then—by some combination of wind and swell—the water gathered in a heap over the bank and burst upward in a leaping spout. It was no place for *Brendan*.

Brendan dropped anchor in a wide bay where there was a short pier for the curraghs to bring their lobster catch. We had landed on the largest of the three main Aran Islands, Inishmore. From the anchorage the ground sloped up, past a small sandy beach at the head of the bay, across a flat shelf of land, and then more steeply it rose to the crest of the hill. There the island ended abruptly, with steep cliffs falling sheer into deep water. It was as if the island had been titled on one edge for our inspection, and from sea level we could admire the pattern of hundreds upon hundreds of tiny fields whose loose stone walls divided up the land like a honeycomb. There are said to be more than 1850 miles of wall on the islands, and the honeycomb effect is all the more striking because the grey walls are not broken by gates. Instead the farmers pull down a section of the wall when they want to drive in cattle, and then build up the stones behind the animals.

That afternoon, after an enormous lunch of crab boiled in a bucket of sea water, we all went ashore and walked up toward the far crest. The sky had cleared, and in the tiny corrals of the fields the turf was sprinkled with thousands upon thousands of spring flowers—buttercups, violets, gentians, and others. We found a narrow track, a "boreen" between the walls, followed it past a cattle pond where a stream trickled into a collecting trough, and finally came out onto open land where the ground sloped steeply up toward the far ridge. Across the hillside the bones of the island lay exposed, enormous slabs of limestone that rain and wind had pockmarked and slashed with scars along the fault lines. These too were filled with wildflowers or little pools of rainwater. Here the stone walls of the small fields were more tumbled down, until suddenly the eye picked out a pattern, and we saw that we were walking through the concentric rings of stone ramparts that encircled the hilltop.

The boreen had turned into an ancient roadway which led straight to the last and most important rampart sitting upon the hill crest like a drum. In its side blazed the bright eye of a single entrance, the light pouring through it. This was the gateway to the fort of Dun Aengus, one of the most spectacular sites of prehistoric

Europe. Climbing through the eye of the gate, we came out onto the cleared space inside the rampart, and where the back wall should have been was only empty sky, for we had come to the very lip of the cliff at the far edge of the island. Edging cautiously forward, we poked out our heads over the abyss and looked straight down the cliffs, past the backs of the seabirds wheeling far below us; and to the surface of the ocean two hundred feet below, broken by huge chunks of rocks that had toppled from the cliff edge.

The great fort of Dun Aengus is one of several massive stone fortresses on the Aran Islands, built in the first centuries A.D. by Irish clans. They were constructed before Saint Enda settled his community of monks in modest stone cells down by the seashore, and began the monastic school that was to become one of the most famous and important in all Ireland. In a sense, the massive forts looming over the Christian cells represented another strand to Saint Brendan's quest for the western land, for they reached far back into a Celtic past. Among the old Celtic beliefs had been the ancient idea of a land that lay toward the sunset peopled by departed souls and strange creatures. This theme of the Other World occurred in the early poetry of the pagan Irish, whose bards described the journeys of famous heroes to this destination and their experiences there. Sometimes the hero traveled over the water in a magic chariot; or he dived beneath the waves and found a submarine world of beautiful maidens who wooed him; or occasionally he rode up into the sky to find this strange realm. Usually the Other World was described as a place that was mystical yet attainable. It lay within the grasp of specially fortunate mortals, and this theme passed easily enough to the Christians when Christianity was introduced to Ireland, because many of the Christian priests lived and worked alongside the older order of seers and sages, sometimes in conflict with them but also sharing knowledge with them. As a result the old idea of the Other World became entwined with the new religion, only given Christian garb. The Christians thought of the Other World as peopled with saints and holy men. It became a land promised by God to men of great virtue. Still attainable, it was a reward on earth, a target for men to explore. Even more important, the journey itself became an act of faith, so that the dangers of the venture only enhanced its appeal.

[79]

In short, Christian voyages to seek a far-off land gained their vital motive.

The Christian monks were well equipped to fit this notion of the distant land into a more accurate frame of geography. Irish monks gathered an incredible store of scholarship from all over western Europe. During the troubled fifth and sixth centuries many scholars came to Ireland from the upheavals of the Continent, bringing with them manuscripts and knowledge of the classical authors. Ireland became the grand repository for this intellectual treasure, and the Irish monks copied and codified this information. They wrote commentaries on it, and handed the knowledge on from one generation to the next. They read Virgil and Solinus and, in translation or original, had access to Greek authors. In their geographical concepts the monks understood that the world was round—"like a well-formed apple" was how it was sometimes put. They understood Ptolemy's concept of geography, and could read how the Romans had sent a fleet around Scotland and found islands lying to the north. The flowering of early Christian culture in Ireland, about which so much has been written, was a process that lasted almost five hundred years. Irish monks were acknowledged to be the best-educated and best-informed men in all of western Europe; and in due course they set out to carry their knowledge back into the mainland. They founded schools, advised kings and even emperors (Charlemagne was a great admirer of Irish learning) and established monasteries from Lombardy to Austria. They and their pupils were regarded as Europe's wandering intelligentsia. As a Frankish observer put it, "Almost all Ireland, despising the sea, is migrating to our shores with a flock of philosophers."

This vitality also produced Saint Brendan's *Navigatio.* Here was a story from the very core of Irish tradition, Christian in inspiration and composition, but drawing also upon the old Celtic heritage. Like the heroes of old, Saint Brendan was the hero who set out to find the Promised Land, and experienced many adventures on the way. Only now the saint traveled by a different route, not in a wave-riding chariot but in a prosaic vessel of skins stretched on wood. And now, instead of the imaginary islands of the Celtic heroes, the saint's itinerary could be based on the real geographical knowledge of the monks. Until recently the earliest surviving version of the story was thought to have been written down no earlier than the tenth century, four hundred years after Saint Brendan's death. But new investigations have suggested a date closer to the year 800, and naturally the date of the story's composition could go back even earlier.

I had met the scholar who, as much as anyone, had traced Brendan's *Navigatio* back deep into the golden age of Irish monastic achievement. Professor Jim Carney of the School of Celtic Studies was a brilliant light in the field of early Irish literature. He made sensitive translations of Irish and Latin poems, and his knowledge of the Irish literary background was outstanding. "Of course we don't yet know exactly when Brendan's *Navigatio* was first composed," he told me when we had met in the library of the Royal Irish Academy. "But I've actually come across a reference in a seventh-century Irish poem to the fact that Saint Brendan was known as a composer of poems. So maybe the *Navigatio* is very old."

"What do you think about the theory that the *Navigatio* isn't a Christian work at all, but merely a Christian gloss on an old and imaginary Celtic tale?"

"You mean that it's one of the Celtic voyage-tales, an *imram*. Well, I think it's been shown that most of the surviving *imrama* are either contemporary with Brendan's *Navigatio* or even later. In fact, instead of the *Navigatio* being a copy of them, I think in one case at least the *imram* has borrowed from the *Navigatio*. By the way, there's something about a Christian boat voyage in my book of early Irish poems I've translated. It's a poem dedicated to Saint Columbanus." He riffled through the pages until he found what he wanted, and began reading:

See, cut in woods, through flood of twin-horned Rhine,
Passes the keel, and greased, slips over seas—"Heave, men!"
And let resounding echo sound our "Heave."

With a snap he closed the book and glanced at me mischievously.

"Sounds as if your voyage will be hard work. But if there's any help on the literary side I can give you, let me know. And incidentally, why don't you tell Mairin O'Dalaigh about your plans? She may be able to help you on the linguistic side. She's an expert on the early Irish language."

"Where can I get in touch with her?"

"That shouldn't be too difficult. Try Aras an Uachtararn in Phoenix Park, the residence of the President of Ireland. She's his wife."

So I went up to the Presidential Lodge, set in the elegance of Phoenix Park, and was met on the steps by a jovial equerry. "Are you the madman who wants to sail round the world in a leather boat?" he hailed me. "Just as far as America will do nicely," I murmured. "Oh well, step this way. Mrs. O'Dalaigh has asked if you'd like to join her for tea."

Mairin O'Dalaigh was a most composed and elegant hostess, and we talked about the Brendan project until there was a knock at the door and the President himself came darting in. At once the tranquillity collapsed. President O'Dalaigh was, it turned out, a great supporter of the Gaeltacht, the Irish-speaking area of the west, and most enthusiastic for the Brendan project. He dashed to his bookshelves. "Have you seen this? Or this one?" he asked, pulling down one volume after another in rapid succession. "Ah! And here's another." Soon the floor, sofa, and chairs were covered with opened books as he scurried from one to the next. "And wait a minute, there's something I want to show you." He whisked me off to another wing of the building where the walls were hung with his collection of paintings. "Here we are." We stopped in front of a small painting. It was a picture of a curragh nestling in the cleft of some rocks. "Found that years ago," said the President. "I've always liked it very much indeed. Where do you think it was done—in Donegal, or in the Aran Islands perhaps?"

The memory of President O'Dalaigh's bubbling enthusiasm came back to me during *Brendan*'s stay in the Aran Islands. Everyone on Inishmore seemed equally determined to help us. It was as if the Brendan Voyage had struck a chord in the imaginations of the Irish-speaking peoples of the Gaeltacht, and they associated themselves with the project. *Brendan* was *their* boat. The curragh men came back twice more to present us with more crabs and lobster. The local wives took it in turns to bake us fresh scones, and when I made a phone call, the postmistress interrupted in order to wish us well in the venture.

A bush telegraph was also signaling *Brendan*'s passage along the Irish-speaking coast. Half an hour after we made landfall in Inishmore, there was scarcely an Aran islander who did not know we were there, and later I discovered that schoolchildren had been stationed on headlands all along the coast to look out for *Brendan* and report her progress. Nor was the help limited to the island. A newspaper paragraph mentioned that our radio was not yet installed, and next day a volunteer flew out to Inishmore and busily soldered connections and tested circuits. When I called up to test the radio, the operator at Valentia coast station spent hours patiently listening in to our signals. "What's your call sign?" he asked over the air. "We haven't got one," I replied. "In fact we never even had time to apply for a license."

"Never mind then. We'll call you up as *Yacht Brendan.* That should do."

"Let's make it *Curragh Brendan,*" I responded.

He laughed. "Yes, there won't be any other curraghs with a radio link. Report in daily if you can. Good luck."

Two days of bad weather held us in the Aran Islands, and then the wind eased enough to let *Brendan* slip out from Inishmore, and we headed across the sound for the mainland coast of County Mayo. I didn't want to risk the open sea, for the wind was blowing too strongly and we didn't know how *Brendan* would behave. We hoisted both our flax sails, and soon discovered that it was too much. The mainmast again bent alarmingly, and *Brendan* leaned over so far that I thought we would scoop water aboard. George called out to Rolf to ease away the mainsail, and he lowered the mainyard about three feet. The effect was immediate. *Brendan* came level; the mast straightened; and we ploughed briskly across the channel toward a line of small islands that extended from the shore. At the right moment the sails came tumbling down; *Brendan* rounded the outer reef, and we rowed our way into shelter and dropped anchor.

Brendan had picked our spot for us. Not half a mile away lay a small uninhabited island, which in the sixth century had been the home of Saint MacDara, "son of the fox." We could not have wished for a more perfect example of the chosen retreat of an early Christian monk. Its feeling of isolation was very strong. There was not a house nor a person in sight, and the sea teamed with wild life.

[83]

Where we anchored, a flock of terns was busily quarreling and diving for fish around the boat, quite unconcerned by our arrival. A pair of curious seals surfaced ten yards away and watched us calmly for two or three minutes before they too resumed fishing, and a patient row of cormorants sat on a half-submerged rock keeping an eye on the efforts of three Great Northern divers. In the air above Saint MacDara's Island hovered a mass of gulls, calling and wheeling; and when we landed on the island we found the reason: the place was a thriving gull colony. We picked our way carefully across the boulder-strewn turf to avoid stepping on the gulls' nests, usually containing three brown and black speckled eggs or an ungainly chick crouching in terror while its parents shrieked and mewed their agitation above us. The island had kept its feeling of lonely serenity. We walked the circuit around the stations of the pilgrimage made by faithful devotees who came out in boats on the Saint's day to make a circuit of the island and to pray in the simple grey stone chapel, one of the oldest in Ireland, with its curiously steep roof and one narrow window slit looking out toward the mainland. Near the strand, half sunk in the turf, stood a low stone cross, just like the crosses on *Brendan*'s sails, but no more than two feet high, and on the surface of the cross we could trace its pattern of intricate carving, still visible after a thousand years of wind and rain. As the sunlight faded, the crew of *Brendan* gathered on the rocks above our landing place and quietly watched the idyllic scene. The wind had died away completely; the place was calm and still. Even the gulls had ceased their calling. Silently, George pointed to the rocks beneath our feet. There, undisturbed, was the rarely seen, sleek form of a large otter, quietly fishing along the foreshore.

St. MacDara's Island made it easier to appreciate another strand that lay behind *Navigatio.* Many of the early Christian monks in Ireland had felt an overwhelming urge to seek solitude on the islands of the west coast, where they could contemplate and pray. They took their inspiration from the Desert Fathers of the Middle East, who had retreated into the deserts to serve God as ascetics. But of course Ireland offered no deserts for retreat, and so these hermits had found their isolated homes deep in the forest or on the islands in the sea. They coined a happy phrase for it: they sought, they said, "a desert in the ocean." In cases of extreme devotion some of these men pushed themselves out in small boats, deliberately threw away their oars and rudder, and let the wind blow them where God decreed. There, accepting divine intervention, they established themselves and led their lonely lives, relying upon divine providence to supply them with food, perhaps fish from the sea or, as on Saint MacDara's island, with a supply of gulls' eggs at hand. According to a nice story in Brendan's *Navigatio,* one hermit even depended upon fish brought to him daily by a friendly otter.

Full-fledged monasteries grew up on some islands, and Saint Brendan visited one of them during his long quest for the Promised Land. The *Navigatio* called the place Saint Ailbe's Island, and when the crew landed it said they were met on the beach by a dignified and white-haired old man who bowed to them, embraced each of the visitors, and taking Saint Brendan's hand led the newcomers to his monastery. At the gates Saint Brendan stopped and tried to find out the name of the abbot and where his monks came from. But the old man refused to answer, gesturing with his hand that he and his fellows observed the rule of silence. In a human touch, Saint Brendan, the *Navigatio* says, told his crew to hold their tongues and respect the rule of silence "or you will destroy the spirit of recollection of the monks here with your chatter." At that moment a party of monks arrived in procession bearing crosses and reliquaries, and greeted the visitors with psalms. Then the abbot himself, Saint Ailbe, came forward to invite the guests inside. Brendan and his crew shared a simple meal with the monks, sitting down at the table, each guest next to a monk, eating bread and root vegetables and drinking spring water in time to a bell struck by one of the monks, who was acting as servitor for the day. Later, the abbot showed Brendan around the monastery and took him into the chapel to show him its arrangement of altars, lamps, and a circle of chairs where the monks chanted their litany with the abbot. For more than eighty years, the abbot explained, his monastery had flourished. The only sound of human voices that was heard was the regular psalm-singing, and the monks lived entirely without outside contact.

Stripped of its embellishments, the *Navigatio*'s description of this island monastery is strikingly matter-of-fact. The only miracles are a flaming arrow which automatically lights the tapers, the unseen replenishment of their food supplies, and the longevity of the monks themselves. But even the latter is explained sensibly: their simple diet and contemplative way of life, the abbot explained to Brendan, had kept the monks in excellent health and prolonged their lives in their settlement.

The *Navigatio* does not give enough geographical details to pinpoint Saint Ailbe's Island accurately. It only says that the monastery lay two hundred yards from the only landing place on

Guillemots

the island and that there were two water sources nearby, one clear and one muddy. However, traces of stone-built island monasteries can still be seen on several islands off the west coast of Ireland, on Inishmurray, Tory Island, Inishkea, and Inishglora. The last is known to have been founded by Saint Brendan himself. Traces of Irish religious settlements have also been found in the Hebrides and in Orkney and Shetland, and suggested as far afield as Faroes—all on the Stepping Stone Route toward North America.

Any one of them could have been the monastery attributed to Saint Ailbe, but most important of all is that Brendan's *Navigatio* describes Saint Ailbe's community as a simple fact. It treats of the place, not as some extravaganza, but as a monastery very like the monasteries an Irish priest of the early Middle Ages would recognize as real.

Saint MacDara's Island was the last early Christian church that the modern *Brendan* was to visit in Ireland. Next morning we awoke to a fresh breeze from the south, and despite gale warnings on the radio, we weighed anchor and seized our chance to take the leather boat slanting away on a course which cleared the turning point at Slyne Head. For a few hours we made glorious progress, spinning along at above five knots with the land sliding past. We could not check our speed properly, for the log was malfunctioning. But we did not care. Our fishing lines caught a couple of mackerel which were soon in the frying pan, and also a greedy young seagull which we managed to release unharmed, though Rolf looked longingly at its wing feathers for pipe cleaners. Only Arthur was despondent, for he was still seasick, and the swell around Slyne Head did not help.

But then the weather deteriorated. We lost sight of the lighthouse on Slyne Head in the low clouds. Rain showers began sweeping regularly across us; and it grew colder. By evening we were in the grip of our first gale, and driving faster and faster out to sea. We dragged ropes behind us to slow ourselves down, and took turns to bail the water swirling in the bilges. At the scheduled time I switched on the radio transmitter and tried to get through to Valentia coast station. But I could hear nothing but the crackle of static. Severe electrical storms had broken contact, and on *Brendan* we could see the lightning flashes in the murk. It was useless to waste our battery power, so I switched off the radio; and to avoid tangling our trailing warps, George hauled in the log. Now *Brendan* was not only cut off, but we could not guess how far the storm was driving us out into the Atlantic.

For twenty-four hours *Brendan* ran before the gale. First Arthur and then Peter fell into a semicomatose state and lost all interest in their surroundings. Rolf, George, and I swallowed some hot sweet soup to keep up our strength, and privately I calculated how much drinking water we had on board. Our headlong flight into the open ocean was completely unplanned and we had no reserves of fresh water. If we were becalmed, or if the wind blew us too far from land, we would have to ration our supplies.

Then, after I had calculated that *Brendan* had been driven about a hundred miles off the coast, the wind eased and swung into the west, blowing *Brendan* back toward land and safety. On the afternoon of the second day we were able to cook ourselves a hot meal, and tidy up some of the mess in the cabin created by breaking waves and sodden clothing. As my fingers unthawed, I made notes in my diary about the lessons we had learned: in future, we should never set out to sea without a full water supply; every man needed extra socks and gloves to keep out the chill; our plastic food packs were unreliable, as far too many of our stores were now a soggy mess in the bottom of each packet. From some packets we poured a nauseating stew of sea water, mashed potato flakes, sauce, biscuit crumbs, and dehydrated vegetables. Equally worrying, every box of matches aboard had been ruined and not one lighter worked any longer. We were so worn out when we finally sighted Tory Island on the northwest corner of Ireland during the third night that we were glad when the wind died away to a calm. After half an hour's rowing, which seemed to get us nowhere, we curled up and rested our tired bodies, letting *Brendan* drift slowly down toward land on the tide and swell.

"Can you get out the medicine chest?" Peter woke me just after midnight. "My arm is killing me."

"What's the matter? Where's the pain?" I asked, struggling to sit up.

"I don't know. There's something wrong with my arm. At times it feels as if it's on fire, and sometimes it goes completely numb and I can't feel anything at all."

"You must have strained it when we were rowing," I said. "Here, take these two pain killers and try to relax as best you can. I'm afraid there's nothing we can do until we get enough wind to take us into the land. Then we can try and find a doctor for you."

Peter took the tablets and sat there, slumped miserably against the thwart. His face was ashen, and his eyelids drooped. An hour later he called to me again.

"It's no good. I'm afraid the pain's getting worse. It's spread to

[88]

the whole side of my chest, and I'm finding it very painful to breathe. Please get on the radio and call for help."

I looked at the chart. *Brendan* lay becalmed scarcely two miles from the coast of County Donegal, but we might as well have been a hundred miles away for any hope of getting Peter ashore quickly. We couldn't row *Brendan* against the tide, and Peter obviously needed medical attention. I switched on the radio.

"Malin Head Radio. Malin Head Radio. This is *Curragh Brendan* calling."

"*Curragh Brendan. Curragh Brendan.* Malin Head Radio here. Come in please."

"Malin Head. This is *Brendan.* We are off the Limeburner Rock and becalmed. I've got an injured crew member on board who needs to see a doctor. Can you arrange any help, please?"

Malin Head told me to stand by, and ten minutes later reported that he was sorry but there were no lifeboats available. "We could alert a ship," Malin Head offered.

"No, I think it would be more effective if we could get a local fishing boat to take the crew member off," I suggested.

"Will do, *Curragh Brendan.* Please watch this frequency."

Malin Head broke contact, and half an hour later called me back. "A local salmon boat is putting out from a village called Ballyhoorisky to pick up your crew member. Please show an identifying light. Good luck, *Curragh Brendan.* Out."

"Thank you, Malin Head. We'll let you know how we get on."

An hour afterward we picked out the lights of a small fishing boat coming toward us, and heard the rhythm of her engine. Then the boat closed on us, the engine cut, and across the calm we could hear the soft mutter of voices talking in Irish. A torch was switched on and I could make out the shapes of two men and a boy on board. "Here, catch this!" and a rope came flopping aboard. "We'll tow you in." The fishing boat engine started and we set off toward a seemingly rockbound stretch of coast. At the last moment when I thought we were about to go on the reefs, a spotlight lit up on the boat. Expertly handled, she slid into a tiny cove with *Brendan* behind her. "You'll be all right here," called a voice, and unseen hands moored *Brendan* alongside. Soon afterward the blue light of an ambulance came down the lonely road, and Peter was taken away. "Thank you so much," I said to the muffled figures of our rescuers who had been patiently waiting all this time. "It's nothing," said the older man. "Just you get some sleep now. Come up to the house in the morning and my wife will get you some breakfast." And as if rescuing a medieval skin boat happened every day, the fishermen calmly turned around and went up the track toward their home. So ends the first leg of the Brendan Voyage, I thought to myself. Historians say that medieval life was cramped, uncomfortable, and sometimes dangerous. They are right.

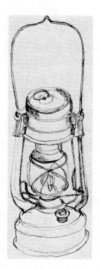

6
Hebrides

For two days we sheltered in Ballyhoorisky, to make and mend, and catch our breath. Our rescuers, the Freil family, epitomized the old saying that there is a brotherhood between all mariners. They fed us, washed our sea-stained clothing, gave us house room, and took me into the market town to buy provisions. There I met Peter, emerging from the hospital gate, looking downcast.

"What's the verdict?" I asked him.

"The doctors said I've strained the muscles down the left side of my chest, and I'll have to have two weeks' rest before I can go back on board."

"Well, that's not too bad. The rest of us can take *Brendan* up through the Hebrides by ourselves, and when you are rested, you can rejoin us in Stornoway or some other northern port, ready for the long hop to the Faroes."

Peter looked even more despondent. "It's no good, I'm afraid. The doctors also warned that the same trouble is likely to recur if I put any strain on the muscles, and if it does, it could be more serious. And the next time we may not be able to get me to a hospital."

This was a blow. In an emergency I needed every member of *Brendan*'s crew to be fit; and Peter was sensitive enough to admit that, once hurt, he would be reluctant to commit himself whole-heartedly for the rest of the voyage. Clearly it was a risk that neither Peter nor I could accept, and in the end there was really no

[91]

choice: Peter withdrew from the crew. Sadly he packed his bags and left us.

Luckily I had a temporary replacement for him in Wallace Clark, past Commodore of the Irish Cruising Club. Wallace had volunteered to help take *Brendan* across from Ireland to Scotland, and he lived only a few hours away from Ballyhoorisky. A quick telephone call, and Wallace duly reported for duty, clad in two pairs of vast woolly trousers, several sweaters, a disreputable stocking cap that would have done service as a pillow case, and a tentlike oilskin smock. In that outfit he even made Arthur look petite.

Meanwhile we profited from the lessons of the storm. First priority was to shift *Brendan's* water ballast farther forward so that her bow dipped down and gripped the water better, and her stern rose more quickly to the following seas. Then Rolf set about making some sense of the hugger-mugger mess of the cooking and eating area, just aft of the main shelter. Until now it had looked like a medieval midden. Every time anyone climbed toward the steering oar, a sea-boot squashed a mug or stepped into the sodden ingredients of the next meal. Now, with odd scraps of wood and string, Rolf ingeniously rigged up a food locker and a couple of shelves to keep our everyday supplies of tea, coffee, and sugar out of harm's way. He had to use string in place of nails or screws because *Brendan's* hull flexed so much that any rigid fastening would have snapped immediately.

On the afternoon tide of May 30 Dun Freil's boat *Realt Fanad*, the Star of Fanad, towed *Brendan* out to the area where they had rescued us, and cast off the line. Once again there was almost a flat calm, and once again *Brendan* hung motionless in the tide, waiting for a wind. But this time there was a completely different feeling on board. *Brendan's* crew was rested and fit, and we had given careful thought to our experiences in the storm. *Brendan* had survived a gale which would have broken and sunk a weaker boat. She had shown us convincingly that, given half a chance, she would carry us safely through high seas and heavy weather—and the result was a marked upsurge of confidence, both in ourselves and in the boat. *Brendan* was certainly not comfortable, and she was extraordinarily difficult to control. Indeed, with such a small crew it was rather like riding a balloon. Once you cast off in *Brendan*, you had to sail in the direction the wind and weather took you. The margin for correction was small, and if the wind turned foul, there was little one could do but hang on and hope. In short, I suspected, we were beginning to appreciate what it was like to have been a medieval sailor, cast out on the seas at the mercy of wind and weather and armed only with patience and faith.

The new spirit of confidence was infectious, and as soon as the wind picked up next morning to a good stiff breeze, George was all for testing *Brendan*'s new paces, now that we had shifted ballast. Under his expert eye, the slanting sails began to draw *Brendan* briskly across the wind. She was still skidding on the surface of the sea, so we could not claim to be sailing against the wind. But we were certainly making excellent progress, and, instead of running downwind away from the waves, we were sailing parallel to them and riding easily across their crests. All that day we managed to keep this course, ignoring the occasional wave which toppled and broke aboard as *Brendan* hurried northwest toward Scotland. It was a new sensation to be at the steering paddle and watch the water sliding briskly past the massive ash blade, and feel the boat responding to the fine adjustment on the helm. At last, I felt, *Brendan* was *sailing*. She was a little cumbersome, it was true, but she handled like a real boat.

Crash! My thoughts were briskly shattered, as the wooden crossyard carrying the mainsail broke free and came hurtling down with a thud, bringing down the mainsail in a flapping mess. The flax rope holding up the yard had snapped, and the entire contraption had come slicing down with its full weight. Had anyone been underneath, he would have been badly hurt. As it was, George promptly swarmed up the mast like a monkey on a stick, reeved a new rope, and we heaved up the sail again and sped on our way. Wallace, whose family had been in the flax business for generations, inspected the frayed ends of the old halliard, and was very scathing. "This stuff is pretty awful. No wonder it broke. There's a lot of rubbish in the thread. Where did you get it?"

"It was all I could find," I replied. "Flax rope is virtually impossible to obtain, and I had to make do with the only sample I could get. It's been giving us trouble ever since we started, and it was particularly useless during the gale when we had to mend the ropes every few hours."

[93]

"I think we had better get you some better stuff than this," Wallace replied. "I'll contact my friends in the flax business, and we'll see if there isn't something to be done. *Brendan* deserves better than this muck."

We made our landfall at the Island of Iona on the second morning, and three hours of steady rowing brought us round to Martyr's Bay, the beach where a raiding party of Vikings massacred thirty monks of Iona's Abbey, and left their corpses to rot on the sand. Until then Iona had been the jewel of the Irish overseas mission. Here in A.D. 563 Saint Columba had landed by curragh after sailing across from Ireland. The little bay where he first set foot on the island is still the Port na Curraich, the Port of the Curragh. According to legend, Columba had then ordered his monks to bury the curragh for fear that he be tempted to return to his homeland. Under the Saint's unswerving leadership, Irish monks proceeded to establish one of the most important Celtic monasteries in the whole of Europe. Iona became the springboard for the Christian conversion of north Britain, sending out missionaries to the west and north of Scotland, and to the people of northern England. On the mainland and throughout the islands, Columba and his successors established daughter houses in the image of the original foundation on Iona. But then came the Vikings. Iona was attacked in 795, again in 802, and again in 806. Under this constant harassment, the monks left the island and moved back to Ireland, where, among other things, they were responsible for the creation of the renowned Book of Kells.

Today, there is once again an abbey upon Iona. It is built upon the ruins of a Benedictine abbey founded there in the twelfth century, and it is the home of the Iona Community, a brotherhood of some 130 members, bound together by a common commitment of Christian prayer and action in the world. This community includes Anglicans, Baptists, and Catholics, and carries its mission overseas and into the industrial towns of Britain. Each year as many of the members as possible return to Iona for a week's retreat, and repledge their commitment. Very kindly, the Warden of the community invited *Brendan*'s crew to lunch in the abbey's refectory, and at the end of the meal presented us with a memento of our visit—a small replica of the magnificent fifteenth-century Irish ringed cross, known as the Cross of Saint Martin, which stands outside the abbey door. It was an apt gift, because Saint Martin's Cross was the cross we had copied onto *Brendan*'s sails.

Iona also gave us a new crew member to replace Wallace Clark, who had to return to his office after the long weekend. Scarcely had Wallace left on the little ferry before a converted, rather battered-looking sailing trawler with a blue hull came into Martyr's Bay and dropped anchor. About an hour later I was accosted on the beach by a fantastic figure.

"I say," he began excitedly, "are you the skipper of that strange-looking boat? I must say, it's fascinating. I'm told you're looking for a crew member."

"Yes," I answered cautiously, looking over the newcomer. He was a big, rather gaunt fellow, with a lock of long hair which kept escaping from under his cap, falling over his eyes, and being

[95]

brushed back with a nervous gesture. His face was dominated by a great beak of a nose, and he was waving his very long arms so that he looked like some sort of strange, flapping predatory seabird. Even more remarkable were his clothes. On his head was perched an army beret, which I recognized from the Officer Cadet Force. His broad shoulders were encased in a shabby naval sweater far too long for him so that it reached to the knees of his frayed jeans, which were embroidered with homemade figures of boats, flowers, and animals. Last of all, his feet projected without benefit of shoes, socks, or boots, and he was apparently oblivious to the fact that he was standing in icy-cold water. I was impressed.

"I'm the captain of that blue yacht out there," hurried on this apparition, with a grand sweep of an arm. "We do charters through the Hebrides. But I'd like to join your crew, if you'll have me."

"What about your boat?" I asked. "What will you do with it? What about your charterers?" I imagined some hapless group of tourists marooned on this spot by this madcap.

"Oh, that's all right," he replied. "I've got two brothers. They can take over for the summer." Then as an afterthought, he asked, "By the way, where are you going in that boat?"

So in this scramble of rag-bag enthusiasm arrived Edan Kenneil, soon to develop into *Brendan*'s jester and resident live wire. With his constant high spirits Edan was a welcome addition. He was one of nature's leap-before-you-look characters whose bravado carried him head over heels through life from one scrape to the next. He could sail and steer, didn't mind cold or damp, and—to my delight—he was willing to share the cooking. Indeed, his only major vice in the weeks ahead turned out to be an enormous and insatiable appetite. His hunger knew no discipline. He would eat virtually anything and everything, and we soon learned that any leftovers on our plates would be speared by his darting fork. His constant hunger and his enormous flailing arms were soon to earn him the obvious nickname of Gannet, in honor of his airborne cousin whose capacity for food is legendary.

Edan needed two days to settle his affairs before joining us, and we agreed to meet at the nearby island of Tiree. So when we slipped out of Iona and turned down the Sound, *Brendan* was even more short-handed, with a crew of only four. As we passed the abbey, the great bells began to ring out a farewell for us and we could see the figure of the Warden standing on the water's edge, waving goodbye until we rounded the headland and struck out for Tiree. We sailed under a sky that seemed to press lower and lower upon us, until we were swallowed up into drizzle and murk, and ploughed forward in a world of our own.

The sea was about to teach us a lesson in medieval navigation. Anxiously I kept glancing at the log ticking off the miles we had covered. I peered forward into the gloom, but could see nothing. Visibility was less than a hundred yards. I glanced at the chart and calculated for the twentieth time the distance between Iona and Tiree. I asked Rolf to heave the lead line, but he could find no bottom. I didn't trust the log, but already it was showing that we had covered the whole distance between the two islands. Perhaps the tide had slowed us down, I thought. Perhaps it had carried us off course, and we were being swirled around Tiree and would fail to see the island. The pilot book warned me that we were approaching a coast foul with off-lying rocks; and the radio began to forecast yet another gale. *Brendan*, I thought, had best be in port as soon as possible.

Then suddenly Arthur gave a shout.

"Land! Land! Dead ahead!" Through the murk a line appeared, a barely visible distinction between sea and shore, not very far away and stretching right across our bows. The wind was blowing us straight ashore.

"Helm up," cried George. Rolf scrambled forward to readjust the sails so we could alter course. With a rattle of its retaining chain, Arthur dropped a leeboard into the water to try to reduce our leeway. *Brendan*'s nose swung northward, but the line of the land followed with her. We were still running toward the shore.

"Can you bring her up any more into the wind, George?" I asked.

"Not without stalling her and drifting down," he replied. "It looks as if we're in trouble." Rolf swung out the lead line.

"Four fathoms!" he called out to me. I peered at the chart. Four fathoms, four fathoms, with land right across our bows. Where were we? Suddenly I saw the answer: blinded by the fog and in the grip of the tide, I had let *Brendan* run into a bay on the southeast

[97]

edge of Tiree. There was no port ahead, only rocks which might puncture our leather hull. If we didn't act soon, we would be trapped and caught, embayed in the classic fashion, and we were too short-handed to row out of trouble.

"Rolf! Boots!" I shouted. "Get to the oar benches. One each side to give her direction. George, if we're lucky, we can scrape her out of the north side of the bay. But it will mean going inside the outer reefs. Keep her as hard on the wind as you can. I'll go forward as lookout."

From the steering position it was impossible to see clearly past the bows. The headsail blocked the helmsman's view. So I scrambled up onto the forward buoyancy deck, grabbed a rope, hauled myself upright, and balanced there, calling instructions back to George, as *Brendan* weaved between the rocks. It was touch-and-go. We had to pick our way deftly between several groups of rocks, partly sailing and partly rowing as Rolf and Arthur heaved away, turn by turn, and George readjusted the set of the steering paddle. We were like a learner skier stumbling down a difficult slope, sliding and slipping between the obstacles, struggling to keep balance and inexorably toppling forward. The sensation on *Brendan* was just the same. The combinations of wind and swell and leeway, of the tide and the backwash were infinite, and it would be disastrous if we blundered, and the hull snagged the rocks.

"Hold her steady, steady as she goes," I called to George, as we slid past the first rock peaks.

"Starboard! Starboard! Rolf, pull away as hard as you can," and *Brendan* rounded another clump of reefs. A startled-looking seal plummeted off a rock as we went scurrying by. Fronds of seaweed swirled on the surface of the water, and showed where the reef lay less than a yard beneath the water. No keel boat would have dared go that way, but *Brendan* drew less than one foot of water, and I blessed the fact. This is how the curragh men manage to maneuver among the rocky shores of Ireland. We were nearing the end of the gauntlet. There was one last group of rocks ahead of us, the waves sucking and swirling majestically around the kelp-covered sides of the rocks.

"Starboard some more, George!"

"No good," he called back. "We can't come any closer to the

wind." Rolf heaved frantically at his oar, eight, nine, ten quick strokes, but it was not enough. *Brendan* started to swing broadside to the rock and drift down on it. In less than a minute we would strike.

"We'll have to risk going inside. Through that kelp," I shouted. "Hard to port, and Boots, give her all you've got."

Brendan began turning. The wind filled her sails, and she surged forward straight at the dark line of kelp. How deep was the reef beneath? Picking up speed, we charged at the gap. The seaweed plucked *Brendan*'s leather skin with a soft brushing sound, and our boat wriggled gracefully over into safe water without a scratch. Boots and Rolf cropped oars and slumped exhausted. I climbed down and joined George at the helm.

"That was a close shave," I muttered to him. "And another lesson. I mustn't let *Brendan* get caught in a bay ever again, or we are likely to lose her."

Tiree was another of the Hebridean islands where the Irish monks had established themselves. In Saint Brendan's time it had been the site of a daughter monastery to Iona. Some say it was founded by Saint Brendan himself, and such is the strength of the Christian tradition in those parts that the Gaelic-speaking islanders still point to one of the rocks in the new harbor and tell their name for it—Mollachdag, the little cursed rock. According to the islanders, this was the rock where Saint Columba, when he came to Tiree, moored his curragh to the weeds. But the weeds broke and the boat drifted away. So the Saint cursed the rock, saying that it would never grow weed again for the rest of eternity. All the other rocks in the harbor, we were told, grow a thick beard of seaweed. But Mollachdag for years was totally bald, and only recently have a few wisps of seaweed begun to grow on it.

The Irish voyager-saints were obviously a cantankerous lot, because similar stories of their short tempers are found throughout the island. On the beach of Tiree, it was also said, Saint Columba slipped and fell when he trod on a plaice lying in the shallows; he condemned the fish to have both eyes on the same side of its head to avoid such an accident in future. And back near Ballyhoorisky an old fisherman had told me why no salmon are ever caught in Mulroy Bay, alone of all the inlets on that coast. One of the saints had sailed into the bay, he said, and asked for fish at a village. But the villagers had refused him the gift, and so he had driven the salmon from their waters forever.

Edan joined us in Tiree and, as we were getting ready to leave harbor, he picked up an oar and took a couple of practice strokes at the water. I had spent three years at Oxford as a coxswain in college rowing eights, and so I knew an oarsman when I saw one.

"Hey, you've rowed before," I called out to Edan.

"Yes, why do you ask?" he replied, looking surprised.

"I expect it'll come in handy. Who did you row for?"

"Oh! I was captain of the Eton Boat when we won the World Schoolboy Championships in Switzerland."

Only Edan, I thought to myself, would have forgotten to mention this qualification before.

From Tiree, we picked our way through a magnificent sunset, northward into the channel of the Minches, which divides the Outer Hebrides from the inshore islands and mainland of northern Scotland. This was a superb sailing ground, for we were sheltered from the full force of the Atlantic by the chain of the Hebrides, and while the gales raged outside, we could sail in comparative peace, and learn more about our strange vessel.

I was worried about the strength of the stitches holding the oxhides of *Brendan*'s skin together. The collapse of our flax ropes had been a dire warning. If the flax threads in the hull were no better than our feeble rigging, then we were sailing a death trap. *Brendan* could fall to pieces without warning. Tentatively I gouged at the sewing threads in the hides. They seemed very soft. I could dent them with my fingernail. But they didn't seem dangerously weak. I knew that they were of a higher-quality fiber than the ropes, but I suspected there was another reason why they were retaining their strength. When we were building *Brendan*, the flax-thread manufacturer had sent samples of his thread to be tested at the laboratories together with snippets of *Brendan*'s oak-bark-tanned leather. The laboratory had made an interesting discovery. As expected, the flax thread was actually stronger when wet than when dry, and it had been more resistant to rot after it had been stitched into the leather. The reason was that the tannin from the leather had migrated into the thread, and in effect had tanned the flax as well. This was a technique which fishermen had known for centuries; and until modern artificial fibers were available, Irish fishermen soaked their nets and lines in tubs of tanning liquor to make them last longer. But what the research laboratory could not explain was the fact that the flax thread when stitched into leather actually became *stronger*. Why this was so was a mystery to the scientists, and as I scratched at *Brendan*'s wet hide, I quietly hoped to myself that this unexplained phenomenon would endure.

My faith in Irish flax received a boost at our next port of call in Loch Maddy on the island of North Uist. There the harbor master delivered to us a coil of new, improved flax rope. An Irish yacht, he said, had come hurrying up from Ulster with the coil, and had asked that it be delivered to *Brendan* with all speed. Later I learned that as soon as Wallace Clark had got home from Iona, he had told the same flax-spinning firm that made *Brendan*'s stitching thread about our difficulties with *Brendan*'s poor-grade rope. Jim Henshall, director of the firm, had bundled a consignment of the stitching thread down to the Belfast Rope Works. Could the ropewalk make the yarn into rope at once? It was badly needed for *Brendan*. Twenty-four hours later the rope was ready, and speeding north by yacht. It bore no resemblance to our previous stuff. The new rope was silky and strong, and a delight to handle. Gratefully we rerigged *Brendan* with less risk of the sails falling on our heads.

We left Loch Maddy with five splitting headaches, the result of too much whisky and a ferocious dose of the bagpipes at short range, because North Uist is a famous breeding ground for Scots pipers. But superb sailing weather soon cleared our heads. There was a fine strong wind blowing clear up the Minches, and raising very little seaway.

"Well, George, here's our chance to see just how fast *Brendan* goes." He grinned with delight.

"Not worried about breaking the mast?"

"No. It's our last chance before the open Atlantic to try out her paces."

"Splendid. We'll put up every scrap of canvas we've got—the lower bonnets and both side panels, and we'll rig a backstay to hold the mast, just in case."

Edan gave a great whoop of joy.

"Now we'll see her go," he said, rubbing his hands with glee,

[101]

Leeboards

and he and Rolf began lacing on the bonnets, the strip of extra canvas on the foot of each sail, which increased our sail area to maximum.

At first we were in the lee of the island, and sheltered from the wind. But once we were clear, the enlarged sails began to drive *Brendan* forward. Smoothly she gathered speed, the water curling back along her leather sides.

"Haul up the leeboards," ordered George, and they came clattering aboard, wet and dripping. With less drag and no keel to hold her back, *Brendan* fairly tore along. I glanced at the log indicator. We were traveling at six and seven knots, and going like an express train. Under George's hand the shaft of the steering paddle was bending noticeably under the pressure of the water

[102]

rushing past. If he turned the paddle slightly, a plume of spray shot up like a tail. Rolf was fairly dancing with delight.

"Look! Look! *Brendan*'s racing!"

A swell was entering the channel between the islands, and when we hit it, we began to sway up and down on the waves. The effect was like riding a roller-coaster at the fairground. *Brendan* began to toboggan on the waves, running down the wave fronts at eight or ten knots. From time to time she actually broke free of the main mass of water and began to surf, up on top of the main body of the wave and racing forward. Then the log would spin up to its maximum of twelve knots, and the needle stuck there, hard against the end stop. The ride was exhilarating and breathtaking. Here was a boat from the Dark Ages sailing as fast as many modern yachts, and the sensation was unique. The flax cords and leather straps of the ancient rigging thrummed under pressure; the massive H-frame of the steering oar clanked and flexed as each wave passed us; and the spread of the sails bulged and trembled under the pressure of the wind. After two hours of this headlong progress, I reluctantly gave the order to reduce sail, for fear we tore the boat apart or ran her under. Later I found out that a coast guard observer had been watching *Brendan* through binoculars as she hurtled up the Sound, diving in and out of the rain squalls of the gale. He telephoned his headquarters with an estimate of our speed, and forecast that *Brendan* would take six hours to reach the port of Stornoway. But as he watched her sliding past the marks, he could scarcely believe his eyes. He checked his calculations again, and then called Stornoway back.

"*Brendan* still in sight," he reported. "But cancel my previous estimate. She'll be in Stornoway in three hours."

We had shown ourselves just what an ocean-going curragh could do under ideal conditions, and our reward was a perfect ending for the dash up the Minch. The wind held with us all the way to Stornoway. We rounded the lighthouse in style, dropped the headsail and glided past the island ferryboat, its rail lined with waving passengers and crew. A figure beckoned us from the fishing-boat wharf, and we curled toward him. A word of command and the mainsail came quietly down. Arthur took two solid strokes on his oar. The tiller came over. And *Brendan* dropped neatly into her berth as though we had been sailing medieval boats all our lives.

"Ye've disappointed us," said a glum-looking figure on the wharf with a doleful Scots face. "The boys in the lifeboat crew were hoping to have a bit of exercise pulling you in. Still," he added, looking down at our strange craft, with splendid Gaelic pessimism, "you'll probably keep 'em busy enough when you try to sail for Faroes. I canna say I would want to sail with you."

7

The Sheep Islands

It is just over two hundred miles from Stornoway to the most
southerly island in the Faroes group, two hundred miles of open
water, exposed to the full sweep of the Atlantic winds. Lying
almost midway in the gap between Scotland and Iceland, the
cluster of eighteen islands which form the Faroes rise abruptly
from the water where the crest of a submarine ridge lifts briefly
above the surface. One of the remotest places in Europe, the
Faroes are in every way the offspring of the sea. The islanders
depend upon the sea for their livelihood; at the age when most
children are learning to ride bicycles, they already know how to
handle the little boats in which they pass from island to island; and
their daily lives are dominated by the huge Atlantic depressions
which revolve slowly over their heads, obscuring the islands in
thick wet clouds for most of the year, and bringing rain on two days
out of every three. Both for Saint Brendan and our latter-day
Brendan, the Faroes were a key point in their journeys. If the
Navigatio did in fact describe the Stepping Stone Route to America
as the Irish monks had used it, then the Faroes were the first logical
long-distance staging post in the chain.

Damp and cloud-hidden, they lie far beyond the horizon from
the Hebrides, and yet the *Navigatio* told how Saint Brendan and
his monks had sighted a remote island and a favorable wind had
brought them to shore. Landing, they set out to explore the place,
and found large streams full of fish, and a great number of flocks of

splendid white sheep, very large in size. They caught one of the sheep to make their Paschal meal, and on Good Friday while they were preparing their service, an islander appeared, bringing with him a basket of fresh bread. He came up to them, fell three times on his face before Saint Brendan, and asked him—presumably in a language he understood—to accept the gift of bread for their meal. Later, the same islander brought more fresh supplies to revictual their boat, and gave the travelers sailing directions for the next part of their voyage. And, in answer to Saint Brendan's questions, he explained that the sheep on the island grew so large because they were not milked, but left alone in their pastures, and that the natural environment was so gentle that they could be left to graze day and night.

Several scholars have pointed out how closely this description of the Isle of Sheep fits the Faroes. The influence of the Gulf Stream produces comparatively mild winters in the Faroes, and the climate and pasture are suitable for sheep raising so that the islands have acquired a reputation for their sheep and wool. In fact, the present name of the islands is unchanged: it seems to be taken from the Norse words *Faer-Eyjaer,* meaning "Sheep Islands." So the Vikings, too, when they reached the Faroes, gave the islands the same name as the Irish or, as likely, picked up the name from the previous inhabitants. As for the islander who gave Saint Brendan the bread, spoke his language, and understood the Christian calendar, there seems a reasonable possibility that he was another of the wandering clerics of the Irish church. The *Navigatio* calls him Procurator, a term applied to an administrator in the monastic hierarchy and usually translated as Steward. Also there is strong independent evidence to show that Irish monks had settled themselves in the Faroes at an early date. In 825 a learned Irish chronicler named Dicuil, who was employed at the royal Frankish court, set out to compile a geography book which he called *The Book of the Measure of the World,* because he intended to put down in it a description of every land known to mankind as described by the ancients. Dicuil had read many classical authors, but he complained that they really knew very little about the islands lying to the west and north of Britain, whereas he, Dicuil, could claim to describe them with some authority, because he had

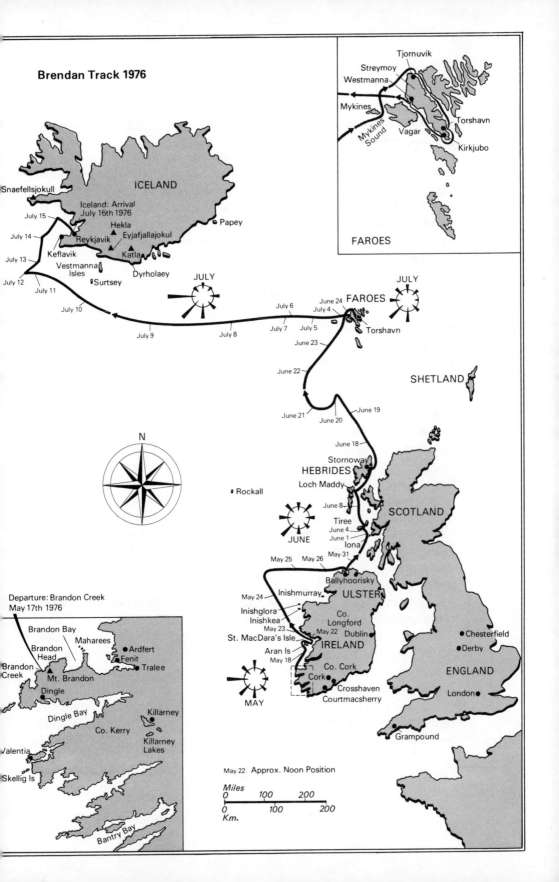

Brendan Track 1976

ICELAND

Iceland: Arrival
July 16th 1976

Snaefellsjokull
July 15
July 14
July 13
July 12
July 11
July 10
July 9
July 8
July 7
July 6
July 5
July 4
June 24

Keflavik
Reykjavik
Hekla
Eyjafjallajokul
Katla
Vestmanna Isles
Dyrholaey
Surtsey
Papey

JULY

FAROES

Torshavn

JULY

SHETLAND

June 23
June 22
June 21
June 20
June 19
June 18

Stornoway
HEBRIDES
Loch Maddy
Rockall

SCOTLAND

June 8
Tiree
June 4
June 1
Iona
May 31

JUNE

May 25
May 26

Ballyhoorisky
ULSTER

May 24
Inishmurray
Inishglora
Inishkea
May 23
St. MacDara's Isle
Aran Is
May 18

Co. Longford
Dublin
IRELAND
May 22
Co. Cork
Cork
Crosshaven
Courtmacsherry

Chesterfield
Derby

ENGLAND

London

MAY

Grampound

May 22 Approx. Noon Position

Miles
0   100   200
0   100   200
Km.

FAROES

Tjornuvik
Streymoy
Westmanna
Mykines
Mykines Sound
Vagar
Torshavn
Kirkjubo

Departure: Brandon Creek
May 17th 1976

Brandon Bay
Maharees
Brandon Head
Ardfert
Fenit
Brandon Creek
Mt. Brandon
Tralee
Dingle
Valentia
Dingle Bay
Co. Kerry
Killarney
Killarney Lakes
Skellig Is
Bantry Bay

N

lived in some, visited others, or talked to Irish priests who had sailed even farther afield than himself, and had read their reports of the farthest islands.

"There are many other islands in the ocean to the north of Britain," Dicuil wrote, "which can be reached from the northern islands of Britain in a direct voyage of two days and nights with sails filled with a continuously favorable wind. A devout priest told me that in two summer days and the intervening night he sailed in a two-benched boat and entered one of them.

"There is another set of small islands, nearly all separated by narrow stretches of water; in these for nearly a hundred years hermits sailing from our country, Ireland, have lived. And just as they were always deserted from the beginning of the world, so now because of the Northmen pirates they are emptied of anchorites, and filled with countless sheep, and very many diverse kinds of seabirds. I have never found these islands mentioned in the authorities."

Dicuil's description could be applied to the Faroes in several points: his "narrow stretches" of water between the islands describe very well the fjordlike channels between the Faroes; the distance by sea-voyage from the Orkneys or Shetlands north of Scotland is feasible in a light boat in good following winds; and the Faroes are renowned for their magnificent variety of bird-life, including enormous colonies of seabirds which nest in the sheer cliffs which surround most of the islands. This remarkable bird-life completes the circle which links the Faroes with Dicuil's northern islands and with the Isle of Sheep in the *Navigatio,* because the *Navigatio* goes on to say that the Procurator directed Saint Brendan to stay at a nearby island which he told them was a Paradise of Birds. There, said the Procurator, the travelers would remain until the eve of Pentecost.

The possible identity of the Isle of Sheep and the Paradise of Birds with the Faroes occupied my thoughts in Stornoway as we prepared *Brendan* for her attempt at the sea passage. The run to the Faroes would be our first long-distance sea crossing, and though two hundred miles on the charts looked easy enough, it could turn out to be at least twice that distance if the winds were against us and *Brendan* had to follow a zig-zag course. No wonder in the old days the Hebridean fishermen had called the Faroes "the Far-aways." If we had really foul winds, then we were quite likely to miss the Faroes entirely. A single bad gale spewed from the prevailing westerlies could skittle *Brendan* past the Faroes and on toward Norway. In the days of sail, storm-driven fishermen from Shetland or Orkney had been carried clear across to the Norwegian coast and been forced to spend days in open boats of the same size as *Brendan* and far handier in sailing to windward than she was. They were the lucky ones: there had been many others who were lost in the fierce storms.

The glum looks of Stornoway's professional fishermen did not help matters as they peered down at *Brendan*, lying in their harbor, and muttered dolefully among themselves. The Doubting Thomas of our arrival was a steady source of gloom. He kept reappearing with sea-wise questions which always ended in the same refrain. Once it was "What do you use for ballast?"

"Water."

"Aye. Stones would be better. There's life in the stones. But water. . . . That's bad. I wouldna want to sail with you."

Or, another time: "How does she sail to wind?"

"She doesn't really," I called back. "We're lucky to get across at right angles to the breeze."

"Not sail to wind. Och, that's bad." He sucked in through his teeth. "I wouldna want to sail with you."

Sotto voce from behind me, Arthur's Irish accent turned Scots for a moment and uttered a mocking warning—"We're all doomed! Aye, we're doomed for sure!"

Edan also banished any despondency. When we were ready to cast off from Stornoway, he suddenly slapped his forehead, cried aloud that he'd forgotten something, and leapt ashore, running off down the jetty with great gangling strides. Puzzled, we waited for nearly an hour. Then he came racing back at full tilt, waving a brown paper parcel.

"What's so important?" George asked him.

"Couldn't go without it," blurted Edan breathlessly as he jumped aboard. "Unthinkable. Sorry I'm late, but I asked every-where and finally got the last one in Stornoway."

"But what is it?" repeated George.

[109]

"A bottle of Pimms!" Edan beamed. "I thought we needed something to mix with our drinks so that we can have cocktails on board."

Sure enough, our Gannet had located the last bottle of Pimms in Stornoway, and his scheme extended to a pan of watercress seeds, which he secreted near his berth in order to grow a little greenery to decorate our drinks. Alas, on the second day he accidentally kicked over the Pimms bottle and spilled its contents stickily into the bilge, and soon afterward a wave deluged his cress tray, drowning *Brendan*'s only attempt at home gardening.

Stornoway's returning trawler fleet gave us a cheerful farewell, tooting their sirens as *Brendan* sailed out and turned her bow northward. By the morning of June 17 we were well clear of the Butt of Lewis, the outer tip of the Hebrides.

Once again we were only four on board, as Rolf had to return home to Norway from Stornoway for urgent personal reasons. So I asked George to draw up a new watch-keeping rota because he, of all of us, put so much effort into his work that no one could begrudge his choice. Watch-keeping ruled our lives, and was the vital framework of our daily existence. Each man exercised strict self-discipline, and made sure he showed up for his watch at exactly the right time. To do less would have been unfair, and could have become precisely the sort of irritant that finally erupts into a blazing quarrel. Each of us knew that we were all living close together under very raw conditions. We were like men locked in a cell measuring thirty-six feet by eight feet—of which less than a quarter was actually sheltered and livable. Potential scope for argument and animosity was almost limitless, and minor irritations could be blown up into a cause for hatred. All of us knew the risks, and an outsider would have noted how, without prior discussion, we all adopted the traditional attitude of live-and-let-live aboard a small boat. By and large, we kept ourselves to ourselves and behaved accordingly. We might discuss modifications to the boat as a group, or make individual suggestions on technical matters. But personal topics were left strictly alone unless offered by the person concerned; and the final decisions in all matters affecting the voyage were left to the Skipper. It was a form of self-discipline which, at worst, might have left hidden grievances to marinate in secret bile; but as it turned out, we were all experienced enough as small-boat sailors to hold our tongues and keep our tempers, and there was no doubt that when we sailed out into the Atlantic, *Brendan* was an efficient and well-integrated boat.

Our daily lives were surprisingly easy. Under most conditions the helmsman's main job was to keep a lookout for changes in the weather, especially for a shift of the wind, and to check that *Brendan* stayed on her set course. But no great accuracy was required at the helm. As the navigator I simply worked out the general direction in which we should sail, and the helmsman lashed the cross bar of the tiller with a leather thong so that *Brendan* stayed within twenty degrees of the right direction. She held her course well, and with so much leeway and the rapid wind shifts it was a wasted effort to be any more accurate. An easy-going attitude also meant that the stand-by watchman, whose task was to readjust the set of the sails as necessary, did not have to go clambering around in the waist of the vessel needlessly, picking his way past the clutter of stores and endlessly fiddling with the ropes or struggling to get the leeboard into a new position. Far better, I had decided, to let *Brendan* sail herself, and to adopt a medieval frame of mind, patient, and unharried. In medieval terms, a week or two added or subtracted to our passage was of no significance, and the benefits of our leisurely outlook were noticeable.

So we lived a relaxed existence. Edan and I divided up the cooking; Arthur and George usually did the dishes in a bucket of sea water. No one bothered to wash himself or to shave, because there was no need, and it would have been a waste of fresh water. *Brendan*'s leather and our sheepskins smelled far worse than we ever would, and it was too cold to relish the prospect of stripping off for a sea-water wash. Sanitary facilities varied according to the weather. One could either hang outboard at the stern, risking a cold slap from a wave, or in rougher seas use a bucket wedged securely amidships. But it was noticeable how reluctant everyone was to use these facilities when the wind blew strongly and the spray was flying, threatening the hapless victim with a cold shower.

Each person had his own area of responsibility. George made regular inspections of all the sailing gear, especially the ropes and halliards, which were subject to considerable wear. We were always digging out our sewing kits to mend tears or to whip the ends of frayed ropes. Every piece of the cordage needed constant

[111]

adjustment, as the flax ropes stretched slack when dry and shrank into iron rods when wet. We found the best technique was to set them up as taut as possible when dry, and then keep them doused with water. Arthur was our rope specialist. His job was to keep the coils of rope neatly stowed and ready for action, and with so much rope on board it kept him busy. In between times he spent hours meticulously cleaning and maintaining the cameras which were recording *Brendan*'s life. Arthur had taken over the photography when Peter retired sick, and our youngest crew member was developing into a first-class cameraman. The delicate cameras seemed desperately fragile in his huge fists, but he had a gentle touch and a born mechanic's skill in keeping them working despite the salt which constantly threatened to clog their shutters.

Navigation, ciné-photography, and radio communications fell within my province. Once every twenty-four hours I switched on the little radio set, scarcely bigger than a brief case, and tried to establish contact with a shore station. On most days we succeeded and, faint but audible, reported our position, which was relayed in turn to the Intelligence Unit of Lloyds of London, who were kindly keeping our families informed. Occasionally, however, we failed to establish any contact, which was hardly surprising as our transmitter operated with scarcely more power than a light bulb and our signals were radiating from a whip antenna tied by leather thongs to the steering frame. Even in a mild seaway, the swell over-topped the antenna. The sole source of power for the radio were two small car batteries, fed by a pair of Lucas solar panels lashed to the roof of the living shelter. These panels were only designed to give a slight charge of electricity, and so our radio time was strictly limited. If I failed to make contact in less than four minutes, I simply switched off the radio and tried again next day. Much of the credit for our successful communications went to the stout-hearted performance of our little radio, and to the skill and patience of the radio operators of the shore stations who kept a special schedule, listening out for *Brendan* at a time when the airwaves were uncluttered by other traffic.

Navigation was simplicity itself. After leaving Stornoway I relied on sun-sights taken with a sextant and cross-checked on radio bearings. But once again there was no real need for great accuracy. We were interested only in keeping a general track of our progress, and allowing the currents and winds to do the rest. *Brendan* was too awkward to allow us to set a fine course or select a precise target. I was content merely if we raised landfalls, roughly where we expected them, along the Stepping Stone Route.

Edan, true to character, provided the light entertainment on board. We all knew when he woke up in the morning by the cries of "Food! Breakfast! How about breakfast!" which came echoing down the boat from his cubby-hole near the foremast. A few minutes later Gannet himself would come clambering into view, eagerly poking his nose into the food locker. His clothes were never the same two days running. One day he had his beret on his head; another a knitted cap; once a knotted handkerchief. His oilskin jacket might be replaced by an old sweater, or a furry diver's undersuit, which made him look like an enormous baby in a pram suit. Once he showed up in a tweed sports jacket and tartan trousers, and was greeted with shouts of delight; another time he arrived in Oriental garb, a flimsy Indian cotton shirt, embroidered, · and with its shirt tail flapping in the breeze like a Calcutta clerk. He must have been freezing cold, for—as usual—his feet were bare. Quite where Edan concealed this extraordinary wardrobe in the tiny space of his sleeping berth, no one could fathom. Yet he still managed to dig out packet after packet of cigars which he had laid in, duty free, at Stornoway. Now he offered them to his shipmates, who looked slightly green at the prospect, but Edan smoked them with jaunty aplomb.

And of course Edan always had his schemes. Each one was more unlikely than the last, but advertised with the same boundless enthusiasm. Daily there was some new dish he promised to cook us—only at the last minute he found he lacked the vital ingredient, or, more likely, there was none left after he had finished "tasting" it in the pan. Twice a day he devised an ingenious new sort of bait for his fishing line which trailed forlornly over *Brendan*'s stern, but the only fish he ever caught was a single limp mackerel, half-drowned by the time he pulled it in, rather to his own surprise. Once he very nearly made his own curtain call, cigar in mouth, when he managed to refill the water jug with cooker kerosene instead of fresh water, and on another occasion he blithely hung up his home-made sleeping bag liner—the product of another scheme—to dry in the riggings only he forgot about it, and saw the liner twitch itself free and go dancing off across the waves like a runaway parachute while the rest of us chortled. Edan, in fact, was our tonic. His bubbling spirits enlivened even the dreariest intervals.

Arthur and Gannet were both avid bird-watchers, and *Brendan* gave them ample opportunity to indulge their hobby. The farther north we sailed, the more varied became the bird-life. Scarcely a day passed without sighting some uncommon species, and the reference book of birds was in constant demand. Halfway to Faroes we had recorded fifteen different species and we spent hours watching the behavior of the gulls and terns which constantly tended us, shrieking and twittering, or staring at us as they wafted past *Brendan* ploughing quietly on her way. Our most elegant companions were the fulmars, the premier aerobats of these waters, who glided in endless loops and circles around us for hour after hour, riding close to the waves on stiff wings, their fat fluffy bodies like huge moths. For some reason we always seemed to attract a pair of Arctic terns which took up their station over us, fluttering nervously and cheeping anxiously to one another as the other seabirds came near them. Occasionally they would break formation to search for fish in our wake, and once we witnessed a terrific air battle when our two small terns drove away a hulking skua which came marauding in our direction. Gallantly the two smaller birds hurled themselves into the attack and drove off the intruder with much shrieking, before they returned to their mast-top station, and we could distinctly hear their chirrups of pride. But their victory was brief. Scarcely ten minutes later, a pair of skuas arrived and this time there was no contest. The two terns fled for their lives, jinking and turning at wave-crest level as the powerful skuas struck at them.

For two days *Brendan* made steady progress northward. The radio continued to give gale warnings, but the wind held fair and my calculations put us halfway to the Faroes. Daily George or I inspected the condition of the leather skin, poking our fingers through the wooden frame to see whether there was any deterioration. By now the leather was completely saturated with sea water, which seeped gently across the membrane and trickled down to join the inch or two of water constantly swirling along the bilge. But the leather itself seemed to be holding up well, except for two patches which worried us near the H-frame. These two patches were in identical places, one each side of the boat, and by sighting along the gunwale I could detect that *Brendan's* curved stern had begun to droop, flattening the profile and wrinkling the skin. This was a pity, for it made the vessel less seaworthy in a storm, and the oxhides in this area were no longer stretched tight over the frame but bagged and corrugated like an elephant's posterior. Prodding a finger against the skin, one could easily pump it in and out like a soft balloon, but this did not seem to affect the material. Our medieval leather was holding up remarkably well, and I suspected that the increasing cold was a help. *Brendan* was now in chilly waters, and the lower temperature would be slowing down the rate of any decomposition in the leather, stiffening the oxhides, and hardening the layer of wool grease into a protective coat. Here again, I suspected, we were learning another reason why the Irish could have chosen to sail to their Promised Land by a northern route: the sea conditions might have been cold and stormy, but they suited their skin boats and made them last longer on sea-voyages. In the warmer waters of a southern voyage, the protective grease might have washed away, and the leather begun to rot.

Our daily inspections also revealed that the sea had been taking its toll on the wooden framework. The steering paddle was held in position by a cross rope which fastened to the opposite gunwale. The strain on this rope was so great that the gunwale of seasoned oak, an inch and a half thick, was literally being torn apart. A jagged pattern of splintering cracks had begun to appear. George lost no time in shifting the rope to another strong point, and he doubled the lashings which held the steering frame together. Later, I crawled forward to inspect the mainmast and found that the main thwart had been bent upward in a curve, probably by the same forces which were causing the stern to droop. It was inadvisable to poke and pry too closely with one's fingers near the mast for the gaps between the thwart and the mast were opening and closing like giant pincers with the motion of the boat, and threatened to crush one's fingers.

Thoughtfully I crawled back and considered our position. *Brendan* was changing her shape. I did not believe it was yet dangerous, but it was very evident that we were dependent on the quality of our basic materials: the timber had to be strong enough to withstand the constant whiplash effect of the flexing hull, and the leather thongs which tied the framework together had to continue to hold. Above all, the leather skin needed to be tough enough to survive the increased sagging and wrinkles, and the miles of flax thread were now under greater strain than ever before, and must not snap. In a strange way I was reassured. It occurred to me that what a medieval boat-builder might have lacked in his knowledge of naval architecture, he gained in the quality of the materials he used, materials which he had selected critically and then prepared with the utmost care. Aboard *Brendan* we were learning this lesson for ourselves in a host of small ways. Item by item, our modern equipment was collapsing under the conditions. Our shiny, new, modern metal tools, for example, had virtually rusted away, despite their protecting layer of oil. After a month aboard *Brendan*, a tempered saw blade simply snapped like a rotten carrot; a miner's lamp, which I had hoped to use as a night light, was useless. Tough enough for a lifetime's use in the mines, its metal gauze had corroded into a solid mass, and its iron rivets dropped streaks of rust. Of our modern materials, only the best stainless steel, the solid plastic, and the synthetic ropes were standing up to the conditions. It was instructive that whenever a modern item broke, we tended to replace it with a homemade substitute devised from the ancient materials of wood, leather, and flax. These we could work and fashion, sew and shape to suit the occasion. The product usually looked cumbersome and rough, but it survived and we could repair it ourselves. Whereas when metal snapped, or plastic ripped, the only choice without a workshop on board was to jettison the broken item.

It all added up to the realization that the sailors of Saint Brendan's day were in fact better equipped materially—as well as mentally—than is usually acknowledged. The early medieval sailors had access to superb materials which lasted well, and, if they failed, could be repaired with simple tools. Even their clothing was admirably suited to the conditions, as all of us on *Brendan* were finding. As the weather turned colder, we had replaced our clothes of artificial fiber in favor of old-fashioned woollen clothes, reeking of natural wool oil. We may have looked and smelled unlovely, but our oiled wool sweaters, thigh-length wool sea-boot socks, and cowl-like woollen helmets were not materially different from the garments available in Saint Brendan's day.

[116]

A calm day, June 19, provided a good demonstration of the short-comings of some of our modern equipment. After breakfast George went forward to dig out the day's food pack.

"Ugh! Look at this!" he called out, holding up the plastic sack with an expression of disgust. It looked like a putrid goldfish bowl, half full of slimy brown water which dripped from one corner. Blobs of food floated by in a soupy mass inside. "How revolting," muttered Gannet, and then more hopefully, "Let's open it and see if there's anything still edible." George ripped open the bag. Despite its double sealing, a leak had somehow developed in the plastic, and the bag had absorbed a couple of gallons of sea water and rain. Disgustedly, George poured overboard a foul-smelling mess of tea-colored water, which splattered out wet lumps of sugar, sodden tea bags, soggy shortbread biscuits and gluey lumps of porridge, all totally ruined. Gannet hopefully seized on a packet that looked less damaged than most.

"Oatmeal biscuits," he exulted. Then he took a bite. "Foch!" He spat out the mouthful. "They're saturated in salt," he complained.

"Well, if you can't eat them, nobody can," remarked Arthur.

"Well, Skip," said Edan as he suddenly realized what might happen. "We will open another bag, won't we? I mean there's nothing at all in that last one."

I laughed. "Okay, Gannet. We're not on short rations yet."

It was another lesson learned. If all our supplies were similarly damaged, we might later run short of food. Indeed we discovered several other bags had also leaked and most of their contents had disintegrated. By far the worst were the dehydrated items which promptly soaked up water, swelled and burst, leaving a putrid mess. Only the tinned items survived, and because we had not had time to varnish them over, labels had been washed off, so we had a guessing game for a hunter's casserole.

"Well, I'm not worried," George summed up, as he inspected a macedoine of instant vegetables swimming in half a gallon of the Atlantic. "These dehydrated vegetables are all right once or twice a week, but day after day is too much. My whole throat tastes of preservative."

The nineteenth and twentieth of June brought us only a moderate advance. The wind headed us for a time, and *Brendan* actually lost ground, ending up thirty miles farther away from the

[117]

Faroes. There was nothing to be done, and we accepted the situation with our newly minted medieval philosophy. Eventually the wind died away completely, and we simply waited to see what Providence would bring. George played Edan at backgammon, and was 15p up in the stakes. Arthur had crawled into the shelter and was dozing. I leaned comfortably against the motionless steering oar, and listened contentedly to the sound of the waves rolling under the hull, the occasional creak from the mast against the thwart, or the H-frame shifting in its socket. Every now and then the log line gave a half-hearted twist as we edged forward over the sea.

"Trawler in sight! Coming down from the north." Anything to break the monotony. The others climbed up to have a look.

"I bet they'll trade for whiskey." Edan was scheming already.

"I doubt it," said Arthur. "They're probably on automatic compass, going home after a fishing trip off Iceland. They won't even have seen us. After all, they're not expecting to meet anything out here."

The trawler kept ploughing steadily toward us. It would pass about half a mile ahead, and there was no sign of life aboard. It was close enough to read the name: *Lord Jellicoe.*

"Here, George. You take the helm. I'll see if I can raise them on the radio."

I switched on our portable VHF set.

"*Lord Jellicoe. Lord Jellicoe. Curragh Brendan* calling. Come in please."

Silence. Only the hiss of the loudspeaker. I tried repeating the call. Again silence. Then suddenly a startled voice crackled back:

"*Lord Jellicoe.* Who's that?"

"*Curragh Brendan.* We're off your starboard side, about half a mile away. Can you give me a position check, please?"

"Wait a minute." *Lord Jellicoe* ploughed on, while presumably her navigator was roused to work out the unexpected request. Just as she was disappearing over the horizon, she signaled the information I wanted, and later that same evening as we listened to the BBC news bulletin, *Lord Jellicoe*'s radio broke in. She was calling up a coast station, and we could hear the flat Yorkshire accents of her skipper.

[118]

14. George at the helm as we ran into our first rough seas; a frightening vista of massive waves, each one capable of swamping, destroying, or capsizing.

15. Preparing lunch. "Why don't we make the Skipper do the cooking?" Peter suggested after Arthur asked how to cook instant mashed potatoes.

16.

16. Rowing into Iona where in the sixth century St. Brendan sailed to meet St. Columba.

17. Plotting a fix. We were unable to sail upwind, and gales drove us in circles or even back on our track.

17.

18.

18.   Jaunty as ever, Edan Kenneil tries his hand at sketching. Note his bare feet. He rarely wore boots, even on the coldest days. **19.**   *Brendan*'s tiny cabin, a mere 6 feet by 6 feet, provided only minimal comfort.

20.   Alive to the sea, *Brendan* rolls easily over the waves. Do you think a big curragh could get all the way to America?" I had asked John Goodwin. "Well now," he replied, "the boat will do, just as long as the crew's good enough."

19.

20.▶

21. A rainbow follows a vicious squall en route to the Faroes.

22. Approaching the Faroe Islands the clouds were so low they almost hid the cliffs from sight. Suddenly, half a mile away, we saw waves breaking against a wall of rock. The gale kept sliding us sideways, ever sideways into the cliffs. Then the clouds lifted and we saw them: thousands upon thousands of sea birds. Was this the Paradise of Birds?

23. The bay of Tjornuvik with its cluster of gaily painted houses was where *Brendan* found shelter from the seething tide race. **24.** *Brendan* ties up by Trondur's home. The Patursson family had lived there, father to son, for 18 generations. No less than three churches surround this holy site, still called Brendan's Creek. Here the Irish hermits are said to have first settled in these remote and magnificent islands.

23.

24.

25.-26.

25. Tim Severin, skipper.

26. George Molony, sailing master.

27. Arthur Magan, photographer.

27.-28.

28. Trondur Patursson, artist.

"Humber Radio, maybe you can tell us something. We passed a strange vessel some time back this afternoon, and I'm told that it's carrying a crew of mad Irish monks, is that right?"

We never heard Humber Radio's reply, because *Brendan*'s crew were doubled up with laughter.

June 21, the longest day of the year, made us realize that we were now in high latitudes. We were enjoying almost twenty-four hours of daylight, and even at one o'clock in the morning I could still read the log book by reflected light in the sky. From that day on, for the rest of the sailing season, we had no need for navigation lights, which was just as well, for I was a miser with our precious battery power. That evening we made the final contact with our friendly coast operator at Malinhead radio station who wished us luck for Faroes in his Irish brogue. As if in response, the winds changed to the south, and *Brendan* began to advance again in the right direction.

At six in the morning, a whale-catcher boat, about fifty feet long, came roaring up, its harpoon looming sinister on the fore-peak.

"Hope she doesn't think we're a leather whale, and take a shot at us," Arthur muttered as the whale-catcher circled us, its crew waving and cheering, and shouting if they could give us any help. We waved back our thanks, and they went tearing off, quartering the sea in search of their prey. Their lookout would not have welcomed the sea fret which quietly closed around us a couple of hours later, and locked us in a white cloud. *Brendan* ghosted along, the mist clinging in thousands of glistening droplets to the fibers of our woollen hats and to our beards like dew on blades of grass in a dawn meadow.

All that day the wind continued light, with just one heavy shower of rain, from which we managed to collect several inches of fresh water as an experiment. Catching the water in a tarpaulin, we drained it into our cooking pots. In an emergency, I calculated, we could just about survive on rainwater in that damp climate.

June 23 answered the question of how the early Irish monks would have located the Faroes in the vastness of the Atlantic. It was an ordinary summer's day for those regions, occasional sunshine and a great deal of cloud. *Brendan* was still more than fifty miles from the Faroes, yet we picked out the islands with ease from the tall columns of cloud building up over them, thousands of feet into the air. The moist southwest wind sweeping across the ocean was deflected upward by the islands, condensed, and built up cloud banks as distinctive as marker flags on a hidden golf green. Picking up the binoculars, I looked more closely at the clouds and saw something which alerted me: the clouds were rolling and changing shape every few minutes in powerful up-draughts, and some of the clouds seemed to be pouring over the hill crests toward *Brendan*. They were the signs of an abrupt change of the weather, and I didn't like the look of the turbulence.

That evening my concern deepened. We had a lowering sunset—a red sky with the purple shadows of the islands in the distance, beautiful but ominous. We were now close enough to be able to identify the individual islands in the group, and I carefully consulted the charts and the pilot book. Our best course was to aim straight for the center of the Faroes, run through one of the narrow channels between them, and then try to duck into shelter on the lee side. But there was one snag—the tidal stream around the Faroes. On every tide the Atlantic sluices through the Faroes in an immense rush of water. The tide gushes through the narrow sounds between the islands with a myriad currents and countercurrents, sometimes so strong that even large ships must take care. The pilot book was a doleful mixture of caution and ignorance. "Little information is available regarding the rate of the tidal streams," it said; ". . . in the channels between the islands, the stream may be very rapid and from eight to nine knots is not exceptional." It also warned the mariner not to sail too close to land for fear of the off-lying rocks called Drangar which lie close off the cliffs on the north and western sides of the group. A medieval sailing boat, I thought to myself, caught in these tide rips would be helpless.

I checked the compass bearings and marked *Brendan*'s position on the chart, just before the storm line hit us. It swept down on *Brendan* from the south, a bank of rain which cut visibility abruptly from twenty miles to three miles in a matter of minutes. The wind force jumped upward. The rain hissed and rattled down, and we pulled on full foul-weather gear.

"Everybody in safety harnesses, please," I ordered, and we

buckled on the belts and clipped lifelines to the boat. "Gannet, you handle the headsail sheets; Boots, take the mainsail, and look after the leeboards. George, you're the best helmsman on board, you take over the steering. I'll handle the pilotage. This is likely to be tricky."

Brendan groped her way in the general direction of the Faroes, heading on the last compass bearing I had been able to take before the rain blotted out the horizon. After an hour, we had a brief glimpse of the islands as the sea-level cloud lifted. At once I saw that I would have to abandon my original plan. The main tide was running in a circular motion around the islands, and had picked up *Brendan* and was carrying her clockwise around the group. There was no hope of getting to the center of the group. We would be lucky to get into land at all, without being gale-swept past the west of the Faroes. Mykines, the most westerly island and closest to us, was out of the question as a landfall. Its only regular inhabitants were the lighthouse-keepers and a handful of crofters, and its landing place could only be approached in calm weather. But Vagar Island, just inside Mykines and separated by the narrow channel of Mykines Sound, had a fjord that offered good shelter and it was worth a try.

By now the wind had risen to a half a gale, and *Brendan* was driving blindly through the rain, closing the gap at a terrific pace with the tide under her.

"Keep as close to the wind as you can," I asked George. All of us were squinting through the downpour for a sight of land. The sea had now turned a nasty grey and was broken into a confusing cross-pattern of pyramids and crenellations. I guessed we must have entered the area of eddies and tidal backcurrents. *Brendan* was going at full stretch. We needed every inch of headway if we were to get up into Vagar, and not be slammed sideways into the sheer cliffs of Mykines. The wind was blowing so hard that although *Brendan* was pointing east she was going almost north, sliding sideways across the top of the water.

"Cliffs!" bellowed Edan. There, half a mile away, was a leaping band of white water where waves were breaking against a sheer wall of rock. It had to be Mykines.

"My God! Look at that lot," Arthur breathed. It was indeed a remarkable sight. The cloud was so low that we saw only down a narrow tunnel, about six feet high, between the cloud base and the grey ocean. Thus the height of the cliffs was reduced to a mere looming black shadow inside the cloud, and our view was confined to the tortured line of water bursting into spray against the rock. At that same moment, *Brendan* entered a back eddy, running against her, so that her forward movement suddenly slowed to a crawl. Yet the gale kept her sliding sideways, ever sideways toward the cliffs. It was like slipping down a tunnel in a nightmare. There was no escape. The cloud base pressed down on us, squeezing us as inevitably as the tide. All of us fell silent. We knew it was a race between our snail's-pace advance and a sideways lurch toward the

cliffs. Hardly breathing, we watched the grey cliffs inch past, yet coming closer and closer.

"I think we'll do it," I said hopefully to George. "I can see the end of the island. Another quarter of a mile and we'll be clear, and Vagar is ahead."

George had climbed up on to the gunwale for a better view and was coaxing *Brendan* forward yard by yard. Edan and Arthur sat calmly in the waist of the boat, huddled in their oilskins and trying to calculate our progress.

"Christ! I hope the mast doesn't go," George muttered. "That really would be curtains."

I glanced up. The mainmast was curved more than we had ever

seen it, drawn down by the intense pressure of the gale on the mainsail, which still carried its bottom bonnet and one side bonnet.

"We'll have to leave the bonnets up," George said. "We need all the driving power we can get to pull free of the tide."

"Keep an eye on the mainmast where it passes the thwart," I shouted forward to Boots. "If it begins to splinter, cut the bonnets free with your knife."

A few moments later, it happened: our world suddenly seemed to stand still. The normal motion of the boat and the waves stopped. It was as though we had gone into suspension. Through some quirk of the tide race in the gale the waves, instead of moving horizontally, simply rose up and down as if marking time. One such wave rose up beside *Brendan*, seemed to jump sideways, and dropped apparently vertically into the bilge. The wave was harmlessly small, but *Brendan* appeared to be hanging motionless to receive it. The boat herself no longer pitched nor rolled, in her normal style. At the same moment, the cloud base rose another thirty or forty feet, and we saw them: thousands upon thousands of seabirds, pouring out from the cliffs of Mykines: gulls, guillemots, razorbills, fulmars, gannets, puffins, skuas, and terns. They came in droves, in squadron after squadron, wheeling and turning, and swooping and dipping down toward the queer, lumpy, contorted sea. Driven by primeval experience, they had emerged to fish in the waters at a time when they knew the combination of wind and tide would bring the shoals of fish close to the surface.

I was awed. If there was any place which fitted the idea of a Paradise of Birds, this was it. "It's fantastic!" I shouted to George above the roar of the wind.

He gave a shout and pointed. "Look! Over there. On the starboard bow. Something big, jumping in the water." I followed the line of his arm. About a hundred yards ahead was a large swirl of water where something had just disappeared. A vast shape heaved beneath the surface. Then it came up again, and this time it was visible, throwing itself clear of the waves—the lurching massive shape of a whale, hurtling out of the depths and leaping into the air again and again as if it were a salmon, only its grey body flopped loosely as it fell back with a burst of white water.

Brendan was at last clawing past the trap where Mykines reached out its heel of cliff toward us. In the space of ten yards we suddenly broke free from the counter eddy, and plunged into the main tidal stream running into Mykines Sound, two miles wide separating Mykines from Vagar Island. *Brendan* shot forward into the gap like a log into the mill race. On each side of us the fjordlike cliffs of the Sound rose up seven or eight hundred feet, funneling the wind into a full gale. Luckily the wind and tide were together, or *Brendan* would have been swamped in the tide rip.

I wrenched out the Admiralty Pilot and glanced at the lines I had underlined while considering *Brendan*'s approach—"The depths in Mykines Fjord are small compared with those northward and south of it," gloomily announced the Pilot, "causing tremendous tide races, especially during gales, in which the waves rise to a great height. . . . There are sudden changes in depth in the fairway; the streams are consequently very strong, and there is violent turbulence, especially during gales, in which undecked vessels will probably founder." There we were in the midst of it, but *Brendan* merely fled into the Sound with scarcely a drop of spray coming aboard. The needle of the log swung smoothly up to six knots, to eight, to ten, to the end stop at twelve knots, and stayed there. The mass of water sluicing through the narrow channel was being accelerated by the gale to six or seven knots, so that *Brendan* was covering the ground at close to twenty knots. I could scarcely believe it. *Brendan* was breaking all speed records for skin boats!

With every gust she leaned over, gunwale almost in the water. The sea swirled by. Heaving on the tiller, George struggled to keep her running straight. If *Brendan* broached, we would be rolled over.

"Ease the sheets. Spill wind," he called to Arthur and Edan. "We have to slow her down." But the moment we slackened the ropes, they began to snap and crack like bullwhips, and I was afraid that someone would crush a hand or finger if they were caught. Abruptly there came a loud report like a rifle shot, quite distinct above the shriek of the wind.

"What was that?" I yelled at George.

"Masthead stay. It's snapped," he yelled back.

"There's no time to fix it," I replied. "Just keep going. We'll have to risk the mast and keep running on. We daren't lose speed in this Sound."

The mainmast gave a groan and dipped forward as its foot

[125]

slipped on the keel plate. Nervously Edan and Boots glanced up and wisely moved over to the gunwhales in case the mast came crashing down.

Brendan careered forward. There was no way we could enter harbor on Vagar. We were right in the grip of the tide race now and fairly flying through the gap. George weaved her slightly from side to side, trying to spill the wind from the bulging sails. But it was not enough. A fierce gust struck, and there was an abrupt ripping noise as the lower bonnet tore free, breaking away from the mainsail. It ripped in an instant, with one continuous crackle of its breaking lashings, a dozen lengths of a hundred-pound codline bursting one after another as if they were threads of cotton. Edan dived for the flailing piece of canvas before it flew overboard.

"Drop the mainsail," I yelled and scrabbled at the halliard. The main yard came sliding down. Arthur pounced on it and wrestled the flapping canvas, spreadeagled across it.

The sail had done its work. Before bursting, it had driven us almost the length of the Sound, and we could see the open sea once again at the far end, the full Atlantic once more.

"I'm glad the sail went then," I commented to George. "It was nicely timed. A little earlier and we would have been in real trouble."

Scarcely had the words left my mouth when a williwaw, a mountain gust, came shrieking across the water. It literally flattened the waves, tearing the surface off the sea into a blinding white sheet. *Brendan* shuddered as if a giant fist had punched her. Under the tiny remaining scrap of our headsail, she plunged away downwind like a frightened colt, while her crew grabbed for handholds.

"If we hadn't got the mainsail down already," I shouted to George, "that gust would have ripped the mast clean out of her."

Even when the tide spat us out of the Sound, *Brendan* was still at the mercy of a full southerly gale, and so I decided to try to lie in the lee of the Faroes, riding to a sea anchor. As soon as we were clear of the tide race, George jury-rigged an oar as a mizzen-mast; Edan lashed on the headsail bonnet as a scrap of riding sail; and Arthur heaved over the drogue. There, in comparative peace, we hung for an hour, brewed up a cup of tea, and relaxed from the excitement.

"Sorry about that, lads," I said. "It looks as though we've lost our chance to land in Faroes. If this gale keeps up, we'll finish up in Norway or Iceland." My companions didn't even flicker an eyelid.

"Great!" said Edan. "We'll just get even further ahead of schedule, and that will give us more time to go to a few parties in Reykjavik."

George put down his tea mug and peered toward the horizon.

"The rain's lifting. And the wind seems to have come round a bit. I think if we go now, we might just have a chance of getting into one of the other islands. But we'll have to act quickly."

We lost no time. Hand over hand, Arthur and Edan pulled in the drogue; up went the sail; and *Brendan* slanted off toward the high cliffs of the main island Streymoy. These cliffs were an awe-inspiring sight, a series of magnificent vertical rock faces with elevations of 1300 feet and more, half-hidden in scudding clouds. As we closed them, we found once again the myriads of seabirds, swooping and soaring in the air currents. Mile upon mile of the cliff face was streaked white with their droppings, and the birds came, unafraid, hovering around *Brendan.*

We failed by half a mile to gain the entrance to Sakshovn, the only shelter facing us on Streymoy, and *Brendan* was swept inexorably round the north tip of Streymoy, its huge wedge of cliffs towering above our heads, riddled with sea caves against whose gaping mouths the tiny white shapes of the gulls tossed like flecks of spume. We ourselves tried to imitate the seabirds, taking advantage of the broken air currents around the foot of the cliffs. George steered *Brendan* until she was no more than fifty feet from the cliff wall, sliding past in hair-raising style, but out of the main blast of the wind. Then we came to the tip of the island, and put the helm hard over to make a ninety-degree turn to starboard, and astonishingly plunged into the grip of another tide eddy running directly against us. Once more, it was an uncanny sensation. *Brendan* was carrying full sail, main and headsail, and they were billowing out, straining on the masts. The rigging was taut with effort; a bow wave curled back impressively; the log gave us a speed through the water of six knots. Yet we were not moving an inch! Fifty feet away, the cliff face was absolutely motionless. The tide race was running against us at exactly the same speed, canceling out our progress. There was nothing we could do. For fully an hour, *Brendan* poised there, as if suspended in the air by a magician. Then the tide changed. The rip slackened, and *Brendan* sailed serenely forward as if released from a spell.

"I don't know how you feel," I said to the others, "but I don't think I expected ever to experience such things in my life—storm and seabirds, leaping whales and such a tide race—and all in the space of twelve hours."

Soon afterwards we spotted a small trawler putting out from one of the channels between the islands. "This should fetch them," cried Edan, and he leapt up on the shelter roof, waving a tow rope in one hand and a bottle of whiskey in the other. The Faroese fishermen altered course, and towed *Brendan* into the nearby bay

Faroes boat

of Tjornuvik, where a cluster of gaily painted houses set into the back of an embayment in the cliffs looked like a child's set of building toys. Arthur and Edan paddled ashore in the rubber dinghy to stretch their legs on land, and to the astonishment of the villagers raced one another, cheering up the steep hillside. Meanwhile a Faroese asked me about our landfall.

"We came through Mykines Sound," I told him, and he looked startled.

"In this gale?" he asked.

"Yes, the wind was behind us, and it was a thrilling ride." He was astounded.

"It's some of the most dangerous waters of our islands," he said. "You were lucky. If the wind had turned against you on the tide, then I think your boat would have been destroyed."

The Faroese were fascinated by *Brendan*. At Tjornuvik the village children put out in their little boats to row around *Brendan* and gaze at her; and when the next day *Brendan* was towed up the narrow Sundini Channel to the capital at Torshavn, entire families came out of their houses to watch her progress. On the green slope, high above the side of the Sound, a line of cars snaked along keeping pace with us, following the road that was etched into the hill, where stream after stream came gushing down from this breathtakingly beautiful land. Each turn of the channel brought more and more hills into view, one rising behind the other, and every slope clothed only in moorland and rock, for native trees do not grow in the windswept islands, and the Faroese hills stand bold and stark to view.

Torshavn's quayside was thronged with onlookers, and when *Brendan* came sailing up toward the pier, out from the harbor dashed the elegant, slim shape of a large rowing boat, manned by a crew of eight oarsmen, all of them rowing in perfect rhythm to a short, quick sea stroke. This superb craft fairly flew across the water, approached us, turned, and then escorted *Brendan* toward harbor. Every line of the classic hull shape indicated her ancestry: she was the traditional sea boat of the Faroese, the direct descendant of the boats which the Vikings had sailed to the Faroes and replaced the Irish occupation. Now lovingly restored and manned by a crew from one of Torshavn's rowing clubs, she led *Brendan*, her predecessor, into port.

Immediately we were deluged with questions, not about the Voyage itself, but about *Brendan*. Every question revealed how strong was the seafaring tradition of the islanders. How was the hull fastened together? What were the dimensions of the frame? What was *Brendan*'s draught and her displacement? Did the side rudder work well in a following sea? It was more like being cross-examined by a board of shipwrights than by ordinary townsfolk.

[129]

Old men wearing traditional red stocking hats with the top turned smartly over one ear hopped nimbly aboard and prodded the leather, clucking with appreciation. Someone thrust a tidal chart of the Faroes into my hand and pointed out the best channels to follow if we were sailing around the islands. Even the local radio station asked me to give an item-by-item account of how *Brendan* was constructed and how she behaved at sea. More than any other people I had ever met, the Faroese understood the sea and showed their appreciation of the endeavor, and once again it was easy to detect the common bond which linked all seafarers in those hostile, northern waters.

And, of course, the Faroese were marvelously hospitable. *Brendan*'s matelots-ashore, Boots and Gannet, were swept into an embrace of comfortable hospitality. When they began to show a strange enthusiasm for doing the breakfast dishes, George and I were suspicious. So we followed our two heroes one morning when they went ashore with the bucket of dirty pannikins, and tracked them down to the seamen's hotel. Sure enough, we found the pair of them sitting at the kitchen table to consume a second—and free—breakfast while an admiring squad of Faroese girls was doing all the work for them.

Saint Brendan's name is familiar to every Faroese who learns in school that the Irish priests were the first people to settle in their remote islands. But no tangible remains of the Irish occupation have yet been found, presumably because the Papars, as the Irish priests were called, left too faint a mark on the islands before the Norsemen overprinted their massive stamp. Recently, however, Faroese archaeologists working at Tjornuvik have dug up cereal grains which indicate that there was agriculture in the Faroes before any record of Viking settlement. And of course there is the enduring literary and traditional evidence of the Papars in the islands. Nowhere is this tradition stronger than on the main island of Streymoy where, it is asserted, the Irish priests established themselves on a small, well-favored creek on the southwestern corner of the island. To this day the creek still bears a significant name; it is called Brandarsvik—Brendan's Creek.

I had made up my mind to visit Brendan's Creek as soon as possible, when I came back from a shopping trip one morning to find a striking couple on board *Brendan* waiting for me. The girl was most attractive. She had beautiful features, large brown eyes, and—for the Faroese, who are very blond—a sallow skin that gave her a gipsy look which was enhanced by her long black hair and a voluminous skirt. But it was her companion who really held my attention. He could have stepped straight from an illustration in Grimm's fairy tales. He was a powerful, thickset figure, sitting motionless on the gunwale. He was wearing very strong boots, rough corduroy trousers, a homemade brown sweater, and had the large, powerful hands of an artisan. But what was really impressive was his head—it was encased in the most splendid growth of hair, so luxuriant that it formed a solid mass extending from his chest to an arc a good three inches out from his scalp. It was a hairstyle worthy of Neptune himself, and from the serious face framed in the midst of this wild tangle, a pair of calm brown eyes gazed steadily at me.

"Hello," I said, as I climbed aboard. "Can I help you?"

The Neptune said nothing, but gazed at me for a full five seconds before calmly looking away at the girl. She spoke for him: "On the radio interview yesterday you said that you had room for one more person on your crew, and you would like someone from the Faroe Islands. This man would like to join you."

Good Lord, I thought to myself, even a Viking raiding party would have thought twice before taking on this fellow.

"Yes, that's right, but I'm looking for someone who's very experienced in a boat, if possible a person who can help take photographs."

"This man is better than that," she said proudly. "He's an artist and a very good one. Also he has sailed his own boat to the Mediterranean, and has been a fisherman on Faroe boats off Greenland. He is a serious man."

I can see that, I thought to myself, as I stole a surreptitious glance at the heavily bearded figure who had still not moved a muscle.

"Perhaps he could show me some of his work?" I inquired tactfully.

Neptune muttered something to his girlfriend.

"His name is Trondur, and he is shy to speak English," she said. "But he invites you to his home tomorrow."

"We'll be delighted to come."

"Good. We will come to collect you in the morning."

Next day they reappeared in a small, battered car. *Brendan's* crew squeezed in, and we rattled off across the spine of Streymoy. Neptune still had not said a word, but scowled solemnly through the windshield, occasionally hauling massively on the handbrake as the decrepit vehicle dived down the hairpins.

"The brakes are no good. This car is too old," said his girlfriend needlessly. Eventually we came to a narrow road which snaked down to sea level. It brought us out into a tiny hamlet on the water's edge. The place was dominated, of all things, by a Viking house. It sat there massively, an overgrown log cabin built of huge and ancient timbers, stained dark brown. Its windows and wooden doors were picked out in red, and on the roof was a carpet of turf like a slab of mountain pasture. A modern wing had been grafted cleverly to one end, but from where we parked the car, the log house was unquestionably Norse and completely authentic.

"This is Trondur's family home," the girl said.

I looked at the house, then past it to a neatly whitewashed church on the edge of the little harbor. In a field to one side, the roofless carcass of an even grander church rose out of the meadow, and its architecture looked late medieval. A strange coincidence occurred to me.

"What is the name of the village?" I asked.

"Kirkjubo," she replied.

"Does it have any other name?"

"Yes, sometimes this place is called Brandarsvik."

So there we were—my silent volunteer was from Saint Brendan's Creek, Faroes.

Bit by bit the details came out, partly obscured by Trondur's natural shyness, partly because no one thought it strange that he should want to join *Brendan*'s crew. It turned out that his family, the Paturssons, were among the longest-established families in the Faroes. Their log house was almost a national monument by Faroese standards, as the oldest continually occupied house in the islands. The Paturssons had lived there, father to son, for eighteen generations; before that it had been owned by the bishop of the islands. No less than three churches stood around the holy site of Saint Brendan's Creek: the roofless cathedral, the white church with its wooden steeple by the harbor, and the stump of an even older church eaten away by landslides into the sea until only its eastern wall remained.

The Paturssons themselves were as traditional and interesting

Brendan's Creek, Faroes

as their own log house. Squads of Patursson children rushed in and out; Grandmother presided as an elegant and stately lady, deferring only to Potl, Trondur's twin brother, and older by quarter of an hour, who was now the head of the family. It was Potl who greeted us cheerfully, dressed in his farming clothes, and half an hour later reappeared in full, traditional Faroese regalia of silver-buckled black pumps, dark blue knee socks with scarlet tabs, blue broadcloth knee breeches, and an embroidered waistcoat and short jacket embellished with a triple row of silver buttons. Totally unself-conscious in this splendid eighteenth-century attire, he stalked ahead of us to the little church, rang the bell to summon the congregation from the hamlet, and led the prayer responses to the austere, white-ruffed Lutheran pastor, while the ribbed wooden roof of the church creaked above us in the gale, like a ship working in a sea.

Afterward we took tea and coffee and cakes with the pastor in the main house, in a drawing room filled with furniture brought back from exotic lands by generations of seafaring Paturssons, and with some of Trondur's pictures on the walls. Then, after a decent interval when the pastor had left, *Brendan*'s crew was entertained to a memorable meal in the old Faroese style. The Paturssons

[133]

maintained the Faroese traditions, and they kept a table which would have done credit to every generation of Paturssons before them. The food put before us was the product of their own labors, from the milk and cream and the homemade rhubarb jam to the potatoes. But most of all they served us the traditional Faroese dishes. There was leg of mutton, killed and then dried slowly in the wind so that it had the consistency and color of Parma ham and a distinctly rank flavour. There were boiled fulmar's eggs, which Trondur and Potl collected from the cliff faces in a perilous exercise which involved dangling from a rope's end over a two-hundred-foot drop. There was even dried whale meat, and a rubbery slab of pure whale blubber with its black rind that reminded one exactly of high-grade tyre rubber. Everything was Patursson-prepared—even the whale, which the Paturssons had helped drive ashore and harpooned to death.

"My word, look at all that," breathed Edan in awe as he looked at this enormous spread. The table itself was a huge lump of timber which had been washed ashore in Brandarsvik some generations earlier with a half-drowned sailor clinging to it. The Paturssons had rescued and revived the castaway, and kept the timber as their great table.

I saw Trondur's eyes twinkle as he pulled out a ferocious knife, and without a word he carved a sliver off the slab of whale blubber. He offered it to Edan, who heedlessly took the blubber in one bite.

"Ugh!" his jaws abruptly froze, and his eyes widened in horror. "Ugh! It's like rubber soaked in cold oil," he blurted out, looking distressed.

"Go on, Gannet, it's rude to spit it out," said George. Edan screwed up his face, took a mighty swallow, and for the first time on the voyage declined a second helping.

After the meal we went up to the small converted farm building where Trondur lived, and saw some of his sketches. Borgne, his beautiful interpreter, was his fiancée and wholeheartedly in favor of the idea that Trondur should go with us. It would give him new material for his drawing and sculpture, she said. And like a true seaman, all Trondur had to do was pack his kit bag, and he would be ready.

Of course Trondur had to join the crew of *Brendan*, and it was one of the best decisions of the entire voyage. From the moment he came aboard, his command of English improved daily. He helped us to prepare *Brendan* for the next challenge—the long crossing to Iceland in the face of the westerly winds. There were several minor adjustments to be made: we smothered the flax ropes in whale fat to make them more supple and waterproof; Trondur and Edan improved the forward tent to make it more watertight; and, farther aft, George and Arthur replaced the ash legs of the steering frame. These had been bending and swaying so alarmingly on the run from Stornoway that I thought they might snap. So we replaced them with heavy baulks of oak, three inches thick, and lashed these new legs into position with leather thongs. Then Potl Patursson towed us round to Brandarsvik where, despite Edan's protests, we loaded Trondur's favorite sailing diet of dried fish, dried whale meat, and yet more chunks of whale blubber. Most of it hung from the rigging, and it gave off a truly medieval smell, strong enough to be noticed above all *Brendan*'s other odors. And so, draped with our new larder, we were ready for the next phase in our adventure.

Patursson family home

8
Faroes to Iceland

The Patursson family made a brave little group as they stood on the quayside at Brandarsvik, with their Norse home and the white church behind them as they waved and waved goodbye to *Brendan*. Their figures grew smaller and smaller, as the magnificent vista of the Faroese coastline opened up on each side, sheer cliffs falling direct into the sea. The sun was setting, and its rays slid from under the Atlantic cloud cover to backlight the silhouettes of the western islands, and here and there strike a patch of color from the rocky hill flanks. Potl was towing *Brendan* with the Patursson family fishing boat, and we were traveling across a calm, bronze, evening sea toward the harbor of Westmanna. The Westmanna or West Men were, in Viking parlance, the men who came from Ireland, the farthest-western land in Europe; and perhaps in Westmanna, too, the Irish or the Norse-Irish had settled. But for *Brendan* it was just a brief anchorage and then away again next day, July 3, to clear the Faroes and set course for Iceland.

Once again we found ourselves afloat off Mykines, our first bird island. Only instead of a raging gale, we now had a slack calm and lay rocking gently on the quiet swell. Trondur at once proved his worth: he taught us how to fish properly. As a five-year-old boy he had learned in the fjords the same skills that generations of Faroese fishermen have practiced off Greenland and on the Grand Banks of Newfoundland. Certainly there was a trick to successful fishing in these depths of water. First Trondur produced a massive lump of lead, perhaps four or five pounds in weight, from his kit bag. This weight he tied to a very long line looped around a curious flat wooden frame which acted as his spool. His lures were three simple hooks with brightly colored rags on them. Splash! The massive weight plunged overboard followed by yards and yards of line whipping over the gunnel. We were in three hundred feet of water. As soon as the weight touched the bottom, Trondur began to pull in the line quite slowly and smoothly, then flick! After about ten feet he gave the line a swift tug, grunted with satisfaction, and began to haul aboard the entire line hand over hand.

"Have you got one?" Gannet asked eagerly.

"Two," said Trondur laconically, as the wet line fell in coils around his sea-boots. Sure enough, up from the sea glinted the shapes of two splendid cod. Splash! Back went the fishing weight. Gather, jerk, and once again Trondur began to haul in.

"How many this time?" asked Edan.

"Three," said Trondur. Again and again he succeeded, and we all wondered how he did it. When I handled the line, even after Trondur told me a fish was hooked, I couldn't feel a tremor. When Edan tried, he raised a fine, fat blister on his hands just by the action of hauling in a single cast of the line. Soon *Brendan* was wearing yet another decoration—a dripping row of fresh-caught fish, hanging like washing on the line, and we were trying out every variation of cod—boiled cod, fried cod, cod in batter, cod stew, cod with rice or potato, or parsley sauce, even a tasty cod spaghetti.

On the second day a fine southeast wind sprang up, and we made excellent progress, fifty miles, in a gentle sea so that we had time to doze and chat and relax. A fog came down at eight in the evening, though of course it was full daylight and we could enjoy the spectacle of the millions of pearly droplets which formed on every surface, from the sails to the fibers of our woollen clothes and, most of all, on Trondur's magnificent head of hair. He was sitting on the stern, sketching in his note pad, and with the wind layering him with fog, he was coated down one side in the most spectacular manner.

Edan, of course, had come up with yet another scheme. This time, it was to launch messages in bottles. For one thing, it gave him an excuse to empty the last few inches of our current bottle of whiskey, and for another it gave him a chance to try out his prose.

[137]

"You never know who might pick up one of our messages," he said, looking hopeful. "I'm sure they'll write back."

George reached over the side and quietly retrieved one of Edan's bottles which was lazily bobbing past in the gentle flow of water along *Brendan*'s leather side.

"Aboard leather boat *Brendan*, west of Faroes," he read aloud from Edan's note. "Dear Reader, I am so glad you have picked up this message, which was thrown into the sea from the leather boat *Brendan* between Faroes and Iceland. Please let me know where and when you found the bottle." Then followed Edan's signature and address.

"I think it's worth a try, don't you?" continued Edan, perking up. "Just think of it. Some delightful girl, strolling along the beach in her bikini, sees this bottle resting on the sand and picks it up, reads my message. I'm sure she will write. That'll show you."

"I have my doubts about the bikini," I said. "You're dropping your bottles into the tail end of the Gulf Stream, and with the prevailing southwesterlies it's much more likely that they'll finish up near North Cape on the Arctic Circle."

"Ten to one the only blond who'll write back to you will be a

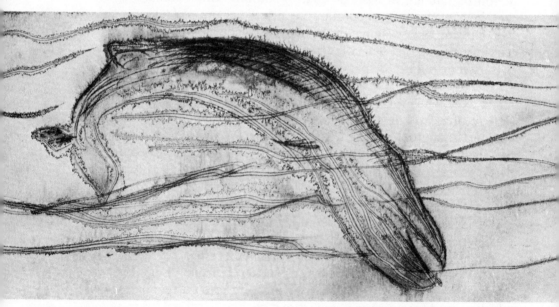

Fin whale

lonely Norwegian fisherman," said Arthur, "six foot tall, fifteen stone, and smelling like a sardine factory."

Whoosh! Just at that moment there was a massive sigh, like a huge gas bag emptying, followed by a gentle rippling sound. "Hval!" cried Trondur with delight, as we all leapt to our feet and gazed aft to where the sound had come from. Whoosh! There it was again, and this time we saw the cause of it, a great, sleek, black island of wet skin which came to the surface not twenty yards from *Brendan*, and wallowed there gently for a moment with the water running off it, and eddying away. "Good, big hval," said Trondur admiringly, as the rest of us gaped at the monster. The whale was certainly big, something like sixty feet long, and perhaps eight or ten times *Brendan*'s weight. It completely dwarfed *Brendan*, and suddenly one had the realization how puny our little, low-slung boat must seem to this huge animal. Apart from that immediate reaction, however, there was no feeling of danger, only a fascination for this huge creature which had deliberately emerged from the depths right beside us.

"He's come to take a close look at us," said George, in a hushed voice.

"Hope he doesn't come too close," muttered Edan. "One nudge from that fellow, and we'll all be swimming."

"No," I said, "he's probably interested in *Brendan* sitting motionless on top of the water. We probably look enough like a whale to make him curious—we're about the right size; curved to something like a whale shape; and, like him, *Brendan* is skin stretched over a skeleton. I wonder what he makes of us."

The whale heaved and sighed beside us, gently and deliberately. Then it sank down, and the next time it surfaced, it was a quarter of a mile away, swimming quietly and without hurry to the north.

I thought back to the visit I had paid in the previous autumn to the Whale Research Unit of the Natural History Museum in London. I was not sure of the reception I would receive, because the meeting was the result of a letter I had sent to a scientist on the Natural Environmental Research Council. Was there any useful work in environmental research *Brendan* could do on her voyage? I had asked. Yes, you might try counting whales, came the unexpected reply. He's pulling my leg, I thought as I read this. He knows the legend of Saint Brendan landing on the whale's back, and this is a

[139]

practical joke. But I went down to the Whale Research Unit, and to my surprise found that the idea was completely serious. "We've been asking selected yachtsmen and the crews of ships to keep a log of all the whales they see on their travels," said the scientist in charge. "The thing is that we really know surprisingly little about the habits of whales on a world-wide basis, where they migrate, what species are to be found in different places at different times, and so forth."

"But how can *Brendan* help?" I asked.

"Well, your boat is going to waters where we receive very few reports, and where one would expect to find a number of whales."

"What sort of whales are we likely to encounter?"

"Oh, almost all types. That's it, you see, we don't really know. But I would expect you to see fin whale, perhaps an isolated blue whale—those are the two largest whales in size—pilot whales, and off Greenland you may even see some of the true Arctic whales. We're interested also in the smaller species such as the dolphins."

"Do you think we're likely to get close enough to identify the particular species?"

"Again, I don't really know. But . . . ," and here he paused, "the minke whale is commonly described as 'curious' and he may come up to take a really close look at you, while the fin whale sometimes rubs himself up against small boats."

Just what *Brendan* needs, I thought, some itchy whale having a good scratch on the leather hull, to say nothing of tipping her over.

But on the voyage itself none of *Brendan*'s crew guessed what was about to happen, not even Trondur, who had a great deal of experience of whales and whale-catching. Day after day *Brendan* was visited by whales, sometimes singly and sometimes in groups. It was uncanny. The conditions were always the same: if the weather was gentle and the sea calm, we could virtually guarantee the appearance of whales close by, emerging from the depths with a great sigh of air, and a spray of water from their blowholes. Then they would stay in our vicinity for half an hour or more. For some reason the whales were drawn to *Brendan*. In all his experience Trondur had seen nothing like it. The great animals seemed to be almost as fascinated by *Brendan* as we were by them. Even when the whales came very close, there was more a feeling of companionship than of risk, and it was noticeable when we finally entered an area of shipping how the whales would dive when the ships were in the area, perhaps frightened by the sound of their engines. But when the ships had gone, the whales reappeared around us, rolling and wallowing in sight of *Brendan*, who was also slopping around on the cold water.

That first day of whale visits was all the more exciting because of its novelty. Scarcely two hours after seeing the first whale, which was probably a large fin whale, Edan was helping Trondur to fix a waterproof collar around the foremast to stop water dripping into the shelter. He was standing precariously on the gunwale, when he glanced down and suddenly let out a cry. "Hey, look at that! There are dolphins under the boat! No, they're not, they're whales and there's a solid mass of them right under us!" Even as he called out and we all rushed to the side of *Brendan*, the distinctive black fin and the boot-shiny back of a small whale broke out of the water just beneath Edan's foot, scarcely three or four feet away, with the characteristic hiss of air from the whale's lungs, and a lazy swirl of water as the animal curved into view. Looking down into the water, we could see the extraordinary pattern of large, moving shadows, as whale after whale moved gently underneath our leather hull, a vast congregation of animals changing places as they rose and fell, a living escort of sea creatures not more than six feet beneath the hull. There were literally scores of them, and we could even pick out the white flash of the bellies of two dolphin who seemed to be traveling in company with the whale school, almost as scouts. Then the whales began to surface around *Brendan*. The air was filled with a constant hissing and sighing of their breath as they came to the surface, some ten or fifteen animals at a time, then sank down and others took their place in a strange marine ballet. "Grind! Grind!" cried Trondur, usually so phlegmatic, but now almost capering with delight. They were pilot whales, one of the smaller species, though the larger members of the school were half as long as *Brendan* and probably weighed as much as our vessel. They were unafraid, and moving very slowly. Trondur seized one of his slabs of whale blubber. "This is grind," he said. "Very good to eat."

"Thank God, you haven't got your harpoon with you," said Edan, "or we'd be eating grind from here till Christmas."

"Or being towed by Moby Dick," added Arthur.

[141]

We calculated that the school contained between a hundred and a hundred and forty whales, and, later in the same day, when another, very large, whale visited us, I watched the huge unidentified creature come up close to *Brendan* and push a massive bow wave of water in front of it as it swam deliberately toward the boat. It was then that I began to wonder about the story of Saint Brendan and the whale. Superficially, of course, it was a preposterous seafaring yarn to think that someone actually could land on the back of a sleeping whale, mistaking it for an island. According to the *Navigatio*, the monks had lit a fire and started to cook a meal, but the heat of the fire had woken the whale, which suddenly began to move away. The monks cried aloud in fright, tumbled back into their leather boat, and the whale swam off into the distance with the fire burning on its back like a beacon.

Yet our experience with *Brendan* and the whales was putting this yarn in rather a different light. There was no doubt now that a leather boat, becalmed on these northern waters, held some sort of attraction for whales. It was not an exaggeration to say that it drew them from the depths. If this was still happening in the twentieth century when the whale population is so sadly depleted, what must it have been like in the sixth or seventh centuries A.D.? In those days it was very likely that there were far more whales off Faroes, Iceland, and Greenland where the animals come to feed off the fishing banks or at the junction of the currents where the masses of shrimps and plankton are found. In the old Viking sailing directions, for example, the sight of whales between Iceland and Faroes was actually used as a position guide, rather like identifying a particular island or headland. How much more impressive it must have been for the Irish monks, drifting quietly across the feeding grounds of these huge animals who, up to that time, would never before have seen a boat or met humans, but remained secure in their own great size and gentle manner. Until then I had been overlooking the fact that the leather boats of the Irish would have been the very first vessels that these whales would ever have seen in these waters. The Irish priests would have been in exactly the same position as explorers who enter virgin jungle for the first time and meet animals totally ignorant of man, animals which are unafraid and curious about the stranger. When one connects this fact with the far greater whale population in earlier centuries, the curiosity of the animals which we in *Brendan* encountered, and the known habit of fin whales rubbing against boats, it was scarcely surprising that the Irish priests came back amazed by the whale life, bearing stories of monsters, of huge sea creatures, of their boat touching the animals. Seen in this perspective and with *Brendan*'s paler experience to underline it, the whale stories in the *Navigatio* increased rather than diminished the realism of the original medieval text.

But not all the sea monsters in the *Navigatio* had been so friendly. After leaving the Island of Sheep and the Paradise of Birds, Saint Brendan's boat was chased by a great animal spouting foam from his nostrils and pushing a great wave ahead of him as he ploughed after the curragh. Just as this animal seemed about to devour the boat, another monster had appeared from the opposite direction in the nick of time, and attacked the first creature. A tremendous battle ensued; the newcomer killed the monster, and its body floated off and was later found washed up on a beach by the monks, who cut up and ate some of the flesh.

On July 7 I felt that this episode, too, had found a possible explanation. That day was another typical "whale day," with *Brendan* becalmed on a light oily swell and under a grey overcast which seemed to merge with the metal-colored horizon. Trondur, who had an almost uncanny instinct for detecting the presence of whale, was sitting on the aft thwart, quietly sketching on his pad. Suddenly he raised his head, and looked north. He seemed tense, which was unusual for him. The others, lounging quietly round the boat, sensed the feeling and we watched him. Faintly, very faintly, I heard the hiss of a whale emptying its lungs. Trondur was already on his feet shading his eyes against the light.

"Spaekhugger," he said flatly. We were puzzled. "Spaek-hugger," he repeated. "In Faroes, we not like this whale. It is not so big, but has big—" and here he was at a loss for the right word, and so opened his mouth and pointed at his teeth. To leave no doubt he drew an outline of the whale with charcoal strokes on his sketch book.

One glance was enough. He had drawn the characteristic shape and piebald blotches of the grampus or killer whale. I was not altogether surprised. From the start of the project I had heard more jokes and quips about sharks and killer whales than I cared to remember. The shark fishermen of Courtmacsherry, my own village in County Cork, had jovially pointed out that *Brendan* leather would make a tasty snack for a shark, drawn to the boat by the smell of her—to a shark—succulent wool grease. "Just like laying a rubby dubby trail across the ocean," they had joked. Personally I discounted the shark danger, particularly so far north, but I was not so confident about killer whales. In the last few years there had been a handful of well-authenticated reports of yachts sunk by killer whales who had battered holes in their hulls. Only the previous summer a big racing yacht off Brazil had been attacked in this way. There was no explanation for these attacks, as the metal or fiberglass hulls certainly were not edible. But it was a different matter with *Brendan*. The killer whale is carnivorous and, quite simply, there was a risk that *Brendan*'s leather skin would be mistaken for a potential meal. A killer whale combines a huge appetite with massive teeth, ten to thirteen of them and up to two inches thick on each side of the upper and lower jaws. These teeth are designed to bite and rend, and were more than capable of ripping *Brendan* to shreds. "As its name implies," said our little handbook about whales from the Natural History Museum, "[the killer whale] is distinguished by its great ferocity, being the only cetacean which habitually preys on other warm-blooded animals." The stomach of one killer whale, I had read, yielded up no less than thirteen seals; and it was often recorded that packs of hungry killer whales attacked and demolished larger whales. Would they now mistake *Brendan* for a dead or wounded whale lying on the surface?

Trondur pointed. There in the distance I could just see the thin line of a black fin lift briefly above the water. A moment later the sound of its hissing breath reached us across the still water. Then another hiss. Trondur's arm swung. A couple of hundred yards to the right of the first spot, another fin lifted from the sea. Then a double hiss. By now my eyes could pick up a pattern, and I looked farther to the right and saw two more fins. "Four—no, five," said George, close by my right ear, as he too stood up to watch. "There's a sixth," called Arthur.

The pack of killer whales was strung out in the classic hunting pattern, line abreast with perhaps one or two hundred yards between each animal so that they covered a front of about three-quarters of a mile. No wonder, I remembered, the Spanish fishermen called them *lobo del mar,* the wolf of the sea. They hunted with the same deadly efficient organization.

The pack swept south, sinking down, then reappearing almost in unison with heavy wheezing breaths. The third time they surfaced, they were close enough for us to pick out that there were five smaller animals and a sixth, much bigger one. This was the bull, the leader of the group. He was swimming two places in from the end of the line nearest us. According to sea lore, the bull controls the movements of the hunting group among these remarkably intelligent animals. The rest of the pack takes its direction from the leader, who is more experienced and acts as a director of the hunt. This pack, I saw, were going to pass well astern of *Brendan* on their present course.

Then the bull sensed us. His fin turned majestically toward us as he left the pack to investigate. We gazed, fascinated by this display of unhurried power. Hiss, ripple, his great bulk surfaced again on a direct course for *Brendan,* and sank down. Puff, a mist of spray and steam leapt a few feet into the air as he emptied his lungs before the water had cleared from his nostrils on his next surfacing. He came up for breath again, and this time he was no more than fifty yards away, and we could see just how massive he was. He was a fully grown killer whale, as large as he would probably ever be, perhaps five or six feet shorter than *Brendan* and three or four times the displacement. Alone, of all whales, he looked totally sinister; he was not like the cuddly, performing creature of the dolphinariums but had the brutal black-and-white ferocity reminiscent of the tiger's stripe. Most sinister of all was the thin, cruel fin which came slicing up every time he surfaced. It looked more like a shark's fin than a whale's fin, for it curved back to a point, and it was so big, a good six feet tall, that it could not support its own weight out of the water, but sagged over to one side. It reminded me irresistibly of the razor-sharp wing of an attack aircraft drooping as it squats on the runway.

The final time the bull killer whale rose beside *Brendan,* the fin was just twenty yards away. It stood above the water as tall as any of us. We heard the full hiss of the creature's nostrils and watched the small cloud of mist which drifted on the boat so we could actually smell the animal's stale air. Then the great back dipped.

Killer whale

There was a flash of the black-and-white flanks where the water sucked back from the massive body pushing through the sea; and the ripples came across and lapped gently against the leather hull. The killer whale had slid right under the boat, all eight or ten tons of him, curious, intelligent, and completely in control. There was nothing we could do. I looked round. We were all absolutely silent. Somehow we had all gathered together near the main shelter. I saw George clip his safety line on the steering frame. If the boat was tipped up, one man at least would stay with her.

We held our breath, absolutely silent, for what seemed like an age.

Whoosh! The great black fin came sliding up out of the water on the opposite side of *Brendan*, the great lungs emptied, and the killer whale began turning ponderously back toward his pack. We, too, all let out our breaths, and Edan with one heart-felt gasp muttered, "Piss off!" We had been inspected, and found wanting, and we were extremely glad.

Later that afternoon Trondur told us why the Faroese islanders so distrust the killer whales. The trouble usually comes, he said, during the pilot-whale hunts. These hunts take place when a school of pilot whales is seen close off the islands. An armada of small boats rushes to the scene and forms a crescent, gently herding the pilot whales toward the killing beaches where the pilot whales are stranded by the falling tide and provide—at least until recent years—an important supplement to the Faroese diet. Sometimes killer whales are also in the area, or, worse still, mixed in with the school of pilot whales. In these cases the killer whales have been known to come up underneath the small boats of the Faroese, smashing the boats, tipping the crews into the water, and men have been badly hurt. Also the killer whales are intelligent enough to rob the islanders' fishing nets as an easy source of food. They chew great holes in the nets to get at the catch, and do enormous damage. Some years ago the United States Air Force was called in to try bombing schools of predatory killer whales off Greenland, but the animals were so intelligent that they swiftly learned to dive out of sight when they detected the presence of an aeroplane. But the most astonishing story of the animals' intelligence came from Trondur. He told us that a Faroese islander had clambered down a cliff to rescue one of his sheep which had fallen onto a rocky sea

[147]

ledge. As the man was on the ledge, a killer whale burst out of the deep water nearby and reached for him as though he were a basking seal. Again and again the whale tried to snatch the man, keeping him trapped against the cliff wall until the whale finally gave up the attempt and swam away.

We ourselves witnessed some evidence of the killer whale's ferocity four days later: most unusually, because it was a choppy day, a school of pilot whales suddenly surfaced around us. They were behaving with great agitation. Instead of their usual placid motion, the animals were greatly disturbed. They surfaced and dived in confusion. Some were darting in one direction, others turning back the way they had come, plunging out of sight without taking breath. A few even leapt clear of the water. Instead of their usual herd discipline, the animals were scattering far and wide into small groups as if in panic. "I think spaekhugger are chasing them," said Trondur, as we watched this display of fear among the whales, and I again thought back to the *Navigatio*'s description of the battle of the sea monsters. Had the Irish priests been worried by a large whale coming up close to their boat, sending before it the characteristic bow wave? And at the last moment had this whale been the victim of a grampus attack? The details seemed quite reasonable: the bow wave sent forward by a large approaching whale and the mist spouting from the killer whale would agree with the medieval description. And what other "sea monster" was there which, when killed, would float away to a beach and make food for the monks? Surely it had to be a whale. Once again the mundane facts, stripped of their fanciful telling, emerged from the Saint Brendan story and made a sensible interpretation.

July 8 we finally received our weather luck. The wind picked up from the east, and *Brendan* began to reel off the sea miles. The wind was exactly what we wanted because it allowed us to steer clear of the long and dangerous coast of Iceland. "The south coast of Iceland is the most dangerous of all its coasts," stated my old edition of the Admiralty Pilot in a welter of gloom. "Should the winds shift to southwest and blow hard, a vessel would be very badly placed on that coast, where to touch the ground is certain loss. . . . The advisability in keeping at a distance from the south coast cannot be too strongly enjoined, and the numerous wrecks of French fishing vessels, whose spring fisheries begin here, demonstrate strongly that navigation must here be carried on with great caution. . . . It is rare that any vessel having incautiously neared the coast in stormy weather can clear it again. . . . Navigators are apt to be deceived. . . . The first warning of its vicinity may be the sound of the surf on it."

The thought of a southwest gale driving *Brendan* sideways onto that inhospitable shore was enough to make me lay a course that headed almost due west, leaving a safety margin seventy miles

Compass and lamp

wide between *Brendan* and the coast. But the gale, when it came, was a blessing in disguise, for it swirled *Brendan* even faster on her way. On the first day we covered seventy miles, and on the second day we went even better. Writing down the log at the end of the day's run, I noticed that in the space of twenty-four hours *Brendan* had notched up 116 miles, even when reckoning by our very ineffective log, which, when the conditions became rough, started to flick its rotor out of the water between the larger waves. A

[149]

hundred sixteen miles was not bad progress, even for a modern cruising yacht, and we were by no means pushing *Brendan* to her limits. After all, the North Atlantic ocean off Iceland was no place to attempt to break speed records in a leather boat.

Then the wind freshened into half a gale, and the seas began to tumble in cold, grey ranks fifteen feet high. We lowered the mainsail five feet on its mast, reefed up its foot, and took down the headsail altogether. *Brendan* began to labor. Her frame squeaked and grunted; the massive H-frame of the steering oar swayed back and forth under the changing pressure; and the rope holding the steering oar in place began to emit the most alarming high-pitched creaks as it was stretched under the increasing pressures.

Sooner or later, we knew, gear failures would begin. The first item to break was one of the splendid new oak posts of the H-frame that we had installed in Faroes. With an impressive groan it cracked just where it passed through the thwart. Hastily we trebled the leather thongs holding it in place and carried on, but the lesson had been learned: the oak was too stiff and resisted the motion of the boat instead of flexing with it, and it could not withstand the strain. The next item to give trouble was at the masthead, where a plain leather strap held the crossyard to the mast. The constant see-saw motion of the yard was wearing through the stitching, and the strap gave way. So it was out with needle, leather awl, and flax thread, and make repairs at sea to keep *Brendan* running briskly on her course. Inside the main cabin the constant dash of spray over the roof was beginning to tell. An ominous damp stain appeared in each corner where the sea was creeping in, and each day the stain expanded a little farther, inching nearer the vulnerable radio set. The rate of the advance increased dramatically when we were eventually forced to bring *Brendan* across the wind. The easterly gale was now blowing us so fast that there was a risk that we would be blown clear past Iceland if we did not claw up to the north. But the new course laid the starboard side bare to the rollers, and the spray collected in the cracks and corners, seeking out *Brendan*'s weaknesses, and steadily trespassing into the living area. A murky tide-line rose steadily along the navigation books stowed on the shelf, and I became accustomed to find my "privileged" skipper's berth nicely wet at each end.

Fortunately we were now completely accustomed to our medie-

val surroundings, and it was remarkable how high was our morale. Six weeks earlier it would have been unthinkable to steer *Brendan* casually across the face of such hostile waves. Yet now we did it without flinching, and scarcely glanced up at the rumbling roar of a large breaker. We had learned that between the roar and any cascade of foam on board, there was a split second to act if we felt the tell-tale thump of the crest butting awkwardly against *Brendan*'s stern. That was the time to duck, or to hunch one's shoulders so that the spray didn't deluge down one's neck. And I noticed that our priorities had altered too. I was cooking up the favorite pudding of dried apricot and mashed biscuits one afternoon when a large breaker hit. A fair-sized dollop of the Atlantic fell right on top of us. Immediately everyone dived to save the pudding and ignored everything else. When it came time to dish up the pudding, we found that the spatula had been washed clear to the other side of the boat.

Nothing seemed to depress our good humor. During the second night of high winds, as I relieved George at the helm, I asked him how his watch had gone.

"Not bad," he replied. "A bit wet here and there, but nothing to worry about."

"Did you have to pump out the bilges at all?"

"Yes, quite a bit now and again. We got one good comber straight over the stern."

"Was that the one which woke me with a crafty squirt of spray in the face?"

"Oh no, a much earlier one. There was about a foot of water where you are standing now, and I was wondering if anyone was actually afloat in his sleeping bag. Good night."

With that, he calmly disappeared into the shelter, and left me to light the pressure kerosene lamp which gave the helmsman some warmth. I worked up a good sweat pumping the wretched thing, turned on the valve, and was rewarded with a mocking water-logged gurgle. The lamp was completely drowned. From inside the shelter George, who hated that lamp, gave a satisfied chuckle.

Each of us was reacting to the conditions in his own way. Arthur had decided that the best place to be in foul weather was warmly curled up in his sleeping bag. But if he curled up, George could not lie down properly, so there was much friendly banter between them as George kept count of how many hours each day Arthur could pretend to be asleep, surfacing only for meals and his turn on watch. Neither did the heavy weather take the edge off Edan's enjoyment of life; though he was complaining that his cigars were getting soggy in the spray. He, alone of us, still liked to take a tot of whiskey in the evening. However much he pressed us to join him, the rest of us had long given up the desire for a drink or even a smoke. Trondur remained absolutely unruffled. He would emerge bearlike from the forward shelter to take his turn at the helm, and on the first wind-swept evening taught us another useful trick. From his pocket he pulled out a pair of shapeless oiled wool mittens. To our astonishment, before he put them on, he leaned over the side and dunked them, warm and dry, into the water, squeezed them out, then put them on half-sodden. "It's better," he said. "Not so cold later." He was quite right; the gloves acted like wet-suit gloves and reduced the wind's chill.

Food became the number-one topic. Every morning George dug out the day's food pack from its place in the stowage area, and each day we watched to see how much of the pack would still be edible after the seas had been washing over it, and our feet had been trampling in the same area. Each bag was sorted through so that the ruined material was thrown overboard and then he brought the salvaged items aft to the cook box. We found that some food was too plentiful. There was packet upon packet of dried soup which we couldn't face eating, too many packets of biscuits, too much sugar, and sad-looking tea bags with half their flavor already washed out by the sea. To save money when victualing, I had bought a supply of very cheap powdered coffee, and this now proved to be false economy. After twenty or thirty cups of the stuff, not one of us could face the revolting brew any longer, and rediscovered the delights of childhood drinks, hot malted milk, chocolate, or meat extract. The main courses of corned beef or tongue or mince were very popular, and there seldom seemed to be quite enough to satisfy all our appetites, so that Skipper's Special, the mush of apricots, jam, and crushed biscuits, was a popular event, besides using up our surplus foods.

By July 11 I was very concerned about *Brendan*'s rapid advance to the west. The easterly winds had abated from gale strength, but were still pushing the boat westward so effectively that I was worried we would miss Iceland altogether. I looked again at the large-scale chart. If the wind kept up, we might even be able to run direct to Greenland in one long haul. But this would mean that we could not pick up the stores waiting for us in Iceland. I calculated our remaining food and water, and did my sums. There were enough supplies to get us to Greenland if we rationed ourselves strictly. But then I remembered the pack ice. There had been reports that the sea ice off Greenland was unusually prolonged that year, and the east coast might still be closed by a shelf of ice. It was not an attractive prospect, and I made up my mind: *Brendan* had to get in to Iceland at all costs.

So we struggled to get north. We set and reset the sails to their best effect. Adjusted and readjusted the leeboards. But still *Brendan* slipped sideways to the west. We put out the sea anchor again, dropped our square sails, and rigged an oar as a mizzen-mast on which we set a bonnet as a makeshift sail to try to keep *Brendan*'s nose up against the wind. But still we were pushed westward, past the Westmann Islands, and past the corner of southwest Iceland. Never again, I thought to myself, would I doubt the theory that many sea-borne discoveries have been made by accident, when ships were driven off course by storms and heavy weather. If a vessel was as responsive to the weather as *Brendan*, then it was very easy to find yourself five or six hundred miles off target after a week of storms.

Then, quite abruptly, the east wind dropped, and we could catch our breath. We knew we were not very far from land because we saw puffins flying past the boat, and these birds seldom range very far from their nesting grounds. Once more Trondur had a new trick to show us. "Crrk!" he called with a low throaty sound as a puffin went whizzing past, looking curiously at *Brendan* but keeping a safe distance. Again, "Crrk!" The bird wheeled in a tight arc and came back. "Crrk!" The bird was being drawn by the noise, closer and closer, until Trondur could keep it patrolling back and forth, puzzled by the strange sound. Seeing our interest, Trondur pointed at the usual pair of terns hovering high above *Brendan*. "Now this bird will come," he told us, and taking a white rag he tied it to the end of the boat hook and waved it in the air. Sure enough, the terns swooped closer for a look. Trondur waved the lure again. Down farther came the terns, until finally he persuaded one of them to land briefly on the sail.

"Pity they're so small," said Edan. "There's scarcely a bite of flesh on them."

"Not so good," said Trondur.

"What sorts of birds do you eat in the Faroes?" I asked him, digging out our bird book and leafing through the illustrations. He pointed out puffins, young gannets, and guillemots. "All good," he said. "We take them when babies from the cliff by climbing or with nets."

"What do they taste like?"

"Very good. Dry or smoked."

"What about these birds—fulmars?" Edan asked carefully, turning to the correct page.

"White bird is good to eat, but black one not good," said Trondur.

"Why not? Do you get sick?"

"I do not know. Only Faroese fishermen say that black one is not good."

Edan looked hungrily back at a noisy flock of fulmars who had settled on the calm waters astern of *Brendan* and were now cackling away, taking experimental nips at the plastic jug bobbing at the end of the safety line. "Do you think we could get any of those?" he asked wistfully. "Some fresh food would be nice after all that dehydrated muck. I can still taste the sulphur and preservatives for hours after every meal."

Trondur reached for a slab of whale blubber, hanging on the steering frame. Edan looked alarmed. "No, no. I'm not that hungry," he said. Trondur grinned as he cut off a little chunk of blubber, strung it on the hook of his fishing line, and removed the lead weight. "For bird fishing," he reassured Edan, and gently dropped the line overboard. The blubber floated down toward the fulmars, and sent out a glisteningly tempting ring of oil. Immediately the fulmars left the safety line and paddled over toward it. One bird took an experimental peck, found the blubber good, and began to feed upon it. Immediately the flock began to fight over the morsel, and squawks of rage and disappointment filled the air as they stabbed away with their beaks and tried to rip the tough blubber to shreds before a neighbor could get a bite. But the blubber was stringy enough to stand the onslaught, and a moment later one particularly gluttonous bird tried to steal a march on his fellows. He bent down, took up the whole lump in his beak, and

[155]

flapped off across the water, trying to make off with the prize. His gluttony was his undoing. The fishing line tautened; the weight of the bird's own rush set the hook firmly into its beak; there was a startled squawk, and Trondur was rapidly reeling in his threshing victim. Five seconds later a fulmar was being skinned, while another lump of blubber drifted innocently back toward the rest of the flock. "Fantastic," gloated Edan, as two minutes later Trondur caught his second victim.

But then the fulmars grew cunning. It took five minutes to catch the third bird, and even longer to catch the fourth. Then the birds simply refused to be drawn. They paddled round the tempting oily blob, came within six inches, but refused to take a peck.

Trondur beckoned to Edan and gestured to him to reel the line in very slowly. The fulmars followed the bait, shearing nervously as they paddled across the swell, trying to keep one eye on the blubber and the other on the strange boat. Thwack! With one clean overhand stroke Trondur brought down the boat hook and hit the nearest fulmar just behind the head, breaking its neck instantly. With a clatter of wings, the flock disappeared leaving five birds, four white and one grey Arctic fulmar on *Brendan*'s thwart. "Who gets the grey 'poisonous' one?" asked Arthur dubiously.

"We'll pluck all of them," I suggested, "drop them all in the pot together, and dish up. And then no one will know who gets which."

I boiled the gulls slowly, prodding them with a knife. They looked like skinny, long-legged wood pigeons and were even more tough. "Shouldn't we hang them for a couple of days to make them more tender?" suggested George. Edan looked agonized at the thought of delay. But after two hours the fulmar seemed to be ready, and I added some dark sauce and a few lumps of dried whale meat to make a gravy. One seagull was dished into each pannikin with some mashed potatoes. There was a moment's pause, a split second of doubt, before Edan took a bite. "Delicious," he announced. "Fantastic." "Still a bit stringy, but jolly good." "Great!" "I thought it would taste fishy, but it doesn't. More like pigeon, or perhaps grouse." Seagull à la *Brendan*, it seemed, was a three-star success. In the next few minutes there was total silence as we ate ravenously, and when the pannikins were collected up, only the bones were left, picked clean. Nor did anyone feel ill, whoever had eaten the grey bird, and thenceforth we agreed we would supplement our diet with fresh seagulls, one of the best foods available. It was yet another example to show how, a thousand years before, the Irish monks could have survived the long passages without difficulty or loading vast quantities of supplies. With a stock of dried meat, oatmeal, and roots, and blubber if they could get it, they could take fish from the rich northern seas and seabirds from the huge stocks of gulls around them, and thus survive almost indefinitely. Fresh water would have been their only limitation, and in an emergency they could have collected sufficient rainwater in those damp sub-Arctic climates to have survived the accident of being blown off course.

As for our own feelings about killing and eating the wild life, no one appeared to have any regrets. For my own part, I regarded it as an exercise in the hunter's skill. We were catching our prey with the most primitive of instruments, and there was no risk that we would deplete the rapidly increasing population of fulmars in those waters. In fact, of all the seabirds, the fulmars attracted the least sympathy. In the Hebrides and Faroes the fulmar population had been expanding rapidly at the expense of the other seabirds. The fulmars were ousting the smaller birds from their nesting ledges. Their unpleasant habit was to spit a green slime at the resident guillemot or puffin, a slime which ruined the waterproofing on the other bird's feathers so that it drowned the next time it settled on the water. Curiously enough, when we caught them at sea, the fulmars either could not spit slime or had shot it all at the hook when they were being reeled in.

It took us nearly six days to creep back into the Iceland coast, gently coaxing *Brendan* through the winds which blew perversely from the north and east. But those days were by no means dull. For one thing we began to see Icelandic fishing boats, a welcome relief from the empty seas between the Faroes and the south coast when we had sighted only two vessels in the entire crossing. The Icelandic fishing skippers would steer close to *Brendan* to look at the strange visitors, and the fishing crews lined the decks to gaze at us and wave. "Can't be much fun earning your living that way," I commented to George, as one Icelandic trawler wallowed past, with the seas breaking clear across her mid-deck as she butted into the rollers. "Just look at that water cascading across her." Then I remembered, and laughed. "I wonder what they're saying. Proba-

Snaefellsjökull

bly much the same thing. Mad to be in an open boat. But just compare the pasting that trawler's getting to the way *Brendan* rolls to the waves and rides the sea. We're scarcely taking a drop of water on board."

The following day a spotter plane of the Icelandic Coast Guard Service roared overhead, not fifty feet above our mast, and our radio crackled into life.

"Hello *Brendan.* This is Icelandic Coast Guard, Sierra Yankee Romeo. Is all well on board?"

"Yes. Fine."

"Are you sure?"

"Of course. Everything is very relaxed and the crew is in high spirits."

"We have a report from the newspapers that *Brendan* is leaking. Can we give any help?"

"No thanks," I replied. "I think the only leak must be among the journalists. If you ever want a leather aeroplane, we'll build it for you."

Mile by mile we crept closer to Iceland's coast. We occupied our time successfully with more fulmar fishing, and using chunks of whale blubber we caught ourselves more seagull stews. And George enlivened one afternoon by boldly plunging overboard into the sea wearing one of our immersion suits. He bobbed gaily round our becalmed boat for half an hour, looking like a bright red tailor's dummy with his feet sticking up in the air. As we were in latitude 62°N, the water was quite cold, yet when he climbed back on board, George was only just beginning to feel chilled. We did not know it then, but those bright red immersion suits were to play a vital role in our struggle for survival off the Greenland pack ice.

The submarine shelf off west Iceland is obviously a favorite area for the big fin whale, because their numbers increased as we approached the land, and as usual the animals visited *Brendan*, sometimes in pods of six or ten animals, including baby ones rolling along in their mother's wake, and—for once—looking comparatively small alongside *Brendan*. We saw, too, the whale-catching boats from Iceland's whaling station which cruise the area on the look-out for their prey, but we never saw them in action, because whenever the whale-catchers appeared, the whales frolicking around us seemed to be warned. They would dive. The catchers steamed past, and half an hour later the whales would reappear, snorting and puffing around *Brendan*.

Finally we had a sight of distant land, the magnificent mountain peak of Snaefellsjökull, the great volcanic cone which stands more than 4700 feet high over the western bay, its peak permanently capped with ice and snow. The white mountain top was the beacon for our arrival, as we began to distinguish the long buttress of mountain ridges running eastward toward the main bulk of land. Snaefellsjökull, too, gave us the wind we wanted. On July 17 *Brendan* began to slant more purposefully towards Reykjavik, and we made a sweepstake on our time of arrival. Just for a moment, as the harbor of Reykjavik came in sight, I felt a flicker of regret. Was it really necessary to be coming in to land with all its problems, its people, and its responsibilities? Life on *Brendan* was so relaxed, so peaceful, and so cocooned inside the leather hull that I was almost regretful that this leg of our voyage was coming to a close.

Yet it was only a passing thought. Our excitement mounted as *Brendan* passed the outer harbor buoy. Trondur, of course, had guessed the time most accurately and won the sweepstake. The Reykjavik pilot boat came chugging out from between the piers, and I looked back over my shoulder. As if to symbolize the new pressure of the land, a large cruise liner was bearing down on us,

30,000 tons or so of tightly scheduled commerce and investment, hurrying to enter the harbor.

"I'll heave to, so that the liner can get past," I shouted to the pilot, as he closed us. "I'm afraid we're not very maneuverable."

"Oh no," he called back. "That ship can wait. We have come out to guide *Brendan* into harbor. That is why we have come. There is a berth in the harbor waiting specially for you, but there is a strong wind inside and I think we should tow you."

"No, thank you," I called back. "We would like to give it a try ourselves. Perhaps you could stand by with a tow line just in case."

I handed the tiller to George, and he excelled himself. *Brendan* glided delicately in between the pierheads, so close that her crossyard almost brushed the legs of the spectators on the sea wall. She turned through an S-bend, and Edan hauled down our sails. Trondur and Arthur stepped quietly ashore with the mooring lines, as unconcerned as if they were stepping off the pavement, and *Brendan* was safely moored. A smartly uniformed Icelandic official picked his way over the greasy leather gunwale, white-topped cap tucked under his arm. He thrust a clip-board and pen into my hand. I looked down. It was a health clearance form, and I duly signed a firm *No* to the question "Are there any rats aboard the ship, or have any rats been seen on board during the voyage?"

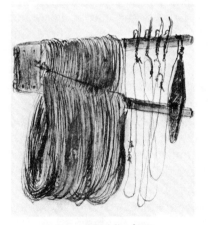

Faroes fishing line frame

9

Island of Smiths

One day, said the *Navigatio*, Saint Brendan and his crew found themselves being blown by a southerly wind toward a stony island "very rough, rocky and full of slag, without trees or grass, full of smiths' forges. The venerable father [Brendan] said to his brothers: 'This island worries me. I do not want to go on to it nor even get near it. But the wind is driving us straight toward it.'

"As they were sailing alongside it, a stone's throw away, they heard the sound of bellows blowing like thunder, and the thud of hammers on iron and anvil. When he heard this, the venerable father armed himself by making the sign of the Cross in four directions, saying 'Lord Jesus Christ deliver us from this island.'

"When he had finished speaking, behold, one of the inhabitants of this island came out of doors as if to do some task. He was very shaggy and full of fire and darkness. When he caught sight of the servants of Christ passing close to the island, he went back into his forge. The man of God blessed himself again and said to his brothers: 'My sons, haul up the sail even higher, and at the same time row as fast as you can and let us flee this island.'

"Before he had finished speaking, the same savage came down to the shore near where they were, carrying in his hand a tongs with a burning lump of slag of great size and heat. Immediately he hurled the lump at the servants of Christ, but it did not harm them. It flew more than two hundred yards above them. The sea where it fell began to boil as if a volcano was burning, and smoke rose from the sea as from a fiery furnace.

[162]

"And when the man of God had got about a mile away from the spot where the lump fell, all the people of the island came running down to the beach, carrying lumps of their own. Some began throwing their lumps after the servants of God, one after another throwing his lump, and always going back into their forges to set the lumps on fire. It looked as if the whole island was on fire like a huge furnace, and the sea boiled as a cauldron of meat boils when it is thoroughly heated up. All day long they heard a great clamor from that island. And when they could no longer see it, the howls of the inhabitants still reached their ears, and a stench came to their nostrils. Then the holy father comforted his monks, saying 'Oh soldiers of Christ, be strong in true faith and in spiritual weapons because we are in the confines of hell. Be vigilant and be brave.' "

Most scholars agree that the *Navigatio* was probably describing the eruption of an island volcano, complete with its shattering bombardment of glowing lava, ash bombs hurling from the crater, the sulphurous stench of the eruption spread by the wind, the thud and rumble of subterranean explosions, and the heavy roar of the surface eruption. But the vital question is whether the author of the *Navigatio* was merely retelling the description of a volcano he had picked up from another source or whether Irish monks had actually witnessed a live volcano in action. On the one hand, the Irish had such an extraordinary breadth of learning that they could have read descriptions of volcanos written by classical authors. On the other, the Irish navigators may have seen the volcanos of Iceland, which lie exactly on the Stepping Stone Route to North America, and could provide exactly the scene found in the *Navigatio*.

As Brendan sailed closer to Iceland, I was thinking over the problem from a practical angle. Certainly the geography of Iceland fitted the tale very neatly: The *Navigatio* states that Saint Brendan approached the fiery Island of Smiths from the south. And there is ample evidence of volcanic activity off Iceland's south shore. The undersea contours on the navigation chart show the cones of numerous extinct submarine volcanos which pimple the sea floor, and the long Reykanes ridge which projects southwest from Keflavik is largely of volcanic creation. In historic times there have been at least six submarine eruptions along this ridge. In 1783, for example, the people on the nearby mainland looked out and saw a new island rise briefly above the waves. But before the new island could be formally claimed and marked with a stone bearing the royal cipher, it was washed away and lost from view. Farther east, in 1973, a great crack opened on the volcanic offshore island of Vestmanna, out of which oozed a broad stream of lava that nearly engulfed the island's only town.

But one island, in particular, held my attention . . . the small island of Surtsey, three and a half miles west southwest of the Vestmannaeyjar group. Here in November 1963 a new sub-sea volcano had abruptly reared up out of the ocean. Everything I had read about that eruption—its 30,000-foot column of steam, the flying bombs hurtling 8500 feet up and splashing back into the sea, the muffled explosions as the sea invaded the underwater vents, the emergence of a new-born island—echoed the volcanic description of the *Navigatio*. The Vestmannaeyjar group had existed in Saint Brendan's day, and once again there was the oddity of their name: they were the West Men's or Irishmen's Islands. The name may have been no more than another coincidence, but in Iceland I wanted to talk to men who had seen the Surtsey eruption, especially to Sigurdur Thorarinsson, one of Iceland's leading volcanologists who had visited Surtsey soon after the island appeared above the sea.

"I remember thinking how accurate was the old Saint Brendan text when I first landed on the new island by rubber boat," said Sigurdur Thorarinsson when I called at his office in Reykjavik's university. "It was not long after the island appeared above the water, and the vents were still throwing out ash bombs. It was remarkable how conditions on Surtsey resembled the situation described in the old Irish story of the monks. As far as I know, there is no similar description by a classical author of a volcano formed by submarine eruption." He paused.

"And there's another point which is sometimes overlooked: Saint Brendan's description makes it clear that the monks came up very close to the source of the eruption. This points definitely to a submarine eruption, as it is hardly possible that they could, in their boat, come so close to an eruption on land. To my mind, I am sure that the monk's description fits only a volcano emerging from the sea floor."

Today Surtsey, even when dormant, still gives some idea of

what the *Navigatio* meant by the "Island of Smiths." Surtsey is low and black, covered with slag and ash, and utterly lacking in any vegetation except for the first few plants now struggling to establish new life. It is precisely like the "Stony island devoid of grass and trees" which Saint Brendan saw; and should a new island appear, it would repeat the pattern of slag bombs, smoke rising from the sea, the fetid smell of sulphur, and the hissing steaming ocean described so vividly by the medieval Irish author.

The submarine volcano which the Irish could have seen poking its tip out of the ocean most likely disappeared long ago back underwater to become a hummock on the sea floor, or it may have been eroded away by the waves. There is no way of telling. Yet until Surtsey erupted, even the most experienced volcanologists had never been presented with a similar opportunity to study a submarine volcano at close quarters. When they did so, there was even a suggestion that the new island should be named after Saint Brendan. Eventually, however, it was named after a Norse giant, Surtur, in an edda poem.

Luckily, the *Navigatio* gives another clue to the location of the volcanic region. On another day, the text states, Brendan and his monks came in sight of "a high mountain in the ocean, not very far to the north, apparently covered in cloud but really in smoke at the summit. Immediately the wind drove them very fast toward the shore of that island until the boat grounded not far from land. There was a cliff so high that they could not see the top, the color of coal, and marvelously sheer like a wall." Here, says the text, one of the latecoming monks leaped out of the boat and began to wade toward the base of the cliff, crying out that he was powerless to turn back and being pulled forward. Demons seized him and, before his companions' eyes, he was set on fire. The other monks hastily pushed off the curragh and, as the wind had shifted, managed to sail away to the south. Looking back, they saw the mountain was no longer covered with smoke, but vomiting fire upward to the sky, then sucking the flames back so that the whole mountain glowed like a pyre.

Again it is obvious that the Irish monks were witnessing a volcano in action, but this time a mountain volcano on land, and apparently a short distance to the north of their Island of Smiths.

[165]

Once more geography corroborates their tale. North and east from Iceland's area of submarine volcanic activity rise the volcanos on the main island. The great volcanos of Hekla, Eyjafjallajokul, and Katla, for example, all lie near the south coast. Hekla and Katla are among the most active volcanos in Iceland, and it may be relevant that here the south shore of Iceland is a long, very gently sloping beach without harbors or inlets, where a curragh would run aground in the shallows if driven on land, just as the *Navigatio* describes. Thus, sailing north from the Island of Smiths, the monks could have seen a distant volcano and been driven ashore against their will by a strong south wind. If so, then, their landfall could have been under the vertical black cliffs of the Reykanes Peninsula, which are fissured into coal-like blocks, or under the steep dark cliff of Dyrholaey, 320 feet high and easily the outstanding landmark on this flat and featureless coast. Even today, the Admiralty Pilot echoes the *Navigatio* when it describes Dyrholaey's dark hill as a "steep *wall-like* projection extending 2 cables south of the adjoining coast." As for the monk seized by "demons" and set alight, perhaps this was the fate of a crew member burned in a lava flow or who rashly trod on the thin crust of surface rock and broke through to the scalding steam underneath.

Fortunately, the *Navigatio* is not the only document to state that Irish monks were sailing to Iceland in the great seafaring era of the early Irish church. Dicuil, the learned monk of Charlemagne's time, records how Irish monks were making regular visits to an island so far north that during the days around the summer solstice "the sun setting in the evening hides itself as though behind a small hill in such a way that there was no darkness in that very small space of time, and a man could do whatever he wished just as though the sun was there, even pick lice from his shirt, and if they had been on a mountain top perhaps the sun would never have been hidden from them." Dicuil's description must mean that his northern island was in the same latitude as Iceland, where the midsummer sun only just sinks out of sight and, almost as Dicuil surmised, parties of sightseers enjoy climbing up to the high Icelandic peaks so that they look north and see the midnight sun just on the horizon, and hold midnight picnics by its light.

Independent evidence for these early Irish visits to Iceland comes from the Norsemen themselves. The *Landnamabok*, the Book of Settlements, written in Iceland in the twelfth century, describes how the Norsemen first reached Iceland from Scandinavia and found already living there "the men whom the Northmen called Papar; they were Christian men, and it is held that they must have come over the sea from the west, for there were found left by them books, bells and croziers. . . ."

The word *Papar* was the Norse word for the Fathers, the Christian priests, and according to the chronicler, Ari the Learned, who wrote the Book of Icelanders shortly before 1133, these Irish anchorites fled from the remote islands when the Northmen sea raiders appeared, because as Christians they did not wish to live near to the heathen. By a happy coincidence the Icelandic scholar who has done most work on the study of the Papars recently was the President of Iceland himself, Dr. Kristjan Eldjarn. Formerly the Director of the National Museum, Dr. Eldjarn searched for ancient ruins on the island of Papey off the southeast coast of Iceland, and excavated the most promising of them. He was one of the first people to greet us at the quayside in Reykjavik when *Brendan* docked.

"We are allowed to believe that the Irish hermits were here," he told me, "but we still have not found any item definitely associated with them. The Book of Icelanders is still thought to be a very reliable historical source; and the place names tell their own story, like Papos, the island of Papey, and Papafjord, and others whose precise location we do not know. We can still believe that they were named after the Papars, the Irish hermits who lived in these places."

I told President Eldjarn a little about our experience in crossing from the Faroes. "*Brendan* has shown how the priests could have made the voyage in their leather boats," I said. "And I find it significant that the Papar names you mention all lie in the southeast of Iceland facing across to Faroes. Under normal circumstances that stretch of coast is exactly where I would expect to make landfall in *Brendan* if I was sailing the shortest route to Iceland. Once again, it seems that geography fits."

President Eldjarn looked wistful. "It so happens that I have not had time to carry on the investigations. We have really only just begun to search for Irish remains in Iceland, and there is much

At Batanaust

ground to cover. One problem should be borne in mind in this connection: In the so-called Viking times there was a lively contact between Iceland and Ireland, and it might be difficult to know whether an Irish artifact, found in Iceland, was brought there by the Norse or by the Papars before them. From the old literature we know that a good many of the Norse settlers came to Iceland via the British Isles, and the study of modern blood groups indicates that a sizeable proportion of Iceland's original population actually came from Ireland and Scotland, either as wives of the Norse settlers, or as slaves and household servants. Iceland and Ireland were certainly very close throughout the early Middle Ages."

Perhaps it was this traditional Irish-Icelandic link that explained the warmth of the welcome which the Icelanders gave *Brendan* and her crew. During the days we stayed in Reykjavik, the offers of help and hospitality poured in. The small boatyard of Batanaust, situated in the next inlet to Reykjavik's main harbor, sent a message to say that we could use their slipway free of charge if we wanted to haul *Brendan* out for inspection. It was an offer I promptly accepted. *Brendan* had been afloat for eight weeks, far

[168]

longer than most people had thought a skin boat could survive without at least a new coat of grease on the leather. I wanted to see what her hull looked like now. So we towed *Brendan* round to Batanaust, and pulled her from the water. She was a reassuring sight. The only damage to her skin were one or two slight gashes near the bow where she had obviously struck sharp edges of flotsam. We examined every inch of the stitching, but not a thread was out of place. The boat was as sound and as tight as the day we had set out from Brandon Creek. Only her shape had changed. On each quarter near the stern two deep wrinkles ran diagonally across the oxhides where the stern had begun to droop, which was allowing the leather skin to slacken and pucker. And on *Brendan*'s starboard side, where she had lain on the beach at Iona, the soft sand had pressed in the leather between her wooden skeleton ribs so that it looked almost corrugated. But what really encouraged us was the way the wool grease was still sticking to the leather. This meant that our vessel still wore its waterproof coat, and that those critics who said that a leather boat had to be beached and regreased every week were wrong. Apart from one or two patches where the grease had been physically rubbed off by flotsam, *Brendan* still bore a good protective layer of lanolin which now had a greenish tinge of algae and in some places even gave foothold to a crust of small barnacles. We cleaned it carefully with wooden scrapers, and checked the leather underneath. Its condition was perfect. Our boat was still in excellent shape for another long ocean passage, and the following day a gleeful troupe of small Icelandic boys had the time of their lives painting a fresh layer of hot wool grease over Brendan's hull, and getting themselves thoroughly sticky in the process.

We also rummaged *Brendan* at the boatyard—the old traditional practice of removing every single item from the boat, cleaning her gear and inspecting the hull. Luckily we had kept the ash legs for the steering frame, and so were able to replace the oak which had cracked. Then, piece by piece we carried the rest of our equipment into the boathouse for store, and as we emptied her, *Brendan*'s leather flanks sucked in a few inches, like a python after digesting its meal. The boatyard cat, however, was dismayed. To the amusement of the shipwrights the cat took one sniff at Trondur's cache of whale blubber and dried lamb, and promptly evacuated the boatyard, not to be seen again until *Brendan* was reloaded and safely afloat once more.

The director of Iceland's telecommunications center also came down to offer his help.

"I think we could improve your radio system," he told me. "I suggest installing crystals for aircraft radio frequencies so that you can try reporting your position to overflying airliners on the aeronautical bands. There are few ships on the way to Greenland, and fewer coastal stations. In fact, once you are out of range of Reykjavik there's only one station in South Greenland before you get to Canada."

"But isn't it against regulations for a boat to use the aircraft frequencies?" I murmured.

He grinned. "Perhaps, but most likely you'll be speaking to Icelandic aircraft, or to our telecommunications center at Reykjavik, and we certainly won't raise any objections."

The next day a pair of white-coated technicians worked on retuning *Brendan*'s radio, and the director had another suggestion. "You'll need a call sign, so what about using ENDA? It sounds as if it's Irish, the Irish call signs usually begin with an E, and the letters are taken from the middle of *Brendan*."

Icelandic officialdom, it seemed, was delighted to bend the rules to help *Brendan*. It was a refreshing attitude, and to our great good fortune, the commanding officer of the Icelandic Coast Guard was the courteous and urbane Petur Sigurdsson. He was a man deeply concerned with the sea and its history, and had been interested for many years in the boats used by the Irish monks. Now, under his personal direction, nothing was too much trouble for the Coast Guard to help us. *Brendan* was given a berth in the Coast Guard base; from Coast Guard stores we were provided with a better anchor, extra warps, a spare car battery for the radio, and an oil bag to spread oil on the water in a storm. "You can never tell; it may come in handy," said Commander Berend Sveinsson, the Coast Guard officer looking after *Brendan*'s needs. "Our lifeboats used to carry this type of oil bag, and maybe it will help in a storm." When I took the oil bag back to *Brendan*, Trondur nodded approvingly. "This is good," he announced. "Oil from fish is needed, but best is whale oil." Twenty-four hours later he turned up with a jerry can of whale oil scrounged from the whale station outside town. It was fortunate he did so. That oil bag was to assist *Brendan* when she was struggling against the Greenland storms.

"If there is anything more we can do to help, just let me know," said Peter Sigurdsson when I visited the Coast Guard headquarters to thank him. In their control room I found myself looking at the big glass operations screen on which they marked the movements of their patrol ships. Still on the screen was the dotted line of *Brendan*'s approach to Iceland. At each noon position an artistic hand had drawn a tiny sketch of *Brendan*, and where we met heavy weather, huge waves were looming over the little boat, menacing her. "When you were coming into Iceland we were keeping an eye on you . . . just in case we were needed," said Petur quietly. I felt very grateful.

But one thing the Icelanders could not do for us was to improve the weather in our favor. We had *Brendan* revictualed within a week and we were ready to set out again, heading for Greenland. But the wind had turned against us. Day after day for three weeks we waited in harbor while the wind blew strongly out of the southwest, precisely the direction we wanted to go. Every afternoon I trudged up to the meteorological station and checked the weather maps. Each afternoon's forecast was the same—westerly and southwesterly winds, usually strong and often gale force. To assuage our impatience, Petur arranged for George and me to go on the ice patrol with the Coast Guard plane that flies off Greenland.

As the plane droned westward at a few hundred feet, I peered down at the Greenland Sea. It was a discouraging sight. Days of southwesterly winds had whipped up a long, rolling sea which left white foam streaks to the horizon. The color of the water was a bleak dull grey-green, chilly and inhospitable; and the sea itself was absolutely empty for mile after mile. Along the path that *Brendan* had to sail, there were no ferries, no freighters, not even a fishing boat to be seen. Instead, about a hundred miles off the Greenland coast, we came to the ice, a great ledge of pack ice extending out from the land and continuing north toward the Pole. From the air the ice looked clean and inviting compared to the foul mood of the ocean. But where the two met, I could see how the great floes dipped and swirled, and their shiny white surfaces suddenly changed to a hostile blue-green as the waves washed over them. Most certainly, it was no place for a medieval leather boat to venture.

When we landed back at Reykjavik, I made up my mind: It would be wiser to winter the boat over in Iceland and return to her the following spring to continue our journey. The season was dangerously late for a westward voyage, and by the time we reached Cape Farewell, the southern tip of Greenland, there was a real risk of autumn gales which could sink *Brendan*. Also there was far too much pack ice even to think of landing in Greenland. I consoled myself that this was what the Irish monks had done. The *Navigatio* made it clear that they advanced season by season, moving from one island to the next. Saint Brendan himself, according to the *Navigatio*, had taken seven seasons to reach the land in the West.

I knew that to delay the Brendan Voyage into a second season would bring practical difficulties, but I told myself that *Brendan* was not in a trans-Atlantic race. Above all, we should not take unnecessary risks. I told Petur Sigurdsson of my decision, and he looked relieved. "I'm sure you're right. *Brendan* has done well to get here, but now the sailing season is too late. Let the Coast Guard look after the boat for you during the winter. You can come back in the spring when we have easterly winds, and continue your voyage."

I assembled the crew aboard *Brendan* where she lay in Reykjavik harbor and, feeling depressed and worried whether the project would hold together, explained the situation to them. "Of course I would like to invite each of you again to be aboard *Brendan* next year. It has been an excellent crew; we all know one another; and I think we all agree that *Brendan* has shown that she can make it to the New World." George, Arthur, Trondur, Edan did not hesitate. Each said promptly that he would be back next year.

Winter nearly broke the back of the venture. We all returned to our separate homes—George to an office in Brighton, Arthur to Ireland, Trondur to begin building a house for himself on the farm near Kirkjubo, and Edan to help his brother overhaul their charter boat for a new season. *Brendan* sat forlornly in the hangar of the Coast Guard airplanes in Reykjavik. But the costs of running into a second season were crippling. The book publishers who had originally advanced the money to help make the project possible agreed to increase their financing. But funds were desperately low. To buy more stores and better equipment, renew insurance premiums, and all the other items of expense, I had to sell my twenty-seven-foot sailing boat *Prester John*—the car had already gone—and scrape the very bottom of the financial barrel. By the time the 1977 sailing season opened in northern waters, I had scarcely enough money to buy the crew's return tickets if we ever did manage to reach North America.

At the beginning of May it was time to muster the crew. I telephoned George and Arthur to tell them a rendezvous date.

Alongside Coast Guard ships

Edan I reached via the harbor master of a small Scottish port, who had to row out to Edan's boat to deliver the message. It turned out that Edan's charter business needed his attention, so while he could come up to Iceland to help us get *Brendan* ready, he decided he could not sail with us. Trondur's summons was suitably matter-of-fact. I telephoned the family farmhouse in Faroes, and when Trondur came to the phone, I said simply "Trondur, this is Tim. Please catch the Tuesday plane to Reykjavik and bring some whale blubber with you."

"Jaoo," he replied simply, and hung up. Five days later the crew contingent from the British Isles was filing past the immigration desk at Reykjavik Airport—George as brisk and efficient as ever; Edan in a shaggy tweed jacket, jeans, and homemade shoes, still without socks; Arthur in a disreputable-looking Irish cap. The immigration official peered doubtfully at Arthur.

"Where is your return ticket from Iceland?" he inquired.

I intervened: "He is a member of the crew of the skin boat, *Brendan*." There was immediate understanding. "Then he won't need a ticket," said the official. "Good luck and have a good voyage!" And he handed back Arthur's passport with a smile. The following day Trondur arrived, as hairy as ever, bearing in one hand a stout brown paper parcel containing about forty pounds of whale blubber and dried lamb, and in the other a harpoon.

We went immediately to the Coast Guard hangar to inspect *Brendan* to see how she had fared the winter. My real concern was the danger from rats and mice. I had heard several stories from tanners about the damage done to leather left in store, particularly if the leather was greased. Rats and mice, it seemed, liked to gnaw the fat for food. But *Brendan* was unharmed. She lay just as we had left her. The Icelandic winter had been exceptionally mild, and the rats and mice had foraged well in the open air. The only evidence of their presence were some mouse droppings and piles of torn-up paper between the double gunwales where several families of mice had built their winter nests.

Brendan was in such good condition that we did not even need to regrease her hull before we lowered her straight back into the water and began loading. After our previous summer's experience, there were one or two changes. We loaded 160 gallons of water, nearly twice as much as before, because there was still no chance that the pack ice would permit us to land in East Greenland and I planned to attempt the voyage to North America in a single long run. We also included two small VHF radios to increase our chances of talking directly to the commercial airliners overhead; and we took much greater care in wrapping our daily food packs, heat-sealing them in double sheets of plastic. Our diet, too, had been altered. After the previous season's trouble with the dehydrated foods ruined by sea-water leakage, I had decided to revert to a more medieval diet. We discarded the bulk of the dehydrated stores, and in its place loaded smoked sausage, smoked beef, and salt pork which a Polish meat curer had prepared specially for me in London over the winter, together with a large supply of hazelnuts, oat cereal, and a splendid truckle of cheddar cheese. These were the foods the Irish monks would have eaten, and I decided to take them too, not for authenticity, but simply because they were the best food for the job. Oat cereal was what Trondur called "good work food," and the smoked and salt meats were to meet every requirement of the voyage. We found it did not matter if they were swamped by a wave or soaked by rain. They survived without special care and tasted just as good. In fact, the medieval content of our diet was to prove a major success throughout the weeks to come.

Our clothing too showed the lessons we had learned. The 1976 season had demonstrated so clearly the advantages of woollen clothing in an open boat in high latitudes that we each brought extra wool stockings, wool hats and mitts, woollen trousers and scarves. Our friendly Icelandic boatyard presented each of us with a superb woollen Icelandic sweater, and now Trondur collected a mysterious-looking package from the airport. "Iceland gave *Brendan* sweaters," he announced, "so Faroes gives clothes too. They send this from factory. This is what Faroe fishermen wear." Digging into the box he pulled out five sets of splendid grey woollen underwear, twice as thick and warm as anything I'd ever seen.

It took only five days to return *Brendan* from her stripped-down state to full seagoing readiness. It was simplicity itself to re-equip a medieval boat. We merely propped the masts in their steps, lashed down the oars, attached the steering paddle by its leather strap, took on food and water, and by May 7 *Brendan* was ready to begin

[175]

the second and major stage of her odyssey. A few minutes past five in the evening, the Reykjavik harbor master's tug towed us out of port, dropped off the line, waved goodbye, and a light wind wafted us gently to the west. We opened a bottle from our fresh supply of Irish whiskey, charged our mugs, and I proposed a toast: "Fair winds!" "Fair winds," the others replied. We knew that the most difficult and potentially dangerous stage of the voyage lay ahead of us.

Dried meat

10
Emergency

The weather treated us almost too kindly. For the first week we had
no more than light airs and calms, and *Brendan* drifted slowly
westward away from Iceland. It was a convenient time to settle
down and readjust oneself to the medieval way of life, remember
the lessons of the year past, and pick up once again the special
rhythm of an open boat in northern waters. At Trondur's suggestion, we adopted the watch-keeping system favored by Faroes
fishermen. We divided into two watches—Trondur with Arthur;
George and myself—and the two watches worked four hours on
and four hours off around the clock. It was a system that allowed
each watch to decide its own arrangements. When the weather was
fine, one man steered the boat while his partner could rest, or read,
or cook a light snack. When the weather grew worse, the two
watch-keepers would take the helm turn and turn about, just as
they saw fit. When it was very rough, as we were to learn, twenty
minutes at the helm was as much as a man could endure before he
became completely numb. Only at noon did we break the four-
hourly pattern. Then we worked two dog watches of two hours
each and prepared the main hot meal of the day, which all four of
us would eat together. And this season we shared the chore of
cooking, which was a far better arrangement.

In some ways it felt as if we had never interrupted the voyage
for the winter. Our old companions the whales promptly paid us a
visit. When we were still well inside the circle of Faxafloi Bay off

Reykjavik a school of minke whale surfaced and blew around us, and a young minke about thirty feet long and consumed with curiosity spent fifteen minutes cruising along up and down each side of the boat, some twenty yards away, puffing and snorting, and rolling under us. Two mornings later, again in a flat calm, a large colony of seals popped up to inspect her, their heads bobbing like sleek footballs all around *Brendan* as the seals gazed curiously at the leather boat. Then, all at once, they sank beneath the water and vanished from view.

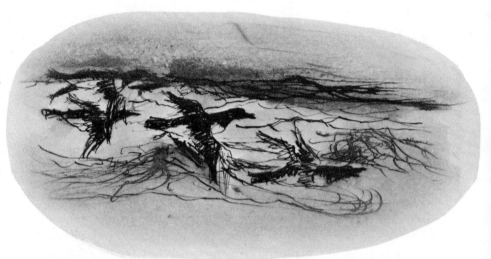

Flying guillemots

We had human visitors, too—a passing fisherman who presented us with lumpfish from his catch, which Trondur skinned and cooked up into fish stew; and a party of hunters in a speed boat. They had been shooting guillemot for the pot, and they also gave us part of their catch, much to Trondur's delight. He plucked, boiled, then fried, and finally sauced the guillemot with sour cream to produce as fine a meal as any French chef. "One guillemot," he announced judiciously as he ladled out our helpings, "is same as two fulmar, or three puffin, all good food."

Trondur was obviously back in his element. He fashioned a new

[178]

fulmar-catching device, a deadly flower of wicked-looking hooks sprouting from a corked float which bobbed along in our gentle wake. Below the surface, at the end of our safety line, he also towed a massive hook-and-feather on a heavy wire trace. It looked big enough to catch a shark. Everywhere one turned, there was evidence of Trondur's activities: coils of fishing line, lead weights, boxes of fish-hooks, chunks of whale blubber ready for fulmar bait, a stone for sharpening fish-hooks, and the occasional loose feather where he had plucked his latest gull prey. Trondur lavished the most care on his harpoon. During the winter he had made a beautiful new one. Its brass shank fitted into a long wooden shaft, and the attack end carried an exquisitely made spear point of steel, shaped like a leaf. This spear point was also set in brass, with an off-set attachment for the harpoon line so that as soon as the harpoon struck, the head broke free and the pull of the line twisted and buried the head in the flesh. For hour after hour Trondur would sit hunched over the harpoon head, lovingly honing it to a bright, razor edge. On the thwart beside him lay the harpoon shaft, its handle wrapped with leather thong for a grip. With the leaf-shaped point in his hands, identical in size and shape to the Stone Age spear heads of flint recovered from archaeological excavations, it occurred to me that the whole picture symbolized nothing so much as age-old Man the Hunter.

Seven miles above our heads we could sometimes see the silver dots of airliners flying between Europe and America, drawing their vapor trails across the sky. In just six or seven hours these aircraft were making a journey that it would take *Brendan* many weeks to complete, if we succeeded in our passage at all. How, I wondered, would those airline passengers comfortably seated in their chairs, with their film headsets and plastic meal trays, react if they knew that far below them four men in a leather boat were crawling at less than two miles an hour across that innocent-looking ocean, only a couple of feet above its surface, and dependent largely for their survival upon skills and materials that had not changed in a thousand years?

In the first four days *Brendan* had progressed so sluggishly that we could still see the snow-capped peak of Snaefellsjokull on the horizon behind us. In the clear northern air it was difficult to gauge just how far from land we had come. This clarity of the air was another factor, along with twenty-four hours of useable daylight in high summer, which must have helped the early voyagers in these northern waters. The Norsemen had used the peak of Snaefellsjokull as their departure point for Greenland. Norse shipmasters would sail west from Snaefellsjokull until the mountain sank below the horizon, and soon afterward, by looking ahead in clear weather, they would have been able to distinguish the first peaks of Greenland. From land to land along this track the distance between Iceland and Greenland is about 250 miles, and the mountains at each end make perfect landmarks, thus reducing a major gap in the Stepping Stone Route westward. On a fast passage the navigator might not be out of sight of land for more than one or two days. Also the phenomenon known as the Arctic Mirage may have helped them still further.

The Arctic Mirage, known in Iceland as the Hillingar effect, is a northern equivalent of the well-known desert mirage. The Arctic Mirage occurs when a stable mass of clear air rests on a much colder surface. The result is to change the optical properties of the air so that it bends the light like a giant lens. Objects far beyond the normal horizon now appear within view, floating above the horizon, and sometimes turned upside down and stacked, one image above the other. Sextant readings become unreliable, and the theoretical horizon may extend for a distance limited only by the resolution of the human eye. Highly favorable conditions for the Arctic Mirage occur over Greenland, where a mass of high-pressure heavy air rests on the great ice cap, while the high-altitude Greenland glaciers supply a bright source of reflected light for the mirage. So it is possible that Irish and Norse mariners, venturing out from Iceland's coastal waters or gale-driven westward, saw this distant light of Greenland well beyond the normal limits of the visual horizon and suspected that land lay in that direction.

Brendan's slow advance made her an easy mark for the patrols of the Icelandic Coast Guard service, whom Petur Sigurdsson had instructed to keep an eye on us for as long as possible. First the Coast Guard spotter plane circled us, then the guard ship *Tyr* came to investigate. As usual Trondur had a fishing line into the water. "We're only fishing for fulmars, not cod," I radioed to *Tyr* as she steamed inquisitively around us. "Jolly good, and good luck, *Brendan*," came back *Tyr*'s reply as she churned off on her duty to protect Iceland's two-hundred-mile fishing limit from poachers. I turned to Trondur. "By the way, did you tell your fishermen friends in Faroes that last year we ate grey fulmars which they say are poisonous?"

"Ya," he replied.

"What did they say?"

He grinned. "They say we are crazy."

Coming from Faroes fishermen, I thought to myself, that was the best compliment we had received so far.

Our next visitor was the patrol boat *Aegir*, which sent across a rubber dinghy. Standing bolt upright in the dinghy was a junior Coast Guard officer, clutching a brown box as if it would explode at the slightest tremor. "The Captain sends this with his compliments. I hope it's all right," he said, gingerly handing over the box. I opened it. Inside was an enormous cream cake, on the cream sailed an outline of *Brendan* piped in red icing. Beside it was an envelope addressed:

HIGH COMMAND OF THE GREENLAND SEA
CAPT. TIM SEVERIN
BRENDAN
ADDRESS POSITION 63° 56'N; 23° 17'V

The letter inside read:

Hello Tim, old boy.

You better start whistling for a wind. For added assurance we will make a powerful woodo [*sic*] dance in your behalf, at the Dance halls in Reykjavik tonight.

Seriously we all here wish you all smooth crossing and may God be with you all on your remarkable journey. The steward sends you a small token of his admiration and wishes you all the best.

Good speed.

Capt. Gunnar H. Olafsson.

As I finished reading the note, *Aegir*'s boat crew was already scrambling back aboard their vessel. The rubber dinghy was whisked aboard; a burst of smoke from her twin exhausts, and *Aegir* went throbbing past us at full speed, her crew waving and three long blasts on her siren to wish us farewell.

The weather continued to be very mild. It was difficult to believe we were in such ill-reputed northern waters. With only a gentle swell on the sea, Trondur could trail astern in the rubber dinghy, sketching *Brendan*, and George was able to clamber around the gunwale, adjusting ropes and leeboards to his precise satisfaction. The sun shone brilliantly through the clean air, and sank down in magnificent sunsets. Only the cutting edge of the wind reminded us that we were less than one hundred miles from the polar pack ice. When the wind blew from the north, from the ice, it sliced through one's defenses. Before emerging on watch, it was wise to struggle first into cotton underwear, then a suit of woollen underclothes, then the heavy Faroes underwear, two pairs of socks, trousers and shirt, and two sweaters, before leaving the protection of the living shelter and tugging on oilskins. The technique was to wear as many layers of warm clothing as possible and to dress up before going outside. Otherwise even a gentle breeze stripped away all body heat in a few minutes, and it was difficult to get warm again. As the temperature dropped each of us produced his own choice of clothing. Arthur sported a selection of shapeless woollen hats and a vast pair of padded Navy watch-keeping trousers. George had stocked up with soft Icelandic woollen socks and gloves. I preferred home-knitted mittens reaching halfway up my forearms. But Trondur outshone us all when he appeared in a magnificent furry Chinese beaver hat, its earflaps waving so that it was difficult to tell where the beaver fur left off and Trondur's luxuriant tangle of hair and beard began.

We were finding that life aboard *Brendan* was much more comfortable with four persons instead of five. The extra space was invaluable. We could stow our spare clothes and equipment properly, keeping out only our personal belongings, safely packed in water-tight kit bags. Also our daily rations, originally packed for five men, now gave us ample food. What with the fulmar that Trondur was catching, and our store of smoked and dried meats, we were eating far better than the previous season, and our morale lifted accordingly, even when we had to chip half-frozen honey from the jar. A constant supply of hot drinks—coffee, beef extract, and tea—kept the watch warm; and our fresh supplies survived well. In temperatures that seldom rose above forty degrees Fahrenheit, nature was providing us with a free cold larder, a fact that

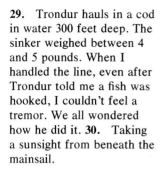

29. Trondur hauls in a cod in water 300 feet deep. The sinker weighed between 4 and 5 pounds. When I handled the line, even after Trondur told me a fish was hooked, I couldn't feel a tremor. We all wondered how he did it. **30.** Taking a sunsight from beneath the mainsail.

31. *Brendan* leaves Iceland and her snow-streaked mountains.

32. Trondur practices with his harpoon. Off the Labrador pack ice he was to score a direct hit on a pilot whale.

31.   **32.**

▲ 33.-34. ▼

33. Outward bound from Iceland the weather treated us almost too kindly. At sunset an illuminated sky seemed to bless us on our way, and for the first week we had no more than light airs and calms. It was a convenient time to settle down and readjust to a medieval way of life, remember the lessons of the year past, and pick up once again the special rhythm of an open boat in northern waters. . . . Our old companions the whales promptly paid us a visit. One young minke whale, about 30 feet long, spent 15 minutes cruising along up and down each side of the boat, some 20 yards away, puffing and snorting, and rolling under us. **34.** Reading by lantern light. We adopted a watch-keeping system favored by Faroese fishermen. It allowed each watch to decide its own arrangements. When the weather was fine, one man steered the boat while his partner could rest. Only at noon did we break the four-hourly pattern.

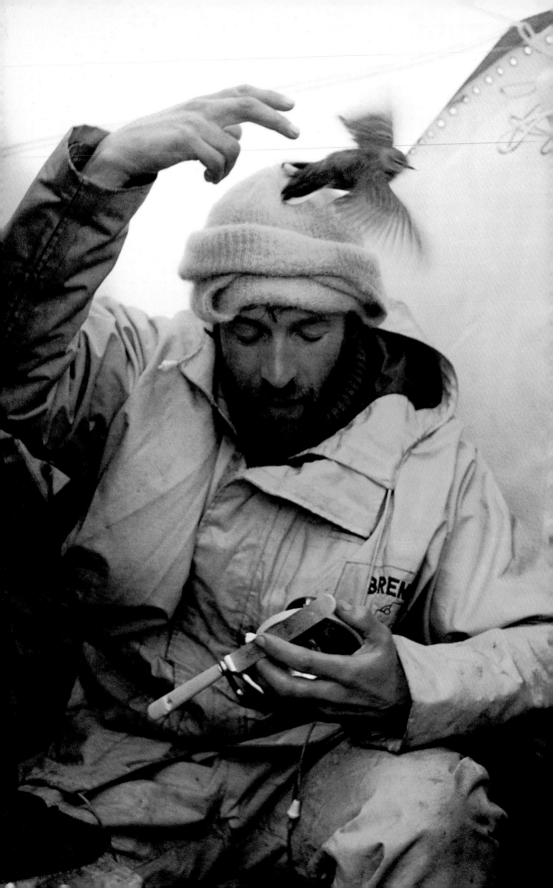

5. A water pipit exhausted on
s migratory flight from North
merica to Greenland tried to
nd on my head during lunch.

6. Adjusting the ties to the
onnet of the mainsail. The extra
anel of cloth meant we could
ncrease or decrease our sail area.

7. Making a daily radio report.

8 (*next page*). A gale roared
ut of the southwest and the
ind was too strong for *Brendan*
o do anything but run away from
. We were being driven farther
orth than I had planned. For the
noment, we had plenty of sea
oom, but a day or two of gales
ould put us into the pack ice. It
as not a prospect I relished.

35.

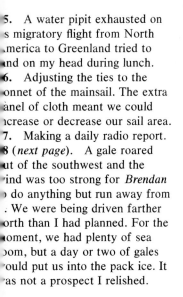

7.   **38 (next page).**

would have been doubly important to the medieval seamen who sailed that way before us and had to rely on fresh provisions more than we did.

On May 12, an exhausted bird arrived on board to remind us that migrating birds also took the same route between the continents. Scarcely larger than a sparrow, we identified it as a wagtail when it fluttered down, totally worn out, and landed on the steersman's head. It refused crumbs and water, but later hopped forward along the gunwale and took up residence in a sheltered hole in the forward bulkhead of Trondur's berth. By next afternoon it had gone, flown on its way, though we jokingly accused Trondur of having eaten it for a midnight snack. The little wagtail's journey lay along age-old migration paths that could have been another clue for the medieval sailors that land lay west of Iceland. But such clues would have had to be treated carefully. Flocks of migrating birds moving high overhead in spring and autumn indicated the direction of distant lands to watchers. But it required special knowledge to interpret these signs correctly. The watchers needed to know something of the habits of the particular birds to know just how far or how directly they flew on their migrations. On *Brendan* we ourselves were witnessing an example of this lore. The previous July whenever we saw puffins flying over the sea, we knew that we were close to land. But now in May we saw flights of puffin one hundred and more miles from the nearest shore. In May the birds were foraging far and wide for food, whereas in June and July, depending on where they laid their eggs, they restricted their hunting to areas close to the nests. On such knowledge could depend the difference between a successful and a futile voyage of exploration.

For our safety, I tried to report *Brendan*'s daily position to the shore radio stations, who passed the information on to the Coast Guard. So whenever the sky was clear, I took sextant readings and calculated our position. To set our course, there was only one golden rule: keep sailing west, always west. With each wind change, we simply altered course to make whatever westing we could manage. If the wind headed us, then we turned north or south, and moved at our best angle of ninety degrees to the wind, until the wind changed again. Calculations of leeway and the effect of ocean current were hit and miss. We judged *Brendan*'s leeway simply by looking at the angle of the safety line to the boat, which could be as much as thirty degrees; and our speed and distance was broadly a matter of guesswork. In light air, *Brendan*, especially when heavily laden, was moving too slowly for the trailing log to be effective, and the log reading was often forty percent wrong. By a simple test we found it equally accurate to throw a chip of wood into the water by the bow, time how long it took to pass the steering paddle, and then calculate our speed.

Friday the thirteenth proved to be our best day's progress to date. A breeze of force 3 or 4 pushed *Brendan* along for sixty miles, and because the wind moved out of the north and into the east, we immediately noticed the rise in temperature. For lunch we ate an enormous cassoulet of beans and smoked sausage, after Boots had scraped the sausages clean of their green fur of mould.

"Let's test some of our dye," I suggested to George as we lounged replete from the meal and wondering what to do to enliven the afternoon. Some bottles of dye powder had been given to us in case of emergency. The theory was to drop the dye into the water where it would be visible to a searching aircraft. "It will color the water an iridescent orange," George read aloud from the label on the bottle. He unscrewed the cap, and tipped the phial of powder overboard. The powder promptly turned green—not much use in a green ocean. "Perhaps the maker was color blind," commented Arthur. "Or his stuff doesn't quite work right in near-freezing water," I added. Five minutes later, however, George himself turned a spectacular blotchy yellow. Some of the powder had blown back and landed on him, and he spent the rest of the day looking like a strange species of leopard.

Next morning brought the first real snag of the second stage of the voyage—the kerosene cooker mutinied and refused to work on either burner. This was totally unexpected. All last season the cooker had functioned perfectly. Now I pulled out a box of spare parts and went to work to strip down the cooker, only to find that most of the spares did not fit. Someone at the factory must have made a slip-up when packing the spares. Superficially, this was merely irritating; but in the long run I knew that it could turn into a major setback. The kerosene was our only source of heat. If the stove failed, we would be left without hot food or drink at a time when a hot meal might make the difference between an efficient

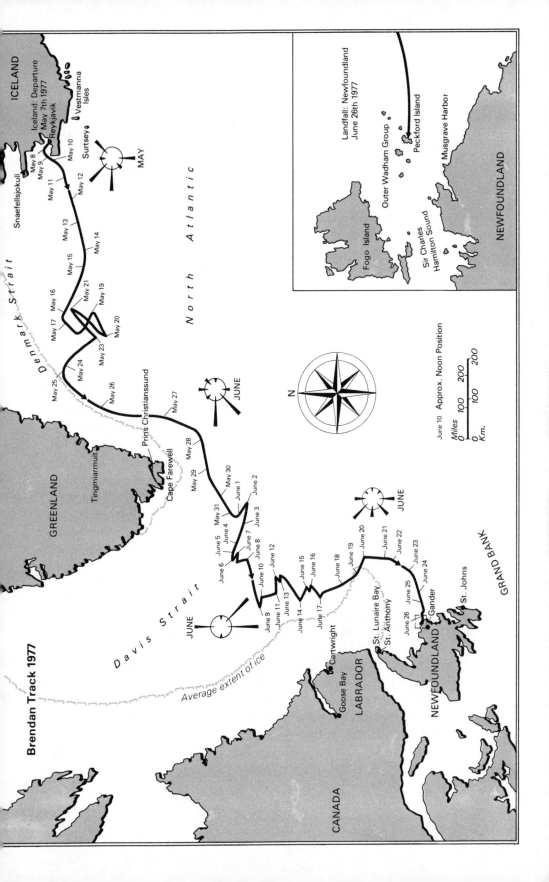

Brendan Track 1977

ICELAND

Iceland: Departure
May 7th 1977
Reykjavik
Vestmanna
Isles
May 8
May 9
May 10
Surtsey
May 11
May 12
MAY

Snaefellsjokull

May 13
May 14
May 15
May 16   May 21
May 17   May 19
May 20
May 23
May 24
May 25
May 26
May 27

Denmark Strait

North Atlantic

JUNE

N

Prins Christianssund
Tingmiarmuit
Cape Farewell
May 28
May 29
May 30
June 1
June 2
May 31
June 3
June 4
June 5
June 7
June 6
June 8
June 10
June 12
June 15
June 16
June 18
June 19
June 20
June 21
June 22
June 23
June 24
June 9
June 11
June 13
June 14
June 17
June 25
June 26

GREENLAND

Davis Strait

JUNE

Average extent of ice

Cartwright
Goose Bay
LABRADOR
St. Lunaire Bay
St. Anthony
NEWFOUNDLAND
Gander
St. Johns

CANADA

GRAND BANK

June 10   Approx. Noon Position

Miles
0   100   200
Km.
100   200

Landfall: Newfoundland
June 26th 1977

Outer Wadham Group
Peckford Island
Musgrave Harbor

Fogo Island

Sir Charles
Hamilton Sound

NEWFOUNDLAND

crew and an exhausted one. Of course we could sail forward, eating only cold provisions, but it was not a cheerful prospect. Even the Eskimos rely on hot food during long journeys; and we still had at least 1500 miles to go in an open boat. After four hours of work crouching over the cooker, I finally coaxed one burner to work on makeshift replacement parts. But the other burner was never to function again, and for the rest of the voyage I was acutely aware of just how much depended upon that single blue flame.

Now the weather, after a spectacular display of the northern lights, began to flex its muscles and behave more as if we were in the far North. The wind swung to the southwest and built up ominous black thunder clouds ahead of us. *Brendan* stopped in her tracks and began to shy sideways, northward, under an overcast sky and steady drizzle. An unfriendly swell heaved up the sea and occasionally splattered aboard as wave crests. Trondur commented on the bilge water which was now surging and lapping under his sleeping bag near the bows. "I hear water," he said, "but it is not wet . . . yet." He was amusing himself by fishing for the cloud of Little Gulls which hovered in our wake. They swooped and pecked at his line, even carrying it with them into the air, but their beaks were too small to be easily caught; and only rarely did Trondur reel in a victim which he could add to the larder of seabirds hanging off *Brendan*'s stern. "Is there any gull you would not eat?" I asked him. He thought for a moment. "The Eskimo, they catch two, three hundred auk. This they put inside dead walrus and bury for many weeks, then they dig up and eat. This I have not tried, but maybe it is not so good." Even so, Trondur looked mildly hungry at the prospect.

Saint Brendan's day, May 16, was the last day of "normal" weather—thick overcast with occasional rain showers that were just short of turning into sleet. It was in stark contrast to our Saint's day the previous year when, nearly thirty degrees warmer, we had waited in Brandon Creek preceding our departure from Kerry. Now in 1977, in the middle of the Greenland Sea but more relaxed and experienced, we toasted the Saint in Irish whiskey twice—once before lunch, and once in the afternoon when the wind turned, briefly, into the northeast and gave us a short push in the right direction. "Ouch!" grunted Boots when he leaned over the gunwale to dip his pannikin into the water for the washing up. "If that's any sign, I'd say we'll see ice at any time."

"Cold, is it?" I asked.

"Bloody freezing," he declared. "I wouldn't fancy my chances of falling into that. It rains just as much here as it does in Ireland, but there's a difference: if you touch metal in this cold, it hurts."

All day long the rain continued to come down, and despite the improvement to the living shelter, the water seeped in. A fine fat puddle formed on the thwart near Boots's berth; every lurch of the boat sent a trickle down on his head. Just before midnight, out of the darkling mist behind us, loomed the patrol ship *Thor*. On Petur Sigurdsson's instructions she had come all the way to check our aircraft VHF radio, which was not giving a proper signal, and how *Thor* managed to locate us in that gloom and swell we never knew. It was near miraculous. She had to come within six miles of us before her radar could pick up an echo from *Brendan*. It was like discovering the traditional needle in a haystack. After an hour in which we tested the VHF set between the two vessels, *Thor* slid away into the darkness. She had come well off her normal patrol route, and I knew that henceforth *Brendan* had passed out from under the umbrella of the Icelandic Coast Guard unless there was a dire emergency. Ahead of us lay only the bleak coast of Greenland, whose only permanent inhabitants in those latitudes were a tiny band of meteorologists at the small weather station of Tingmiarmuit. During the last few years the sea ice had been growing worse and worse, and even the East Greenland Eskimos who had once hunted along the coast had abandoned that region as too inhospitable.

As if to underline my sense of foreboding the weather continued to deteriorate. The next day began with fog, mist, and drizzle, and the barometer began to fall rapidly past 980 milibars. A sullen swell from the southeast warned us that heavy weather was on the way. George and I made ready. We dug out a tarpaulin, and stretched it as tightly as possible over the waist of the boat. Two oars acted as a ridge pole, and left a tunnel underneath the tarpaulin just big enough for a man to crawl into if he had to work the bilge pumps. The Irish monks carried leather tents and sheets of spare leather aboard their curraghs and presumably rigged themselves a similar shelter to throw off the breaking seas, otherwise a severe gale would have filled and sunk their boats.

By noon our lack of freeboard was growing dangerously apparent. *Brendan* was so heavily laden for the long passage direct to North America that, as the wind and waves increased, she promptly heeled over and began to scoop water aboard. Bilge pumping became a regular chore; and when the watches changed, Arthur and George climbed forward to reduce sail, rolling up the foot of the mainsail and tying in the reefs. Then we ate a hot stew of sausage, and waited for whatever the gale would bring.

By now I had abandoned any attempt at a westward course. The wind was too strong for *Brendan* to do anything but run away from it. On the charts I could see we were being driven farther north than I had planned. In a sense we were being embayed, just as we had been embayed on Tiree in the Hèbrides. Only now it was on a giant scale. Ninety miles ahead of *Brendan* lay the pack ice off the east coast of Greenland. From there the ice edge ran north and then curved east, sweeping back toward Iceland, so that we were being pushed into a great embayment of ice. For the moment, we had plenty of sea room, but a day or two of gales would put *Brendan* into the pack ice. It was not a prospect I relished, but there was nothing we could do about it while the heavy weather lasted.

We were not the only victim of the strong winds. Another migrating bird landed on *Brendan*. This time it was a small brown-and-white water pipit traveling its long migration route to a summer home in Greenland. The high winds must have sapped its strength, because the exhausted creature dropped into the sail, slid down, and lay quivering on the cabin top. It was too tired to protest when George picked it up, and put it out of the wind until it regained its strength. When the bird felt active enough, it hopped curiously about the steering area, perched briefly on George's hat, and then, still wary of humans, decided to spend the night on a coil of rope lying on top of the cabin shelter. There it stayed all night, where the helmsman could see it, balancing and bobbing to the swing of the boat, and unperturbed by the slap and rattle of the mainsail above its head. The little fluffy shape made a companionable fellow creature in the dark loneliness of the night watch; but the bleak conditions were too much for it. By dawn it was stiff and cold, dead of exposure.

Our next radio contact was encouraging. My radio call to Reykjavik was picked up and answered by the coast station at Prins Christianssund on the southern tip of Greenland. Prins Christianssund is a lonely outpost lying only a few miles from Cape Farewell and it handles the radio traffic for vessels rounding the Cape, so *Brendan* was now, in radio terms, at the halfway point between Iceland and Greenland. The weather also gave us a brief respite. The wind eased, though it left a heavy swell behind it, and we could prepare another hot meal. As I reached for the pressure cooker, Boots called out from the cabin, "Careful of the camera!" I thought he was talking in his sleep because as usual he was snug in his sleeping bag.

"Watch out for the camera," he called again.

I stopped, puzzled. "What do you mean?" I asked.

"It's in the pressure cooker."

"What!" I couldn't believe he was properly awake. "What did you say?"

"In the pressure cooker," he repeated as if it were the most natural place in the world to keep his camera. And in a sense it was. I removed the lid of the cooker, and there nestling in the vegetable cage was his precious camera, dry and safe, if smelling of onions. Thenceforth no one filled the kettle or put a saucepan on the stove without first checking that it did not contain our photographer's equipment.

Soon, for the third time in as many days, the wind turned against us, and picked up strength. Our spirits fell with the barometer. For three days now we'd been struggling in circles, covering the same patch of ocean with no progress. It was very disheartening. Enhanced by the almost constant rain, the sea took on a permanently hostile look. From one point of view the huge swells were impressive. They came as great marching hills of water, heaped up by the wind blowing counter to the main ocean current. They were grand monuments to the power of Nature. But seen from a small open boat, they depressed the spirit. It was difficult to judge their height, but whenever *Brendan* sank into the troughs, the swells were far higher than her mainmast. The entire mass of the wave loomed over us, and became as much of our

[189]

surroundings as the sky itself. If I was talking to George at the helm, it was disconcerting to see a great slab of water loom up behind and above his head not more than twenty yards away as if to topple on him. Ripples wriggling down its face, the water wall rushed toward the boat; then George's head would suddenly begin to lift against the backdrop as *Brendan* rose to the swell. Abruptly the skyline would appear, and all at once there was the broad unfriendly vista of Atlantic rollers stretching all the way to Greenland, before *Brendan* sank once again into the next trough and the grey-blue water closed in about us.

At 6:20 A.M. on May 20, we picked up a faint signal from Prins Christianssund which gave the weather forecast I had been dreading: we were due for a southwest gale, force 8 rising to force 9 of about forty-five miles an hour, precisely from the direction in which we were headed. We scarcely needed the warning. The ugly look of the cloudy wrack ahead of us was enough to advise us that we were in for heavy weather. Sure enough, within an hour, we were struggling first to reef the mainsail, then to lower it altogether and lash it down. Only the tiny headsail was left up to draw us away downwind and give the helmsman a chance to jockey the boat among the ever-larger seas which now began to tumble and break around us. Even as we worked to belay the mainsail, it was clear that we had left one precaution too late; the heavy leeboard should have been taken in earlier. Now the weight of water had jammed it solidly against the hull. Each time the boat heeled to the pressure of the wind, the leading edge of the leeboard dipped into the sea and, like a ploughshare, carved a great slice of water from the ocean, over the gunwale, to pour solidly into the bilges. In ten minutes the water inside the boat was swirling above the level of the floorboards, and the watch—George and I—could feel *Brendan* growing more and more sluggish. This was dangerous, because she was no longer rising properly to the seas; and the loose water was heaving back and forth, unbalancing her.

Clearing the leeboard was typical of the workaday chores aboard. George and I scrambled forward. The holding thongs of the leeboard were taut from the tremendous strain of the water, and the knots defied our efforts to clear them with marlinspikes. Water continued to pour in with every roll of the hull. George pulled out his knife and slashed through the thongs, while I hung onto the leeboard to stop it being swept away. Lurching and clumsy in our heavy clothing, we man-handled the unwieldy leeboard into the boat. The work was slippery and dangerous. We knew a single misstep could send either of us sliding overboard with no chance of survival in those chill waters. Next we tugged the tarpaulin into place to shoot off the breaking seas that leaped the gunwale. Ten minutes pumping and the water level in the bilge was down to a safer margin.

Then it was time to pay out the main warps in loops from the stern to slow *Brendan* down. I was fearful that she would somersault or slew sideways and roll clean over if she went too fast down the face of a wave. Finally we poured whale oil into our oil bag, pricked holes in the canvas, and dangled the bag from a short stern line. The oil bag left a streak of oil in our wake which partly quenched the worst of the wave crests directly behind us, but it was all the helmsman could do to keep *Brendan* running directly downwind of the slick where it would do any good. Each wave swung the little boat out of control; she threatened to broach and spill, until the trailing rope loops took hold with a thump that shook the steering frame, and literally hauled her straight. Looking back one could see the tremendous strain on the ropes, literally tearing across the surface of the sea under pressure, the spray rising from them like smoke. In this fashion we fought the gale, and in the next five hours of flight we squandered every mile of hard-earned progress from the previous day. And there was no end in sight for the gale.

Arthur was off-watch, asleep in the main shelter, when the first drenching took place. George was at the helm; I was crouched under the forward tarpaulin steadily pumping out the bilge water. As if in slow motion, I felt *Brendan* begin to tip forward, bows down. The boat seemed to hang there at a weird angle. Curious, I thought to myself, she usually levels off more quickly than this. Then George bellowed, "Pump! Pump as fast as you can!," and I heard the heavy onrush of water down the length of the boat. *Brendan* squirmed like a gaffed salmon and began to level off. Water bubbled and gushed out of the floorboards beneath me. Frantically, I redoubled the speed of pumping, and heard the thump, thump, thump of George briskly operating the bilge pump near the helmsman. Trondur emerged from his shelter, crawled to the starboard midship's pump, and aided in emptying the boat. When the water level was under control I climbed back and peered into the shelter.

There I saw Arthur sitting, disconsolate. On all sides he was surrounded by sodden clothing. His sleeping bag was sopping wet and his hair plastered to his scalp. "I'm afraid half the shelter is soaked, and my cameras have been drenched," he said.

"A big wave broke over the stern and traveled up the boat. It pushed in the rear flap of the shelter and poured on top of him," George explained. "Did it drown the radios?" I asked anxiously. "I don't think so," Arthur replied, "though there's spray all over them." I removed my wet oilskins, crawled into the shelter and dabbed carefully at the sets with a strip of dry cloth. Then I tentatively flicked on the power. To my relief the radios came to life. "Better sponge up the puddles as best you can," I advised Arthur. "There's a spare dry sleeping bag which Edan was using. Meanwhile, I think I'd better put extra plastic bags around the radios in case we get pooped by another wave."

It was lucky I did so. When the watches changed, George and I peeled off our oilskins, crawled inside, and lay down in our sleeping bags. Trondur and Arthur took it in twenty-minute spells to nurse *Brendan* through the seas.

George and I were half asleep, when out of nowhere there came a thunderous roar, an almighty crash, and a solid sheet of water cascaded into the cabin. It brushed aside the rear flap, slammed over the thwart, and hit with such force that water sprayed onto the shelter roof lining. The water was icy, straight from the East Greenland current. Underneath us in our sleeping bags, the sheepskin mattresses literally floated off the cabin floor. A moment later, there was the frigid shock as the water soaked through the sleeping bags. "Pump her! Quick, pump her! She's heavy!" somebody shouted. Frantically, George clawed out of his sleeping bag and raced out of the shelter, wearing only his underwear. In the same movement he had scooped up his immersion suit, which was hanging on the steering frame, zipped himself into it, and was swarming forward to get to the bilge pumps. At the helm Arthur was desperately wrestling with the steering paddle, trying to keep *Brendan* straight to the waves. Trondur, his oilskins glistening, was peeling back the small awning over the cooker and getting ready to bail. For want of a bucket, he had grabbed up the largest saucepan.

Ankle-deep in water in the cabin, I took a quick look around to see if anything could be saved from the water. Virtually all our gear was saturated. A book floated forlornly across the floor; the sleeping bags lay like half-submerged corpses. Water was sloshing everywhere. Quickly I jotted our last estimated position, tore the leaf from the message pad, and stuffed it in my pocket. If *Brendan* filled and sank, our only chance was to broadcast a MAYDAY with an accurate position advice. I thrust the small VHF transmitter, spare batteries, and a microphone into a satchel which I placed, ready to be grabbed, on top of the radio board. Then I, too, clambered into my immersion suit and went forward to help George, who was ratcheting away, flat out, at the port midship's pump. As I passed Trondur, I could see what a shambles the steering area had become. He was standing up to his knees in water, steadily scooping away, while around his legs bobbed pots and pans, jars of food, empty sea-boots, and wet rags. This was a full emergency.

Pump, pump, pump. The two of us heaved back and forth at the pump handles, sending two feeble little squirts of water back into the ocean. Curled up in the wet darkness beneath the tarpaulin, one had a heightened sense of the crippled motion of the boat. *Brendan* lay almost stopped in the water, dead and sluggish, while the water inside her swirled ominously back and forth. She was so low in the sea that even the smaller waves lapped over the gunwale and added more water to the bilges. It was a race against the distinctive rhythm of the sea. As I heaved frantically at the pump handle, I wondered if there was another wave waiting to break and fill her. Would she stay afloat? And what a Godforsaken place for this emergency to happen—halfway between Iceland and Greenland. What had the experts said? Survival time in this near-freezing water was five minutes or less.

Pump, pump, pump. A glance through a chink of the tarpaulin revealed the cause of our distress. The full strength of the Atlantic was showing itself. Whipped up by the gale racing clear from Greenland, the waters were thrashing in wild frenzy. The main

[193]

motion was the steady pounding of huge waves from the south-west, overtoppling their crests in a welter of foam. Flickering across the surface as far as the eye could see were spume streaks drawn out by the gale across the skin of the water. Here and there cross waves slid athwart the main wave direction, and collided. When they met, they burst upward as though cannon shells were landing. It was an awesome sight.

Pump, pump, pump. It took forty-five minutes of non-stop work with pumps and Trondur's saucepan to reduce the water in the boat to a safer level, and lighten *Brendan*. Then we could assess the damage. Structurally *Brendan* seemed as tight as ever. The steering frame was still in place, and the seams of stitching had held. It was easy to see where the wave had struck. It had come aboard at the unprotected flank of the boat, through the open gap beside the steering paddle. Right in the wave's path stood the metal cooker box. It had taken the full brunt of the wave. One side of the box was stove in and completely twisted. The retaining clip had been

[194]

smashed open, and its rivets sheared off cleanly by the force of the blow.

The scene inside the cabin was heartbreaking. Everything on floor level, which was most of our equipment, was awash in water trapped on top of the plastic sheet we used as a base for our living quarters. We opened the flap that led forward beneath the central tarpaulin, and one by one I handed through to George the dripping floor mats, sodden sleeping bags, sheepskins oozing water, soaked clothing. Everything was saturated in icy, salt water. Only the radios and equipment perched above floor level had been saved, together with the contents of our personal kit bags, which, thank heavens, had remained waterproof. Our spare clothes, at least, were dry.

George was shivering with cold and pulled on proper clothing at last. "Christ," he muttered as he struggled into a sweater, "I hope your theory is right that body heat will dry out our sleeping bags. I don't fancy being this wet for the rest of the voyage." As soon as the shelter was clear of gear, I concentrated on trying to get rid of the water on the floor, mopping up puddles and stabbing drain holes in the plastic floor with a knife. After half an hour's work it was obvious we would have to be content with the glistening wet interior. The shelter would never become any drier. Back from the tarpaulin tunnel, George passed everything we had evacuated, except the three sheepskins and one sleeping bag. These were so saturated that even after we had tried to squeeze them dry, the water poured out in rivulets.

Exhausted, George and I crawled back into the remaining two sleeping bags, trying to ignore the fact that we were drenched to the skin and the sleeping bags lay clammy upon us. For nearly thirty-six hours we'd been working with scarcely any sleep.

Boom! Again a heavy wave came toppling over the stern, smashed aside the shelter door and poured in, slopping over my face as I lay head-to-stern. We sprang up and tried to save the sleeping bags from the flood. But it was too late. In a split second the situation had returned to exactly where it had been before. Water was everywhere. The bilges were full, and the cabin was awash. *Brendan* was near-stationary before the breaking seas, and George and I were wading around the cabin floor with icy water soaking through our stockinged feet.

[195]

Once again it was back to the pumps for an hour, rocking back and forth at the pump handles, hoping silently that another wave would not add to the damage while *Brendan* was handicapped. Then back to the same chore of stripping out the cabin contents, squeezing out the sodden items, mopping up and returning everything to its place. I flicked on the radio. There was a heart-stopping moment of silence before I realized that the radio had been knocked off-tune in the hectic scramble. As soon as I had corrected the fault, I put out a call to try to report our position in case of disaster. But no one was listening. We were many miles off any shipping lanes, and with the radio's tuning unit drenched with water and the waves over-topping the aerial more than half the time, I thought it was very doubtful that we were putting out a readable signal. The little VHF set had fared even worse. Water had got into it, and it would only squeak and click in frustration. I switched the set off before it did itself an electrical injury.

"We've got to do something about those big waves," I said. "We're exhausting ourselves pumping and working the boat. This can't go on. The cabin will soon be unlivable."

The crew looked at me with eyes raw-rimmed from exhaustion and the constant salt spray. The wind buffeted the mast and plucked at the tarpaulin; the waves kept up their ceaseless rumble and roar; and for a moment I seriously wondered what on earth the four of us were doing here in this lonely, half-frozen part of the Atlantic; cold, drenched, and very tired, and out of touch with the outside world.

"I propose we put up an oar as a mizzen-mast," I went on. "Rig a mizzen staysail and put out the sea anchor so that she rides nose up to the waves. It means taking a risk when we peel back the tarpaulin to dig out the oar—a wave might catch and fill her—and it will be a dangerous maneuver trying to turn the boat around. She could be caught broadside. But the curragh men of Aran ride out heavy weather, head to wind, hanging onto their salmon nets as sea anchors."

I saw Trondur was looking very doubtful. "What do you think, Trondur?" Of all of us, Trondur had by far the most experience in these heavy northern seas.

"What we are doing now is right," he said. "It is better that *Brendan* is this way to the waves. Now she can move with them."

He twisted his hands to imitate *Brendan* zig-zagging down the combers. "If we have sea anchor," Trondur continued, "*Brendan* cannot move. When big wave hits the bow, I think tarpaulin will break and we have very much water in the boat. Water in stern of *Brendan* is not so much problem. Water in bow, I think, is big problem. Now we must stop water in stern and in cabin."

But how? What we needed was some way of closing the large gap between the cabin and the helmsman's position. But even if we cut up a sail as an awning, or used some of the forward tarpaulin, which we could ill afford to do, I doubted if they would withstand the pressure if we rigged them over the gap. We needed something extremely strong, yet something which we could erect at once in the teeth of the gale.

Then I had it. Leather! Under the cabin floor lay a spare oxhide and several slightly smaller sheets of spare leather. They were intended as patches if *Brendan* sprang a leak or was gashed. Now they could be used to plug a far more dangerous hole in our defenses. At the same moment I remembered, absolutely vividly, an encyclopedia illustration of the Roman army *Testudo*, the "tortoise" under which the Roman legionnaires advanced against a town rampart, holding leather shields overlapping above their heads to ward off missiles thrown by the defenders. Why hadn't I thought of it before?

For the third time, I began emptying out the contents of the cabin, peeled back the floor sheet with a sticky ripping sound, and prized up the leather sheets where they had lain on the deck boards. "Get a fistful of thongs," I told George. "I want to lace the hides together." He crawled forward.

I shoved the leather sheets out of the cabin door. They were stiff and unwieldy in the cold. So much the better, I thought, they will be like armor plate.

Quickly I pointed out to Trondur what needed to be done. Immediately he grasped the principle, nodded his understanding, and gave a quick grin of approval.

Then he was off, knife in hand, scrambling up onto *Brendan*'s unprotected stern where the waves washed over the camber of the stern deck. It was a very treacherous spot, but it was the only place where the job could be done properly. With one hand Trondur held onto his perch, and with the other he worked on the leather sheets

[197]

we passed up to him. Every now and then, the roar of an oncoming breaker warned him to drop his work, and hold on with both hands while *Brendan* bucked and shuddered and the wave crest swirled over the stern. Meanwhile, Arthur at the helm kept *Brendan* as steady as he could, and George, balancing on the port gunwale, pinned down each sheet of leather to prevent it being swept away by the gale. Trondur's job was to cut a line of holes along the edge of the oxhide in the right place for the leather thongs to lash down and join together the tortoise. With the full power of his trained sculptor's hand, Trondur drove his knife point again and again through the quarter-inch-thick leather, twisted and sawed, and carved out neat hole after neat hole like a machine. It was an impressive display of strength. Then George fed the leather thongs through the holes, tied down the corner of the main hide, and laced on the overlapping plates.

In less than fifteen minutes the job was done. A leather apron covered the larger part of *Brendan*'s open stern, leaving just enough room for the helmsman to stand upright, his torso projecting up through the tortoise. Leather cheek plates guarded the flanks.

Boom! Another breaker crashed over the stern, but this time caromed safely off the tortoise and poured harmlessly back into the Atlantic; only in one spot did it penetrate in quantity, where I had plugged a gap beneath the leather apron with my spare oilskin trousers. So great was the force of the water that the trousers shot out from the gap, flying across the cockpit on the head of a spout of water.

The tortoise won the battle for us that night. Several more potentially destructive waves curled over *Brendan*, broke, and shattered themselves harmlessly against our leather defenses. Only a fraction of that water entered the bilges, and was easily pumped back into the sea. Poking up through his hole in the leather plating, the helmsman had a hard and bitter time of it. Facing aft and steering to ride the waves, he was battered achingly in the ribs by the sharp edge of the tortoise while the wind scoured his face. From time to time a breaker would flail his chest, and it was so uncomfortable that each man stayed only fifteen minutes at the helm before he had to be replaced, his hands and face numb in the biting cold.

But it was worth it. Even if we were losing the distance we had made and were being blown back in our tracks, we had survived the encounter with our first major Greenland gale. We had made *Brendan* seaworthy to face the unusual conditions of those hostile seas, and we had done so with our own ingenuity and skills. Above all, we had succeeded by using the same basic materials which had been available to Saint Brendan and the Irish seagoing monks. It was cause for genuine satisfaction.

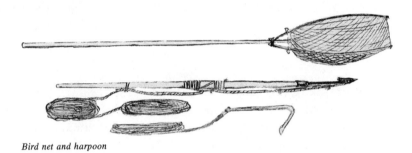

Bird net and harpoon

11
Greenland Sea

By eight o'clock next morning the gale had eased enough for us to begin sorting out the jumbled mess in the cockpit created by the waves that had washed aboard. Shelves were knocked askew; canisters of food had leaked. The lids had sprung off plastic boxes, and their contents now swam in murky puddles. When the salt container was tipped, its contents ran out as a liquid. All the matches we had been using, and the lighters, were ruined; to light the stove we had to resort again to special lifeboat matches which ignited even when damp. Sea water had burst into the kerosene lamps so that even the mantle had been broken behind the glass of the pressure lamp. Gloves, socks, scarves, hats, all were soaked, and there was no way to dry them except by body heat. The pages of my daily journal, which were written on waterproof paper, had been so badly soaked that most of the allegedly indelible ink had run. Each page had to be mopped off with a rag. Nor could I raise contact on the main radio with any shore station until that evening our signal was picked up by one of the Icelandic Airlines regular flights between Reykjavik and Chicago, and the pilot promptly relayed our position report to his air traffic control center, who in turn passed on the message to the Coast Guard that we were safe. That at least was one worry out of the way: the last thing I wanted was for our friends in the Icelandic Coast Guard to start searching for us on a false alarm. They had been magnificently generous in offering to keep track of *Brendan*, and I had the reciprocal responsibility not to put them to unnecessary trouble.

The wind dropped, but the weather did not really relent. It produced rain, fog, a brief calm, then more rain, and more fog. For half a day the wind obliged us by going into the northeast, and we bowled along sometimes at six or seven knots, rapidly picking up valuable mileage in the right direction. But then it turned again into the south and we were forced to slant even closer to the ice edge. All this time we kept up our efforts to dry out—mopping up again and again, sponging and bilge pumping, trying to beat back the water.

Whether the medieval Irish seafarers had to endure such bleak conditions is doubtful. Most historians who have studied climate agree that the climate of the North Atlantic between the fifth and eight centuries was often warmer than it is today. But they are cautious about the precise details. Quite simply, too little is known about the reasons for climatic change, and the experts are still gathering evidence of exactly what happened. The leading English historian of climate, Professor H. H. Lamb, had studied the early chronicles for references to floods, harvests, and other records of climatic change. "Briefly, there is good reason to believe," he had written to me, "that there were periods, particularly between A.D. 300 and 500 or perhaps as late as 550, and again between 900 and 1200, as well as a briefer period coinciding approximately with the eighth century A.D. in which there was an anomalously high frequency of anticyclones about the 50 latitudes and sometimes higher latitudes which must have reduced the frequency of storms and made the possibility of safe voyages to Iceland and Greenland higher in those times than in most others. However, it is quite clear that the variation of climate was not sufficient to rule out the possibility of a disastrous storm at any time."

Professor Lamb's conclusions were supported in part, though not in every instance, by the recent analysis of ice-core samples drilled out of the Greenland ice cap by Danish and American scientists. The horizontal layers in these ice cores represent annual snowfalls in Greenland extending back for more than a thousand years. A technique has been devised to calculate the temperatures in those years by measuring the amount of the heavy oxygen isotope trapped in each layer. Again, the evidence shows various warmer periods in Greenland's history, including one between A.D. 650 and A.D. 850.

[201]

Several scholars had already pointed out that the weather was much more suitable for trans-Atlantic voyages when the Norsemen were reaching Iceland and then went on to colonize Greenland. But there were at least two other favorable intervals, sometimes overlooked by the historians: a period in the eighth century just before the time Dicuil had been writing of the Irish voyages to Iceland; and an earlier opportunity in the sixth century closer to the time of Saint Brendan himself. Dicuil's information also throws a revealing sidelight on the more general climatic picture provided by the scientists. Dicuil declared that in about A.D. 800 the Irish monks had been setting out on regular voyages to Iceland *in February*, a time of year which modern sailors would certainly not recommend as the best season for the passage. But wind and weather in February, in Dicuil's day, were suitable for the voyage, more evidence that the early medieval climate was not the same as it is in the mid-twentieth century.

Of course the air temperature over the North Atlantic in early medieval times was only one factor in the problem of climatic history and the Irish voyages. Nothing is known of such vital matters as the prevailing wind direction, or the frequency and seasonal distribution of storms in those earlier centuries. However, it does seem likely that there was less sea ice on the Greenland coast for most of this time. The Norse sailors who voyaged from Iceland to the Greenland settlements in the early years were not unduly hindered by the Greenland ice. And it is reasonable to suppose that with higher temperatures at the time of the Irish Christian voyages, the sea ice would not have presented the problem it does today. Appropriately enough Páll Bergthorsson, a meteorologist at Iceland's Weather Center, had checked back through the Icelandic records and shown how the variations in winter temperatures could be directly related to the amount of sea ice appearing off Iceland. Now Páll and his colleagues were watching the Greenland weather maps on behalf of *Brendan* and, whenever possible, sending us weather forecasts by radio.

An improvement in the climate of the North Atlantic in the Middle Ages may explain why the *Navigatio* had so little to say about bad weather during Saint Brendan's epic voyage. In general, his curragh seems to have been troubled as much by calms as by gale-force winds. But this was due in part to the Saint's good sense in restricting the main stages of his voyage to the summer, though there was one occasion when he was taken by surprise by the weather: After their narrow escape from the hostile sea monster who attacked them, only to be defeated and killed by another sea creature, the travelers beached their curragh on an island. Here they found the carcass of the dead monster where it had been washed ashore, and Saint Brendan told his men to cut it up for food. This gave them extra supplies for three months. But the travelers had to spend all three months stranded on the island because foul weather at sea, with heavy rain and hail storms, kept them from putting out in the curragh. Some commentators had suggested that this unseasonal bad weather indicates that the monks had landed in South Greenland, where the weather can be notoriously foul even in summer. A bad Greenland summer, it is claimed, would have caught the Irish monks unawares because they were accustomed to better summer sailing at home.

A more intriguing clue to the possibility that the Irish navigators landed in Greenland is to be found, once more, in the writings of the Norsemen themselves. When the Norse first discovered Greenland they reported coming across "human habitations, both in the eastern and western parts of the country, and fragments of skin boats and stone implements." The eminent American geographer, Carl Sauer, argued that these skin boats and stone dwellings were much more likely to have been left behind by Irishmen than by the Eskimo, because at that time—as far as all research can show—there were no Eskimos living in South Greenland. The Norse settlers in South Greenland did not encounter any living Eskimo, nor have archaeologists found Eskimo relics of that time in that area. What the archaeologists have found is evidence that the only Eskimos in Greenland when the Norse arrived belonged to the Dorset culture whose early traces are confined to the north of the country. Just as important, the only habitations, other than tents, known to have been used by the Dorset people were very characteristic subterranean burrows, sometimes roofed with skins. These burrows would certainly not be described as "habitations of stone."

This being so, Carl Sauer asked, then whose skin boats and

stone habitations did the Norsemen find in South Greenland? Surely the Irish, because cells are typical structures built by Irish monks all over the west coast of Ireland and in the Hebrides.

Had the Norsemen stumbled across the traces of the Irish monks who fled there as refugees from Iceland when the Norsemen drove them on? Or were these relics left by Irish hermits who had voyaged direct to Greenland from the Faroes or from the Hebrides? The Norse sagas do not give any more information about the size or shape of these "habitations of stone," but with *Brendan*'s experience to help, another point now arose: the "skin boats" the Norsemen found were not likely to have been Eskimo kayaks, because the skin cover of a kayak will perish if it is not regreased and looked after very carefully. The skin has not been tanned in the true sense, as *Brendan* was, and will disintegrate when abandoned any length of time on the shore. By contrast, the oak-bark-tanned leather of the Irish curraghs was extremely stable and durable, and could last for a very long time indeed. Perhaps, then, the skin boats of pre-Norse Greenland were Irish ocean-going curraghs.

As we now struggled toward Greenland's coast, *Brendan*'s modern weather-luck was causing me real anxiety. The gales had not only forced her around in a futile circle in the Greenland Sea, but the boat was being pushed much farther north than I had anticipated or wanted. To clear Cape Farewell and its eighty-mile-wide shelf of pack ice striking out from South Greenland, *Brendan* needed to head southwest. But she was being frustrated by the constant foul winds. So I decided to take a gamble: We would steer close to the ice. There the local wind often blows parallel to the ice edge, and *Brendan* might find the wind she wanted so desperately. But the danger was obvious; if we were caught by an easterly gale, *Brendan* would be driven headlong into the pack ice with very little chance of anyone reaching us in time if we got into trouble. Petur Sigurdsson of the Coast Guard had told me not to be worried by the ice. "We call it the Friendly Ice," he had said with a twinkle in his eye. "Coast Guard patrol ships have found shelter many times from the storms by entering the ice. The sea is always calm there." But he was speaking of steel-built ships, and I was not so sure that *Brendan*'s leather hull would withstand an ice collision.

I did not have to explain the risk to *Brendan*'s crew. They watched the pencil line on the chart, which showed our daily progress, inching nearer the Greenland coast. Each man kept his own counsel but it was clear that they appreciated the importance of every slight variation in the wind direction. The foul weather continued to afflict us all the next week, and began to take its toll. There can be few places where the daily fluctuations of weather have a greater and more immediate effect than on the crew of an open boat in such waters. Whenever it rained—which was several times a day—we spent our time off-watch huddled in the shelter or under the tarpaulin, patiently trying to stem the trickles of water. When the air temperature hovered within a few degrees of freezing and the wind got up, the wind chill was harsh enough to restrict us to our damp sleeping bags as much as possible, despite the fact that the sleeping bags were still clammy. The trick, we found, was to keep rotating the bags so that the bottom side of the bag, which oozed a film of water, was periodically turned uppermost and had a chance to dry out. Grudgingly, we hoarded our last remaining dry clothes. The near-swamping had taught us to keep some dry clothes in reserve in case they were needed in a real emergency, and so we continued to wear our damp garments, even though it was a penance to pull on wet socks and trousers, push one's feet into wet sea-boots, and squelch to the helm on a rainy cold night.

Yet under these conditions, we remained remarkably cheerful, provided only that *Brendan* was making progress in the right direction. Sails were carefully adjusted; arms plunged into the icy water to haul up the leeboards; the helm painstakingly set to just the right angle. It was when *Brendan* was stopped or being driven back by headwinds that life became wearisome. All of us knew that the only answer was to be stoically patient, to watch and wait and bide our time until the winds turned in our favor. There was nothing else we could do.

Each man reacted in his own way. As sailing master, George must have felt the most frustration. With the wind against him—or no wind at all—there was little he could do to help us reach North America. Yet he never lost his meticulous sense of care for *Brendan*. He checked and rechecked ropes for wear, readjusted lashings, stripped down and reassembled the steering frame when it became slack, moved the leather chafing pads to fresh positions. Inside the shelter, he was equally careful about details. With his

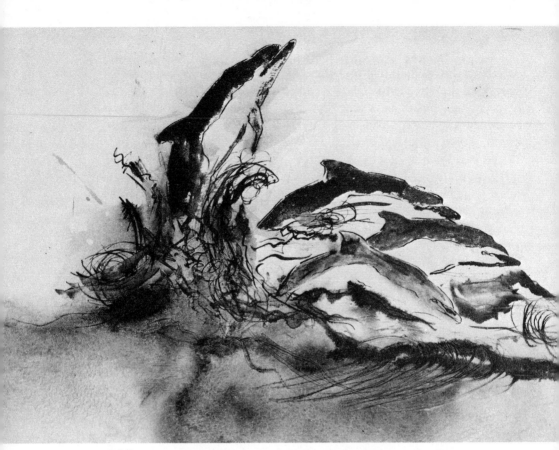

Dolphins

army training he always left his sleeping bag neatly rolled, his gear carefully wrapped and stacked and out of harm's way, and one could set a clock by his well-regulated watch-keeping routine.

Arthur was the complete reverse—a rumpled, chaotic, easy-going shambles. Arthur's sleeping bag, if Arthur was not in it, was usually serving as a squashed-up cushion. His stock of sweaters and scarves ran loose and turned up in strange places, until we finally banished his sodden naval trousers from the cabin, when they threatened to take over the entire living space. It was a standing joke that Arthur never remembered a hat. Invariably he lurched out of the shelter to begin his watch, and a minute later his head would pop back with a plaintive "I say, could you pass my cap, please. I'm not sure where it is, but it should be somewhere."

Arthur always had the bad luck. If a sneak wave broke unexpectedly over the gunwale at mealtime, it was Arthur who was sitting in the wrong place so that he received the cold sea water down his neck or in his pannikin. When it began to rain heavily, it always seemed to be as Arthur was about to start his watch. "Arthur!" George would sing out cheerfully. "There's a thunder cloud ahead. It must be time for you to take the helm!" With unwavering good nature, Arthur remained unruffled by his mishaps. Only his suit of green oilskins suffered. They seemed to wilt under Arthur's tribulations, and adopt their own personality. The rest of our oilskins hung heatly over the steering frame ready for use; but Arthur's green jacket and trousers were always to be seen, crumpled, battered, and inside out in a corner of the cockpit. "It hardly seems worth putting them on," Arthur would say as he poured a cupful of sea water from his jacket hood and shrugged his way into the soggy garments. And likely as not, he would discover that the inside of his boots were full of water, too. And there was no mistaking which were Arthur's sea-boots; his feet were so large that he was obliged to wear agricultural rubber boots, specially ordered from the makers, and their ribbed soles had treads like tractor tyres.

Trondur had spent so much time at sea in boats that he had developed his own brand of patience. "When do you think the wind will change?" I would ask him. Trondur would look at the sky, at the sea, and pause. "I say nothing," he would announce calmly, "sometime north wind." And when the weather was really atrocious, with driving rain, poor visibility, and an unpleasant lumpy sea that had *Brendan* staggering to the waves, he would say "Is not so bad. It can be worse than this in winter," and go about his work with such calm assurance that he raised all our morale. Trondur always found something to keep himself busy. If he was not fishing for fulmar, he was sketching shipboard's scenes or working over his drawings, sometimes using the frayed end of a match stick to spread the ink wash. The inside of his berth under the bow tarpaulin was a vertible artist's atelier. He had rigged up a hammock of fishnet which contained his paper and pens, his ink bottles and pencils, and the inevitable box of fish-hooks. Drawings and half-finished studies were hung up to dry, and one could sometimes see a needle and thread scrapings of leather where he had commandeered a spare bit of oxhide and was stiching up some knick-knack, perhaps a little box for his ink bottles, or a leather pendant carved with a Celtic cross.

On the whole, there was little idle conversation among the crew. Like dry clothing, we tended to dole out our thoughts and our comments little by little, knowing that there was much empty time ahead. One side effect, George noticed, was how our conversation actually slowed down. George was using a tape recorder to make a sound track for a film about the voyage, and when he played back the day's recording he found it was very frustrating. One person would ask a question. There would be a long pause; and then the reply would come back. Nor did George's tapes reveal much of our thoughts. By and large, each member of *Brendan*'s crew kept his opinions to himself, and in an old-fashioned way concentrated on running the boat and minding his own affairs. By unspoken agreement it seemed the best way of enduring our ordeal.

Sailing aboard *Brendan*, we were finding, was becoming a very personal experience despite our shared adventure. Each man reacted in his own way to events, and his experiences did not necessarily mix with the ideas of his companions. Nowhere was this more true than on watch. Then the helmsman was often the only man to see the distant single spout of a whale, the sudden jump of a dolphin, or a changing pattern in the sky. Some incidents passed in a flash before there was time to rouse the other crew members—others happened so slowly and gently that they were only perceptible to a man obliged to wait by the helm for two hours at a stretch.

Watch-keeping in a gale was perhaps the most personal experience of all, because then the helmsman was acutely aware that the lives of the other three depended on his skill. Every big wave during his watch brought a challenge which only the helmsman could judge and meet. Each wave successfully surmounted, and rolling safely past under the hull, was not noticed by the rest of the crew. But to the helmsman it was a minor victory, only to be forgotten in the face of the next on-rushing wave behind it.

Some moments, by contrast, were seared in the memory of the man concerned. One such incident occurred on May 23, when *Brendan* was yet again running north. It was the dusk watch, and although the wind was only about twenty-five knots, it was blowing counter to the East Greenland current and kicking up a short, breaking sea, with an occasional rogue wave which raked the boat. We were all very tired. The day-long moan of the wind and the roar of the combers sapped one's concentration. Watch by watch we had been climbing into our immersion suits, strapping ourselves to the steering frame with our safety lines, and holding onto the tiller. George happened to be forward under the tarpaulin, pumping out the bilge; Arthur and Trondur were in the shelters in their sleeping bags; I was alone at the tiller, steering through yet another maelstrom of sea, cliff after cliff of water rising up behind the boat. Each wave demanded a heave on the tiller bar to bring *Brendan* to the correct angle to her adversary.

Almost casually I happened to glance over my shoulder, not toward the stern to where the waves were coming from, but to port and away from the wind. There, unannounced by the usual crashing white mane of foam, was a single maverick wave. It was not particularly high, a mere ten feet or so, but it was moving purposefully across the other waves, and now reared nearly vertical along *Brendan*'s length, while *Brendan* was already locked solid in the crest of a regular breaker. "Hang on," I yelled at the top of my voice, and grabbed at the H-frame.

Brendan began to tip away from the face of the new wave. She leaned over and over until, on the lee side, I found myself looking almost straight down at the water and still hanging on to the upright of the H-frame. "My God, she's going to capsize!" I thought. "She can't possibly hold this angle without tipping over. What's going to happen to the men in the shelter and under the tarpaulin? Will they be able to get out?" It was a long, very unpleasant, moment. Then instead of capsizing, *Brendan* began to slide sideways down the face of the wave.

The next instant, the wave covered *Brendan*. It did not break in a spectacular roar of white water or tumble over her in impressive foam. It did not even jar the boat. It simply enfolded her in a great mass of solid water which poured steadily across *Brendan* like a deep steady river. Sea water swept across the tortoise and plucked at my chest. Looking forward, *Brendan* was totally submerged. Not two yards away, the cabin top was completely covered. The life raft, which was strapped on top of it and stood twenty-one inches higher, was under water. Only the masts could be seen,

[209]

projecting up from the water. *Brendan* seemed to have been absorbed into the body of the wave. In a curious distraction, I thought how her long, low profile and the two stubby masts looked exactly like a submarine with its periscopes hidden in the wave. And like a submarine emerging, *Brendan* struggled up from the sea. The air trapped under the tarpaulin and in the shelter simply pulled her up out of the wave. The water swirled off quietly, and *Brendan* sailed on as if nothing had happened. I was amazed. At the very least I expected the whole cabin to have been twisted and all the tarpaulins split. But when I clambered up on a thwart to survey the damage, everything was still intact.

The only casualty was my peace of mind. From my vantage point at the helm I knew exactly how close we had been to capsizing. And when my watch ended and I crawled into my sleeping bag, I found that I could not sleep although I was bone-weary. The rumble of every big wave sweeping down on the boat made me tense up to await a certain disaster. I did not get a moment's rest, and when the watches changed again, I mentioned the rogue wave to Arthur. "Yes," he said. "Everything inside the cabin went an underwater green." And that was where, by tacit agreement, we left the subject; and did the same a couple of days later when George had a similar bad experience thinking that *Brendan* was about to roll over during his watch. Such episodes in our lives seemed best left without discussion.

Only seventy or eighty miles from the edge of the Greenland pack ice we were at last rewarded with a break in the weather. On the morning of May 25 a much-needed calm succeeded the high winds, and we could enjoy the revival of sea life around us. On the horizon great flocks of gulls were circling and diving. As they flew closer, we made out the bursts of white spray beneath the birds where a school of dolphin was hunting the same shoal of fish from below. Then a separate, excited group of dolphin approached. They were escorting one single, very large, very fat fin whale. As usual the whale changed course to visit us, and brought his dolphin escort with him. When he was close, the whale gave a deep puff, sank down, and swam under *Brendan*'s hull. But his dolphin escort stayed at the surface, leaping and jumping, twisting and turning all around us like gamboling dogs. Glancing astern of *Brendan* we could see the turbulence thrown up by the whale's broad flukes, coming to the surface and flattening the small waves, so that for a moment it looked exactly as if *Brendan* had her own propellers churning up a wake. Then the big whale surfaced, blew twice, and circled round us for one last look before he puffed off to the east, his spout visible for four or five miles.

It was, in fact, a typical "whale day." George was leaning over the gunwale to scoop up a pot of salt water to boil the lunchtime potatoes when he glanced up and said in a matter-of-fact voice, "There are five big whales watching us, just astern." "What sort are they?" I asked. "I'm not sure; they seem different," George replied. Trondur stood up and looked over the stern. "These are sperm whale," he said, and we watched as yet another of the whale species cruised quietly up to *Brendan* to take a look at her, their strange blunt heads shoving steadily through the water. One member of the pod swam to our bow to have a closer inspection and then all five moved majestically on their way, not bothering to dive but wallowing on the surface.

The calculated risk of running close to the ice edge paid off. On the afternoon of May 25, the wind began to blow steadily from the northeast, and *Brendan* started to move parallel to the ice edge, heading toward Cape Farewell. Prins Christiansund Radio

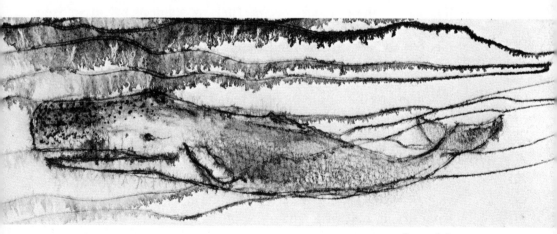

Sperm whale

broadcast a gale warning, which proved to be correct. All that night the wind stayed near gale force, and the night watch awoke to the chilling sound of hailstones crackling off the tarpaulins like the sound of crumpling cellophane. There was another gale warning the following morning, and the morning after that, too, and also on the third and fourth days. But now the wind always came out of the north or northeast, and *Brendan* fairly scampered along, helped by the East Greenland current which pushed her even faster, giving us an extra twenty or twenty-five miles a day. On May 26 *Brendan* put up her best performance, 115 miles on the log in twenty-four hours. This equaled her best day's run the previous season, and would have been a respectable achievement for a modern cruising yacht.

The scrawled comments on the daily log sheets summed up the conditions of those Greenland days; "fog," "drizzle," "thick mist," "gale warning" were repeated monotonously. Under such adverse conditions, Arthur's cameras began to give trouble. The salt atmosphere was penetrating their delicate mechanisms and the shutters seized up. Painstakingly Arthur disemboweled the cameras into dozens of little pieces on the shelter floor, cleaned and oiled the bits, and from two camera bodies salvaged one camera which worked if he gave it a hearty cuff between shots. We had now been more than three weeks at sea and our fresh food supplies were running out. We ate the last of the apples, and regretfully finished off the cheddar cheese. There was still plenty of smoked and dried meats, but our German black bread was a disappointment. It had turned sour, and there was green mould on every slice when we opened the packets. But the reduction in our stores and the amount of water we had consumed now meant that *Brendan* was nearly a third of a ton lighter, and she was beginning to ride a little more easily.

Living conditions daily grew more basic. The contents of the cabin had been stripped down to essentials—there remained only our sleeping bags, a kit bag of clothes for each person, radio, sextant, a bag of books, and the cameras—nothing else. Also the shelter was beginning to smell strongly with the permanent smell of wool drying out, of leather, and of damp, unwashed bodies. We were growing accustomed to living with permanently wet hair, wet shirt sleeves where the water oozed past the cuffs of the oilskins, wet socks, and wet sweaters. Fortunately no one suffered any illness, not even cuts or sprains. The only problem was Trondur's hands, which puffed up with fat red swellings on knuckles and fingers with a pitted sore in the center of each swelling. But Trondur only shrugged and said it was a normal affliction for fishermen who handled nets and lines in cold water. The rest of us merely came off watch with fingers like dead white cucumbers, grained with cracks of grime, and it took a couple of hours for the normal color to return.

We began to treat the daily gale warnings from Prins Christianssund with a certain downbeat humor. We joked among ourselves that the wind never seemed to reach the ferocious speeds that were forecast, though our little barometer agreed with the pressure readings that were being broadcast. A series of low pressure centers, sometimes as low as 970 millibars, were rubbing shoulders with the Greenland high pressure gradient where the gale winds blew. We wondered whether we were avoiding the worst of the winds because *Brendan* was so low in the water and sheltered by the troughs of the waves. Certainly we did not feel the full blast of the gales, and we were surprised when we received a worried message from Páll Berghtorsson to say that a ship, not sixty miles from *Brendan*, was reporting a wind speed of force 10, full storm. The message was relayed by an Icelandic fishery research boat, *Arni Fridriksson*, which was operating to the north of us, and when *Arni Fridriksson* finished her tour and left for home, our radio link with Reykjavik was broken and we felt even more isolated. The high winds and poor visibility grounded the aircraft in South Greenland, and even the Ice Patrol plane, which was supposed to look for us, was unable to fly due to bad weather.

On May 29 *Brendan* at last cleared the tip of the ice ledge extending south from Cape Farewell and we breathed more easily. We were now crossing the wide approaches to the Davis Strait which divides Greenland from North Labrador. Here, to our frustration, we came into an area of calms, light airs, and pea-soup fogs. Almost every wind, when it did come, arrived from the south and west, and *Brendan*'s advance slowed to a crawl. Once again, the pencil line of our course again began to zig and zag and make erratic circles on the chart.

"May 31st" read a typical day's entry in the journal. "Began calm, but a northwest wind by noon, and we altered the course more directly for Newfoundland. Then the winds turned southwest, and we are virtually hove to, lolling through the water. Nothing of interest."

Tedium became our new enemy. Once or twice we glimpsed enough sun to make it worthwhile to hang the sleeping bags in the rigging and to try to dry out our clothes. But usually the weather was too foggy or too damp for any success. And it was so cold that the next migrant to land on *Brendan*, another water pipit, also failed to survive the night and perished. To pass the time, there was a shipboard craze for fancy rope work, and *Brendan*'s rigging sprouted complicated knots and splices, intricate lashings, and every item that could possibly be embellished with a Turk's head was duly decorated. To add to the boredom, there was an increasing sense of remoteness brought about by our limited horizon, which seldom exceeded three or four miles because of constant fog. Often the fog banks closed in so thickly that we could see no more than fifty yards in front of the vessel, and it was impossible to distinguish the line between air and sea, so that *Brendan* seemed to be suspended in a muzzy grey bowl. The only consolation was that there was very little chance of being run down by a ship. These were desolate waters, crossed only by an occasional fishing boat on its way between North American and the Greenland fishing grounds. Nor were there many coast stations either, and so *Brendan* gradually fell into a gap in the communications network.

The radio voice of Prins Christianssund grew fainter and fainter until finally it could only just be heard. Then came the day when their signal vanished entirely and we still could not make contact with the Canadian stations ahead of us. Above, we heard the airliners reporting their positions to air traffic control, but they did not reply to *Brendan*'s calls and we seemed very alone.

On June 11, we picked up a Canadian Coast Guard radio station broadcasting an advisory message to all ships, giving *Brendan*'s description and announcing that as nothing had been heard from *Brendan* for sixty hours, any vessel sighting her or hearing her signals was to report to the Coast Guard. Frustratingly, we could not reply ourselves to the message because of heavy atmospheric interference. But on the following day a sudden improvement in conditions allowed both the Canadian and Greenland radio stations to pick up our position report and the Canadians advised us of the position of the main pack-ice edge off Labrador. According to their observations, the main pack ice was retreating steadily northward, and from the chart it looked as if *Brendan* would be clear of the Labrador ice. Only a week earlier the Canadian news bulletins had been describing the fate of the ferryboat *Carson* about two hundred miles east of us. The 8273-ton *Carson* was built as an icebreaker, but on her first run of the season up to Goose Bay, she had hit ice and sunk. Fortunately the weather was ideal and she was close to shore. Military helicopters had rescued her passengers from the ice floes without loss of life, but her sinking was a grim warning.

Thirteen seemed to be our lucky number, because on June 13 we finally got a favorable wind, and *Brendan* ran up the miles all that afternoon and the following night. During the evening watch George mentioned that he was disappointed. "It seems a pity to have come all this way, and never to have seen any ice. I don't expect I'll ever be up here again," he said. Next morning at dawn, George was making himself a cup of coffee. "Hey!" he called in delight. "Ice. I do believe it's ice." There, floating by like some strange Chinese carnival dragon, was a queerly contorted chunk of ice, bobbing gently like a child's toy. "There's another chunk, just ahead," George said. We all lined up to watch. *Brendan* was beginning to slide past humps and bits of loose ice. They were extraordinarily beautiful, lurching and dipping and occasionally pieces splitting away and breaking free. And then the whole chunk of ice would revolve as its balance changed, spinning over to reveal some entirely new profile. All the while the constant surge and wash of the swell on the ice came to our ears as a low, muted roar.

Trondur beamed with pleasure. "Good," he said. "Now we see more birds and more whales. Near ice is good fishing."

I pointed away to the east. "Trondur, what is that white line over on the horizon? It looks like ice blink, according to the description in the pilot book. Do you think there is pack ice in that direction?"

"Yes," he said, peering in the direction I was pointing. "Yes, there is much ice."

I was puzzled. According to the latest information, there should not be any ice in that direction. "I expect it's a big isolated raft of ice broken from the main part," I said confidently. "According to the most recent ice report we should be clear of the main ice, and there shouldn't be any pack ice in this area. I expect we've come between the land and some stray drifting ice."

I was wrong. Unwittingly, I altered course to starboard to pass inside the ice "raft" and sailed down toward the ice blink. As we came closer, the ice edge became more definite. It was an awesome sight. The solid edge of the ice was made of brilliant white floes, which shimmered in the strong sunshine. Every hundred yards or so, the carcasses of larger and thicker floes had been driven in the lighter floes and jammed there. These larger floes were made of multi-year ice, ice from several years of freezing, and broken chunks of icebergs. These larger pieces stood above the general level in strange sculptured shapes, some soft and round like melted butter, others grotesque and jagged, all sharp edges and spines. A fringe of smaller ice debris drifted along the main edge, and into *Brendan*'s path. We wove our course between them, innocently admiring their shapes. They looked like little boats, pieces from a jigsaw or sea serpents. One small floe was banana-shaped and was promptly dubbed the "ice curragh."

Treacherously the wind began to shift into the northwest, and try as we might, we could not prevent *Brendan* from sidling closer to the ice edge. The sun clouded over from time to time, and the pretty shapes looked less enticing. "The swell is really grinding the ice," commented George. "Look at that big, dark-colored floe over

[216]

there. Look how it's lifting and falling." He was pointing out a sizeable block of ice, perhaps the size of a two-storey house, which had a distinctive, ugly grey band along its lower edge. Each time the swell moved it, this chunk of ice rose up ponderously, tilted, and then came smashing down with its dark underbelly so that the water gushed from the undercut edge. "It wouldn't be very pleasant if *Brendan* got driven under the edge of that one," I commented. "We'd be pulverized as if by a steam hammer."

Steadily we glided past the ice edge, keeping it to port. Arthur was taking photographs; George steering; and Trondur sat on the shelter roof, gazing at the marvelous vista. In the distance, across the hummocks and rifts of the lesser ice, we could distinguish the massive shapes of true icebergs locked in the depths of the ice field. "I don't think we're going to clear the tail of the ice raft," said George in a worried tone; "it seems to stretch a long way ahead, and we're drifting down toward it rather fast." A nagging fear took shape in the back of my mind. We were about 160 miles from land, and a long distance from where the main pack ice was reputed to be. But this ice looked remarkably solid. George spoke again. "What if we're just running ourselves into an ice bay? I can't see how we would get out without being crushed."

I glanced inquiringly at Trondur. "*Brendan* must find a hole in the ice. There is safe," he said and, pulling out his pencil, sketched what he meant—*Brendan* should try to find an open patch within the body of the pack ice and lie there as if in a lagoon. But the ice edge was unbroken. There was no gap and no haven, least of all for a skin boat. Just at that moment George exclaimed "A ship!"

It was the first vessel we had seen since the patrol ships of the Icelandic Coast Guard. Low on the horizon she looked like a fishing boat skirting the edge of the ice raft. "I'm afraid she won't see us against the ice," I said. "White sails against white ice, and even our radar reflector will just look like a small blob of loose ice."

Suddenly George had a brain wave.

"The signal mirror!" he exclaimed, and quickly dug out the little metal mirror from its storage place.

Blink! Blink! Blink! We took it in turns to focus the sunlight on the distant ship. When first sighted, she had been heading almost straight at us, but then she had turned aside to steam parallel with

[217]

the ice edge. Blink! Blink! Blink! "Let's hope we can get some fresh food," Arthur muttered longingly. "I rather fancy some fresh milk and bread." Blink! Blink! "She's turning, she's seen us!"

Quarter of an hour later the boat was almost within hailing distance. George peered through the binoculars. "Her name is *Svanur*, and hey! Trondur, I do believe she's a Faroese boat." Trondur beamed with anticipation. He cupped his hands and bellowed a string of Faroese across the water. His shout was greeted with a mass of waving arms from the boat's crew, who were lining the rail. "I wonder what they're thinking on *Svanur*," George said, "meeting up with a leather boat off of the ice."

"One thing is sure," I replied, "when they hear Faroese coming from *Brendan*, they'll know it can only be Trondur Patursson."

In fact the Faroese fishing boat knew all about *Brendan*, not only from our visit the previous year to the Faroes, but also via the mysterious network of sea gossip which links the fishing boats and small freighters plying the far North Atlantic. The voyage of the leather boat was a topic of conversation in the Icelandic and Greenland ports; and *Svanur* had just come down from Greenland, loaded with a cargo of shrimp to be landed at Gloucester, Massachusetts. All northern ships, her skipper later told Trondur, had been asked to keep a special watch for us, and Greenland radio had been broadcasting our last known position. Nevertheless, had it not been for the bright flash of the signal mirror, *Svanur* would never have spotted *Brendan*. Her captain had already changed course away from the ice when the mirror had caught the attention of the watch and *Svanur* closed to investigate.

Trondur pumped up the little rubber dinghy and paddled across to *Svanur*. After ten minutes he came back. "The captain says there is very heavy ice all ahead of *Brendan*. *Svanur* has been steaming six hours and could not find a way through the ice. Also he has heard on the radio from another ship which cannot get through. He says the ice is very thick." I saw that *Svanur*'s steel bows had ice dents in it. If *Svanur*, a well-built fishing boat designed for those waters, was backing off the ice, then it was wise for *Brendan* to do the same. It seemed that the ice had moved since the last reports and was a good deal farther south. Trondur continued: "*Svanur*'s captain said if you want, he will pull *Brendan*

[218]

around the corner of the ice where we can pick up the wind again. *Svanur* is going this way."

"Please tell him that I accept his offer."

Trondur paddled back with a tow line and soon *Svanur* was plucking us out of danger. More Brendan Luck, I reflected, that the first boat in three weeks should show up just when *Brendan* was blundering into an ice trap. Doubtless we would have been able to work ourselves clear of the ice once the wind had changed, but in future I would be more wary of the ice reports. The pack could move and change its boundaries faster than the Ice Patrol could keep track of it, and next time, I promised myself, I would keep *Brendan* to seaward of it. I did not know what a broken promise that would soon turn out to be.

It took only three hours for *Svanur* to pull *Brendan* out of her predicament, and then she cast us off. Trondur, who had stayed aboard *Svanur* for the tow, came back with a bag of frozen bread, a sack of potatoes, the supply of milk which Arthur had wanted, and a great box of frozen shrimp.

"That's a splendid haul," I grunted, taking the box from Trondur's hands. "Yes," he replied, "*Svanur*'s captain lives not so far from us, on the island of Hestor." Only the wandering Faroese fisherman, I thought, could make so light of a chance meeting off the pack ice.

We were still busily stowing this welcome supplement to our rations when George exclaimed, "Good Lord—it's another ship." Sure enough, rolling down from the north was a grey-painted vessel. She had a strange profile, with a cut-back icebreaker bow and a crow's nest fixed to her foremast. "This place is like Piccadilly Circus," I said. "Two ships in a day. Everyone has to come round this corner en route to or from the Arctic."

"Let's hope that ship has seen us," muttered George. She's bearing straight at us."

The look-out aboard the newcomer had spotted *Brendan*. The vessel slowed down and then stopped about two hundred yards from *Brendan*. She was the U.S. Navy ship *Mirfak*, and we could see her deck officers leaning over the wingbridge to gaze curiously down at us.

"What ship are you?" *Mirfak* asked by radio.

[219]

"*Brendan* out of Reykjavik and bound for North America," I replied.

There was a long pause.

"Can I have that again?" came a puzzled voice.

"*Brendan*, out of Reykjavik and bound for North America. Our boat is an archeological experiment. She's made of leather and testing whether Irish monks could have reached America before the Vikings."

Long pause.

"Say that again."

I repeated the information. Another pause, as the khaki-clad officers peered at us.

"I had better take this down in writing," said *Mirfak*'s radio operator. "Where did you sail from?"

"Reykjavik, this season."

Another incredulous pause. "Where?"

"Reykjavik in Iceland. We've had pretty good weather this side of Greenland, but we took a battering between Iceland and Greenland."

"I should say so. Things can be pretty bad in this steel tub. I can't imagine what it's like in your little boat."

Mirfak, as it turned out, was a U.S. Navy supply vessel returning from Sondrestrom Fjord in Greenland and a regular visitor to Arctic waters. Meeting *Brendan* was a complete surprise.

"Can we give you any help?"

"Some fresh vegetables and meat would be very welcome if you can spare any. We ran out of fresh food a little while back."

"That's easy. But how will we transfer the stuff to you?

I smiled to myself at the thought of a leather boat advising a navy ship. "That's easy. We'll send you a boat." I turned to George. "Your turn in the dinghy."

So *Brendan*'s little rubber dinghy paddled off again, a tiny dot against *Mirfak*'s tall flank. We saw crewmen lowering sacks on the end of the line to George, who was heaving up and down on the swell. Then George gesticulated upward.

Ten minutes later he pulled back to *Brendan*, the dinghy low in the water. "I had to stop them," he puffed. "They gave me so much food it would have swamped the dinghy." Piled around his legs were sacks of oranges, apples, yet more milk, tins of coffee, slabs of meat. It was an incredibly generous haul.

"Look at that lot," said Arthur. "Marvelous! We ought to set up a corner shop at the ice here and trade with passing vessels. We'd never starve."

"And I left behind three more sacks of food they had ready on deck for us," George added.

As *Mirfak* picked up speed to continue on her way to Bayonne in New Jersey, I made one more request. "Could you give us a position check, please?"

"Yes," came the reply. "We're getting a read-out from the satellite now."

That was a nice touch, I thought to myself—a medieval leather boat receiving her position from a twentieth-century navigation satellite. Then *Mirfak* was gone, and *Brendan* was left rocking on the swell. The wind had died completely, and the sun went down in a spectacular mauve-and-orange sunset, the sky streaked with radiating patterns of high clouds that complemented the brilliant white of the ice field stretching away on our starboard side. We ate a delicious supper of Greenland shrimp and turned in that night, listening to the ceaseless mutter and grumble of the ice floes rubbing against one another on the Atlantic swell.

12

Puncture in the Ice

That evening George finally gave up the unequal contest of trying to compete with Arthur's flailing knees and elbows inside the confines of the main shelter, and he moved his berth forward to a spot under the bow canvas. We slept with the tent flaps open because the weather was so still, and it was a surprise to find a rind of ice covering *Brendan* in the morning. We were now some 1600 miles along our route from Iceland, and across the icefield lay Labrador, only 200 miles away. Moreover our encounter with *Mirfak* and *Svanur* had put *Brendan* back on the map for the outside world. The Canadian Coast Guard radio stations now arranged a special listening watch for us; and on the afternoon of June 15 a small plane flew over the boat for five minutes and took pictures. By radio the plane warned that large areas of pack ice lay to the south and west of *Brendan*. But there was little to be done. *Brendan* was still becalmed.

At quarter past three the next morning, however, I was awakened by the sound of water sliding past the leather hull. That's odd, I thought to myself, *Brendan* is not heeling to the wind. Nor can I hear the sound of waves. On my last watch the weather had been very settled, and there had been a flat calm and no sign of wind.

Then I heard Trondur and George speaking softly, and some sort of commotion, punctuated by light thuds and the flapping of a sail, and several splashes. What on earth were they doing? Was George helping Trondur restow some of the stores? But that was

[222]

ridiculous; it was dark, and George was off-watch, and should be asleep. Finally, I could contain my curiosity no longer, and called "What's going on? Do you need any help?"

No answer. Then abruptly, the thuds and splashes stopped. I heard the others moving back down the boat.

"What's up?" I asked again.

"Oh, Trondur just lost a pilot whale he had harpooned," came back George's casual reply. I pulled on a sweater, and listened to their story.

Trondur had been on watch by himself when a large school of pilot whales surfaced around *Brendan*, splashing and puffing. Although it was dark, this was the opportunity Trondur the Hunter had been waiting for. Without bothering to wake up anyone, he clambered forward to his cabin, unshipped his harpoon, and scrambled up onto the very bows of the boat where he could get a clear throw. George was awakened by the sound of Trondur clambering across the thin tarpaulins just over his head. George got up, and emerged just as Trondur saw his chance—a pilot whale of the right size swimming near the boat.

Chunk! From a kneeling position on the bow Trondur tossed his harpoon three or four yards to starboard, and made a clean hit. It was a classic shot.

Immediately the harpooned animal dived. There was a tremendous flurry among its closely packed companion whales. The water churned as the animals thrashed in panic. The shaft of the harpoon snapped under the press of bodies, and then all the whales were gone, leaving the stricken animal to its fate.

Fascinated, George watched as Trondur began to play the whale like a fisherman with a salmon on the end of a line. At first the thirty-foot harpoon line was pulled out taut to its fullest extent. Trondur had tied the free end of the line to the foremast as a strong point, and the harpooned whale began towing *Brendan* briskly along. If the whale had been any larger, this could have been dangerous, but Trondur knew what he was doing. He had selected a whale of the right size, about fifteen feet long, small enough to handle from *Brendan*. As the whale grew tired, Trondur began to haul in on the line. The animal darted back and forth underneath the bows, trying to rid itself of the clinging harpoon. Flashes of foam and phosphorescence rolled up off its body and fins as it

[223]

fought to escape. Inexorably Trondur continued to haul in. As the line shortened, the pilot whale began to weave up and down; its tail scooped dollops of water aboard *Brendan* as it fought to resist. Trondur's strategy was to pull the animal high enough to the surface so that it could get less grip on the water. At the crucial moment, however, when the whale was right alongside the boat, the harpoon head pulled free. A second later, the animal was gone.

"Harpoon too far back in whale," said Trondur, sadly shaking his head. "More forward and it would have been good."

I wondered to myself what on earth we would have done with a fifteen-foot pilot whale on *Brendan*. We didn't have that much extra space. But Trondur the Hunter had done remarkably well to harpoon the animal in the dark. "Never mind," I said, "you picked a good whale. It was towing us in the right direction at a good two to three knots."

Our adventures and misadventures all seemed to be happening in the dark, or at best, in the last hour of daylight. On June 18 the barometer began to fall rapidly. So did the temperature. Then the wind backed into the northwest and blew strongly, bringing driving rain. In short, it was a thoroughly villainous evening, and it was lucky, in view of what was to follow, that Trondur and Arthur unlashed and stowed the bonnet from the mainsail before they ended their watch at dusk. George and I took over on a foul, black night, rigged an awning over the cooker, lit the kerosene lamp, and huddled over it for warmth, taking an hour each at the helm. Our only consolation was that *Brendan* was thrusting briskly through the murk, sailing at a good pace. At 3:00 A.M. it was my turn to seek the shelter of the cabin, and I crawled in thankfully. I had just pulled off my wet sea-boot socks when suddenly there was a high-pitched crackling sound, rather like stiff calico tearing. "What on earth was that?" I exclaimed, poking my head out of the cabin. George was already standing up, flashing a torch on the sails. "I don't know," he replied. "Everything looks okay. The sails seem all right." "Perhaps a bird was flung into the sail by the high wind, and was thrashing to get out," I suggested. "No," said George, "I thought the sound came from the hull—still, there's nothing we can do about it in the dark," and he settled back down on the thwart.

Crack . . . crack . . . crack. There it came again, something weird was happening, a strange snapping noise, this time much louder. George was right. The noise was coming from the hull. George was back on his feet, peering into the darkness, trying to see a few yards in the pitch black. Hastily I began to put on my outer clothes again, knowing by instinct that we had a crisis on our hands.

"It's ice!" George suddenly shouted. "We're running into ice! I can see lumps of it all around." Crack . . . crack . . . crack, we heard the sound again and realized without looking what it was. *Brendan* was hitting lumps of ice at speed, and they were swirling and bumping along her flanks so hard that they rattled and crackled along the oxhide skin.

"Drop the sails," I yelled. "If we collide with heavy ice at this speed, we'll knock her to pieces. Our only chance is to stop and wait for daylight."

George moved into action. By the time I had struggled into my oilskins, he had lowered the mainsail and scampered forward over the icy tarpaulins, and already had the headsail halfway down. I went forward to help him secure the sodden canvas. It was perishingly cold. In an instant our bare fingers were numb as we secured the lashings on the sails. Neither George nor I said a word as we worked frantically. We could glimpse indistinct shapes in the water, and felt under our feet that *Brendan*'s hull juddered softly against unseen obstacles. We hurried back to the helm and took out the two most powerful hand torches. They were the only spotlights we had. We switched them on, one each side of *Brendan*, and shone them over the water. Their beams penetrated only fifty yards through the spray and sleet which hissed down in white streaks through the shafts of light. But fifty yards was far enough to reveal a sight which brought the adrenalin racing. All around us floated chunks and lumps and jagged monsters of ice. This was not the same ice we had seen a few days ago. In place of the well-defined ice edge, there was now a nightmare jumble of ice floes of every size and description, with channels of clear water opening and closing between them as the floes moved with the wind. But this ice should not be here, I told myself. I knew the ice chart by heart. That same day I had painstakingly marked in the ice boundaries according to the latest information radioed by the ice information service. *Brendan* should be at least sixty miles clear of the nearest ice. Yet here it was; and with a morbid feeling of satisfaction I knew exactly what had happened. The same northwest gale which had been spinning *Brendan* so happily on her way had swept over the main ice sheet and burst it open. The compact ice raft we had seen two days ago was now sprayed like shrapnel right into *Brendan*'s path. Later I learned that the entire pack-ice front had advanced across a broad front so that the Straits of Belle Isle, well to the south of *Brendan*, were nearly closed to merchant shipping.

Our torch beams showed us that *Brendan* had blundered into a type of sea ice known as Very Open Pack, and that most of the ice was rotten. Very Open Pack would have presented no problems to a large ship, which would have been able to shoulder forward, driven by powerful engines. But it was a totally different matter for *Brendan*. How much of a battering would her leather hull withstand, I wondered, and what would happen if a couple of ice floes bumped together, and *Brendan* was caught in the middle? Would she burst open like an overripe banana? And just how much sailing water was there among the ice floes which lay ahead? The devil of our situation was that there was no way to plan a strategy. We might only be in a small zone of ice, a temporary obstacle which we would soon clear. Common sense said that it was far more likely that we were in a major area of ice and that sooner or later we would find massive rafts of consolidated ice still frozen together. We had already seen the grinding action of the giant ice floes on a relatively calm day. I shuddered to think of what would happen to *Brendan* if she was blown into that sort of obstacle in the dark. She would be fed in like mincemeat. For about an hour George and I tried to keep the boat out of trouble. Without her sails, *Brendan* was still moving through the pack ice at one or two knots, driven by the pressure of the wind on the masts and hull. But sail-less, *Brendan* was at her worst—slow to maneuver and only able to turn through a very small arc. If too much helm was applied, she merely drifted sideways, out of control.

Everywhere the torch beams probed, white lumps of ice winked back out of the dark. Painfully, we wallowed past them, heaving on the tiller, and silently hoping that *Brendan* would respond in time. Smaller floes bumped and muttered on her leather skin; and out of the darkness we heard the continuous swishing sound of the waves breaking on ice beyond our vision.

George hoisted himself on the steering frame to get a clearer view. "There's a big floe dead ahead," he warned. "Try to get round to port." I pulled over the tiller as far as it would go. But it was not enough. I could see that we were not going to make it. "Get the foresail up," I shouted. "We've got to have more steerage way." George clipped on his lifeline and crawled forward along the gunwale. Reaching the foremast, he heaved on the halliard to raise the sail. It jammed. A loose thong had caught in the collar that slid up and down the mast. "Trondur!" shouted George. "Quick, pass me up a knife." Trondur's berth was right beside the foremast, and he began to emerge like a bear from hibernation. But it was too late. With a shudder from the top of her mast to the skid under her, *Brendan* ran her bow into the great lump of sea ice. It was like hitting a lump of concrete. The shock of the impact made me stagger. "That will test medieval leather—and our stitching," I thought. Thump! We struck again. Thump! Once more the swell casually tossed *Brendan* onto the ice. Then ungracefully and slowly, *Brendan* began to pivot on her bow, wheeling away from the ice floe like a car crash filmed in slow motion. Thump! The boat shivered again. We had a feeling of total helplessness. There was nothing we could do to assist *Brendan*. Only the wind would blow her clear. Thump! This time the shock was not so fierce. *Brendan* was shifting. Scrape. She was clear. "Is she taking water?" George called back anxiously. I glanced down at the floorboards. "No, not as far as I can see back here," I replied. "Try to clear the jammed headsail. I'll get Boots up as well. This is getting dodgy."

Scarcely had I spoken than a truly awesome sight loomed up out of the dark just downwind of us—the white and serrated edge of a massive floe, perhaps the dying shard of an iceberg, twice the size of *Brendan*, and glinting with malice. This apparition was rolling and wallowing like some enormous log. Its powerful, squat shape had one great bluff end which was pointing like a battering ram straight at *Brendan*, and it was rocking backward and forward with ponderous certainty to deliver a blow of perhaps a hundred tons or so at the fragile leather.

George took one look at this monster and leapt up the foremast to try to clear the jammed sail and give us steerage way. It was a slim hope. "Hang on tight!" I bellowed at him as the swell gathered up *Brendan* and pushed her at the great ice lump which heaved up ponderously to greet her. Crack! Thump! The whole boat shook as if she had struck a reef, which indeed she had, but a reef of ice. The impact flung George backward from the mast. "Christ, he's going to fall between *Brendan* and the ice floe, he'll be crushed," I thought, horrified. But George still had the jammed halliard in his hand, and clutched at it desperately. The rope brought him up short, and for a heart-stopping moment he dangled backward over the gap like a puppet on a string. Now the wind was pinning *Brendan* against the great block of ice so that she was nuzzling up to it in a deadly embrace. The next impact was different. This time the ice floe rocked away from *Brendan* as the swell passed beneath us. *Brendan* swung over a broad spur of a wave-cut ledge projecting from the floe. The spur rose under us, caught *Brendan* with a grating sound, and began to lift and tip the boat. "We're going to be flipped over like a fried egg," I thought, as *Brendan* heeled and heeled. Then, with another grating sound of leather on ice, *Brendan* slid sideways off the ice spur and dropped back into the water.

Crash. The next collision was broadside, halfway down the boat's length. The leeboard took the impact with the sound of tortured wood.

This can't go on much longer, I wondered. Either *Brendan* will be blown clear of the floe, or she will be smashed to smithereens. As I watched, *Brendan* jostled forward another six feet on the next wave, and there was a chance to gauge the rhythm of destruction. It was obvious that the next blow would strike the steering paddle and snap its shaft. That would be the final problem: to be adrift in the pack ice with our steering gear smashed. Now the great floe was level with me where I stood at the tiller bar. The face of the floe stood taller than I did and in the light cast by my torch, the ice gleamed and glowed deep within itself with an unearthly mixture of frost white, crystal, and emerald. From the water-line a fierce blue-white reflected up through the sea from the underwater ice ledge. And all the time, like some devouring beast, the floe never ceased its constant roar and grumble as the ocean swell boomed within its submarine hollows and beat against its sides.

Here comes the last blow, I thought, the final shock in *Brendan*'s ordeal. I felt a wave lift the leather hull, saw the bleak edge of glistening ice swing heavily toward me and—feeling slightly

[228]

foolish—could think of nothing else to do but lean out with one arm, brace against the steering frame, and putting my hand on the ice floe I pushed with all my strength. To my astonishment, *Brendan* responded. The stern wagged away and forward from the ice wall, and instead of a full-blooded sideswipe, we received a glancing ice blow that sent a shiver down the hull, but left the steering paddle intact. One wave later, the great floe was rolling and grumbling in our wake. It had been a very close call.

Trondur and Arthur were soon up and dressed in sweaters and oilskins ready to help. I should have called them earlier, but their off-watch rest had seemed too precious. Now their assistance was needed, because I planned to try to get *Brendan* through the ice by increasing speed, which in turn meant that we might be blundering into the main consolidated pack ice and wreck the boat. But it was a risk we had to take. It was better than gyrating into loose floes and being broken up. "Boots! Trondur! Go forward by the fore-mast and stand by. We'll raise and lower the foresail as we need it, and trim the sail to port or starboard, depending on the position of the bigger ice floes. We're going to run through this ice. George, could you act as look-out, and sing out the bearings on the larger floes?"

George climbed up on to the shelter roof, wrapped an arm round the mainmast for support, and from his vantage point spotted the approaching dangers.

"Big one dead ahead! Two floes on the port bow, and another on the starboard side! I think there's a gap between them."

As he called the position of each floe, he aimed the beam of his torch at it to identify the hazard for me at the helm. In turn I called out instructions to Boots and Trondur to raise and trim, or lower, the headsail to catch the wind and pick a route through the ice. "Up foresail . . . down!" We slipped past a white shape of ice, ghostly in the dark. "Up foresail . . . sheet to starboard," and I hauled over the tiller bar so that *Brendan* slid past the next floe. It was a crazy scene, an icy toboggan run in the dark, with a minimum of control, no way of stopping, no knowing what lay fifty yards ahead. From where I stood, I could see the shape of George's body clinging to the mast, the gale plastering his oilskin to his back; then the line of the midships tarpaulin running forward to where Arthur and Trondur stood, one by each gunwale. They had opened a gap in the tarpaulin, and the upper halves of their bodies poked out like

[229]

the crew in an open airplane of First World War vintage. Only the hoods of their oilskin jackets now made them look more like monks in cowls, and the impression was heightened by the red-ringed cross on the foresail, which raised and lowered and bellied out with a thundering clap above their heads. Beyond them, still farther, was the blackness of the night out of which loomed the eerie white shapes of the ice floes, occasionally illuminated by George's torch beam through which still flicked the streaks of rain and spray.

After three hours of this surrealist scene, the gloom began to lift. George switched off his torch, and found he could detect the white flashes of the ice floes without help. Dawn lightened the horizon, and we started to identify ice patterns beyond our

immediate orbit. We were surrounded by pack ice. Off to one side
was floating a huge, picture-postcard iceberg, a sleek monster of
ice sloping spectacularly to the ocean with virgin white flanks. But
the berg was no danger, for it was at least a mile away. Our real
troubles lay ahead and around us in the contorted shapes of the
floes which had ambushed us in the night. Now we could identify
them by type. There were "bergy bits" broken from the dead
icebergs, ice pans of assorted sizes, and "growlers," the unstable
chunks of hard ice which twisted and turned in the water and
threatened to do most damage to *Brendan*'s quarter-inch-thick
leather hull. Now with enough light we could see to avoid these
obstacles. Surely the way ahead must be clear, I thought to myself.
Brendan had shown her worth yet again. Her leather skin and

[231]

hand-lashed frame had survived a battering. No more could be expected of her. "Is there any water in her yet?" George asked again.

"No," I replied. "She came through like a warrior."

But my hopes were soon dashed. Ahead we began to discover mile upon mile of ice, floe after floe, oscillating and edging southward under the combined effects of gale and the current. *Brendan* could neither hold her position nor retreat. Her only course was forward and sideways, hoping to move faster than the pack ice until we eventually outran it and emerged somewhere from its leading edge.

All that day we labored on, trying to work our way diagonally across the pack ice and find its limits. It was a nerve-wracking business, trying to pick our way from one gap to the next. Planning ahead was impossible, because the ice floes changed their position, and our horizon was very limited. From time to time fog banks gathered over the ice and visibility was often less than a mile. Our only advantage was that the water was very calm within the pack ice. As we penetrated deeper, the wave action died away even though half a gale was still blowing. The great carpet of ice muffled the waves like an enormous floating breakwater, leaving only a powerful swell which rocked and spun the floes. Sometimes we came across patches of open water, dotted with only a few lumps of rotting ice. Here we sailed without hindrance for a few minutes. Sometimes ice barriers and ice ridges rose ahead of *Brendan* where the floes stretched right across her path, forming an impenetrable wall which had to be avoided at all costs. Once or twice there loomed out of the mists the magnificent shape of the great icebergs, one hundred feet high and more; and as we drew closer to them we could discern ominous cracks riven through the ice blocks where the bergs would split and calve. Such bergs had to be avoided because downwind of each one lay its attendant cluster of broken ice. Even more awkward were the patches of consolidated pack ice, the larger relics of the old ice sheet. This consolidated ice floated in broad jumbled rafts, heaped and contorted where one floe had piled upon another, and then frozen into one mass, like a breaker's yard where every block weighed a score of tons or more.

Brendan's ability to maneuver past these dangers was so limited that virtually every floe had to be skirted on its leeward side. This meant sailing directly at the floe, putting over the helm at the last moment, and skidding around the lee of the ice where the scud and foam sucked and spread as the floe rocked in an endless see-saw motion to the swell. Our advance was a cross between bumper cars at a fairground and a country square dance, except that our dancing partners were leviathans of ice as they dipped, circled, and curtsied. Again and again we slithered past floes, listening to the bump and crunch as ice brushed the leather hull, the sharper tremor and rattle as we ran over scraps of small ice, the shudder as ice fragments the size of table tops and weighing a couple of hundred pounds ricocheted off the blade of the steering paddle.

"Well, you wanted to see ice on this trip, George," I said. "You can't say you've been disappointed."

"It's fantastic," he replied ruefully, "I'm glad I've seen it. But I don't think I ever want it again."

The strain on the crew was terrific. When daylight came, we tried to revert to our normal watch-keeping system and get some rest. But it was impossible to relax with the clatter of the ice reverberating through the little thin hull so close to one's head. And time after time every man had to be called into action—raising and lowering the sail to vary our speed, hauling and readjusting the sheets to alter the slant of our course; and, when the worst befell, leaning out to poke and prod with boat hooks to fend off the boat, or, once or twice, even sitting out on the gunwale, putting feet on the floe, and kicking off with all one's might. Once again I was reminded of the early voyages—this time of a famous picture of Elizabethan sailors fending off the heavy ice from their ship with just the same simple technique. But I had to confess to myself that I had not expected to find *Brendan* in quite the same predicament.

All that day, June 18, we were kept so busy in the pack ice that there was no time for proper meals. At noon Trondur cooked up a hot mush which we spooned down between emergencies, and there was just enough time for two cups of coffee later in the day. But breakfast was a failure—I found my pannikin of cold cereal at tea time. It was still sitting untouched, in a safe place under the thwart.

It had to be admitted that the ice had a certain lure and majesty. The ice was rotting and disintegrating into thousands upon thousands of weird shapes and sizes, odd corners and pillars, which floated low in the water and speckled the surface as far as the eye could see. The colors were entrancing—opaque whites, deep greens of undersea ledges, transparent flecks the size of cabin trunks, vivid blue glacier ice, dirty ice coated with ancient dust and grime. Once George reached out and broke off a morsel of blue ice from a passing floe, and popped it in his mouth. "Delicious," he quipped. "Please pass the whiskey."

But each color signaled its own danger. The least worrying was the transparent dead ice in the last stage of melting. This ice was riddled with myriads of tiny air pockets so that the outer layer crushed on impact with *Brendan*'s hull and cushioned the shock. Its only disadvantage was that this type of ice floated so low in the water that it was hard to spot in time to avoid. Most of the big heavy growlers were equally difficult to see because they revealed only a small portion of their bulk above the surface, usually a sleek, round lump of opaque white dipping innocently below the swells. But under the water the growlers could be massive—great blocks of menace that heaved and churned in the current. They could deal a tremendous blow to a small boat. The snow-white surface floes, though thinner and lighter, were awkward because they tended to form up in strips and block our path. Our only chance was to bear down on the line, hoping to pick out a gap at the last second, and slither through. It required judgement, skill, and a lot of pure luck that a gap would open at the right moment. Usually *Brendan* bumped and weaved her way through safely, but occasionally she would run her bows right onto the floe. Then for a moment or two, we would ride on top of the ice, waiting for the wind to catch *Brendan*'s stern and lever her back into the water, pirouetting away in her strange ice dance. "It's easy to follow our path through the ice," Arthur remarked, "just follow the line of wool grease marks on the edges of the floes in our wake."

The two colors we treated most warily were the deep green of the underwater ledges, which threatened to gouge upward into *Brendan*'s hull as she glided over them, and the stark diamond-white and blue of the floes made of very old ice. The latter had been born many years earlier as snowfalls in interior Greenland and Baffin Land, compacted, and squeezed out as glaciers and finally spawned into the ocean as icebergs. This ice had scarcely begun to melt at all. Its floes were sharp and hard and utterly uncompromising.

Bump, slither, swing sideways, charge at the gap, don't think about the quarter inch of leather between yourself and the icy sea, ignore the rows of stitching offered up to the constant rubbing of ice along *Brendan*'s flanks; fend off with the boat hook. Helm up, helm down, search for the space between ice floes ahead; calculate, calculate. Wind, leeway, current, ice movement. For hour after the hour the ordeal continued, until by dusk, with the wind still blowing half a gale, the ice seemed to be thinning out. And this time we really did seem to be nearing the edge of the pack.

Then Brendan Luck finally ran out.

We were in sight of relatively open water and passing through a necklace of ice floes when two large floes swung together, closing a gap *Brendan* had already entered. The boat gave a peculiar shudder as the floes pinched her, a vaguely uncomfortable sensation which was soon forgotten in the problem of extricating her from the jaws of the vise. Luckily the two floes eased apart enough for *Brendan* to over-ride one ice spur, and slip free. Five minutes later, I heard water lapping next to the cooker and glanced down. Sea water was swirling over the floorboards. She was leaking. *Brendan* had been holed.

There was no time to attend directly to the leak. The first priority was still to get clear of the pack ice while there was enough daylight to see a path. Otherwise we would find ourselves in the same predicament as the previous evening, blundering into ice floes in the darkness. "One man on the bilge pump, one at the helm; one forward controlling the headsails; and the fourth at rest," I ordered, and for two more hours we worked *Brendan* clear of the pack until there was enough open water to run a fairly easy course between the ice floes, and set the mainsail, double reefed. The helmsman still needed to be vigilant, but the man at the headsail could at last be spared; and after twenty-four hours of sustained effort, we could revert to our normal two-man watch-keeping system. The risk, it seemed to me, was as much a question of human exhaustion as of the frailty of our damaged boat.

"We can't tackle the leak tonight," I said. "There's not enough light to trace it, and then to try to make a repair. Besides, we are all too tired. But it's vital to learn more about the leak. I want each watch to work the bilge pump at regular intervals and record the number of strokes needed to empty the bilge and the time it takes to do so. Then at least we will know if the leak is getting worse and gaining on us. If we've torn the stitching somewhere, then more stitches may open as the thread works itself loose, and the rate of leakage will go up."

Trondur tapped the leather at the gunwale. "I think stitching is broken by ice," he said calmly.

"It's very possible," I replied, "but we can't be sure. We've simply got to find out all we can."

"Ah well," said Arthur cheerily, "that's what the right arm is for—pumping. It's our watch, Trondur, I'd better get to work." And he crawled forward to get to the bilge pump. It was none too soon. Even as we had been talking, the water level on the floor by the cooker had risen noticeably. The water slopped back and forth around our boots, and would soon be lapping into the lee side of the shelter.

Pump, pump, pump. It took thirty-five minutes of non-stop pumping to empty the bilge. *Brendan*'s bilge, though shallow, was broad and relatively flat in profile and so held a great deal of water. Just fifteen minutes after being pumped out, the water level was as bad as ever, and threatening to get worse. Pump, pump, pump. "How many strokes to empty her?" I asked. "Two thousand," Arthur grunted as he collapsed, exhausted. I did a rapid sum. Two thousand strokes every hour was within our physical limit, but only temporarily. One man could steer, while his partner pumped and kept *Brendan* afloat. But this system would work only while our strength lasted, or, more likely, we ran into bad weather, and waves began once again to break into the boat. Then we would no longer have the capacity to keep emptying *Brendan* fast enough. It was a tricky situation: In slanting out of the pack ice and clawing to seaward, I had brought *Brendan* out a full two hundred miles from land, and even then the nearest land was the thinly inhabited coast of Labrador, from which little help could be expected. We were running before half a gale, and now the damping effect of the pack ice was gone, the waves were beginning once again to break and tumble around us. Nor were we entirely free of ice danger. Here and there we could see in the darkness the occasional white shape

[236]

of a large growler, stubbornly refusing to melt. "We've got six hours before daylight," I said. "There's nothing for it but to husband our strength until dawn and then tackle the leak. It's best if one man in each watch keeps pumping continuously, turn and turn about. If we can keep the bilge empty, *Brendan* will ride lighter and take fewer waves on board."

That night was the most physically tiring of the entire voyage. It was difficult to rest or sleep properly. On watch one stood for half an hour on the helm, then went forward to take over the pump, scarcely having time to nod to one's partner as he struggled wearily back, to go to the helm. There, peering through the murk, one tried to decide whether the white flashes ahead were the manes of breaking waves or the telltale sign of a growler lying in *Brendan*'s path.

As soon as the first watch ended, I called the Canadian Coast Guard radio station at St. Anthony in Newfoundland. "This is the sailing vessel *Brendan*," I reported. "We have been in open pack ice for the last twenty-four hours but now seem to be clearing the ice. We have suffered hull damage and the vessel is leaking. In the next twelve hours we will attempt to trace and repair the leak, but it is important to note our estimated position, which is 53°10'N., 51°20'W. I repeat, this position is only an estimate, as we have lost our log line sheered off by the ice, and due to poor visibility have had no sight of the sun for two days. We are not in immediate danger. But could you please investigate the possibility of air-dropping to us a small motor pump, with fuel, in case we cannot contain the leak. I will call again at 14.15 hours GMT to report progress. If no contact is made at 14.15 hours or 16.15 hours, we may have activated an emergency locator transmitter on 121.5 and 243 megacycles. Over."

"Roger, Roger," replied the calm voice of the radio operator at St. Anthony, and he confirmed the details I had given. Then he advised me that he would inform the Rescue Coordination Center at Halifax, and listen out for *Brendan* on the next schedule. Later I learned that the Canadian Coast Guard responded unstintingly to our request for standby help. An aircraft was readied at Halifax, and the Operations Room at St. John's calculated that a Canadian Coast Guard icebreaker could reach us from Goose Bay in twenty-one hours. "But to be honest," said an officer who was on duty that night in the Operations Room, "we didn't know how our ship would be able to locate you in time. And after the loss of the *Carson*, which sank in the same ice not many days before, when we heard that a leather boat was in trouble in the ice, we rated your chances of getting out as nil. How could a leather boat survive when a steel icebreaker went down?"

Nevertheless, at the time of our ordeal, it was very comforting to know that someone, somewhere, was informed of our plight and, if worst came to worst, we could call for help. Partially relieved by this thought, I sat hunched in my sleeping bag and tried to concentrate my mind. *Brendan* was leaking at the rate of two thousand pump strokes an hour. This represented a sizeable leak, and obviously we had to track it down without delay at first light. But how on earth would we find the leak? It could be almost anywhere in *Brendan*'s hull below the water already filling up the boat. We would have to shift all our gear, section by section, along the vessel; lift up floorboards, remove the fresh-water storage tubes from the bilges—and where would we store the drinking water temporarily?—and then try to trace the leak by following any current or bubbles in the bilge. All this would have to be done in a rough sea.

And if we were lucky enough to trace the leak, what then? Suppose we had cracked the skid keel under the boat when *Brendan* rode upon an ice floe, or pulled its fastenings through the leather hull? At sea we could neither refasten nor mend the skid. And what if we had gashed the leather skin or ripped the flax stitching? Then, I feared, we would be in an even worse way. I could not imagine how we would ever stitch on a patch under water, it would be impossible to reach far below the hull, and equally impossible to work on the inside because there was not enough space between the wooden frames and stringers to put in a row of stitches. The more I thought about our straits, the gloomier I felt. It seemed so futile if *Brendan* were to sink so close to the end of her mission. She had already proved to her crew that an early medieval Irish skin boat could sail across the Atlantic. But how could people be expected to believe that fact if *Brendan* sank two hundred miles off Canada? It would be no good to say that there

[238]

was less pack ice off Canada and Greenland in early Christian times, and that the Irish monks would probably not have faced the same problems. To prove the point about the early Irish voyages, *Brendan* had to sail to the New World.

To clear my mind, I took up a pen and made a summary of our position:

1. *Brendan* is leaking fast. We can keep her afloat for two days, or less, in bad weather; indefinitely in fair weather but at great physical cost.
2. First priority is find the leak—skid fastening? Burst stitches? Hull gash?
3. If we cannot trace and mend a leak, the Coast Guard may get a motor pump to us. Do they have a suitable pump? Can their plane find us? This will depend on visibility and sea state.
4. No pump—we MAYDAY and abandon ship.

It was a grim scenario, and the situation did not become any more cheerful during that night. Driving rain reduced visibility to a few yards, and with an increase in wind strength, the helmsman no longer had the option to dodge potential growlers in the water. *Brendan* could only flee directly downwind, and we trusted to luck that we did not hit isolated pieces of ice, or worse yet an iceberg recently set free from the pack.

All of us were desperately tired. The constant strain of bilge pumping was a stultifying chore, which battered mind and muscle. First there was the awkward slippery climb along the gunwale to go from the steering position to the midship's lashing in the tarpaulin. There you had to open the lashing with half-frozen fingers, drop into the dark slit, turn around to unclip your lifeline, duck under the tarpaulin, and tug the tarpaulin shut. If you did not, the next breaking wave would cascade into the midship's section and drop even more water into the bilge. Once under the tarpaulin, you had to strip off your oilskin jacket or wriggle half out of your immersion suit. Otherwise the next half hour's work would drench your clothes in sweat. Now it was time to squirm down the tunnel under the tarpaulin to reach the handle of the bilge pump. Grasp the handle with the right hand, lie on one's left side on top of the thwart, and pump four hundred to five hundred strokes. By then the muscles of the right arm and shoulder would be screaming for relief; and so you reversed position laboriously, lay on the other ribs, and pumped for as long as possible with the left arm. Then reverse the procedure, and begin all over again, pumping and pumping, until at last came the welcome sucking sound of the intake pipe, and you could begin the laborious return journey to the helm, put on oilskin top, unfasten and fasten the tarpaulin, clamber back to reach the helm, and arrive just in time to find that the water level had risen to exactly the same place as when you had started the whole operation. Only now it was the turn of your watch companion to empty the bilge.

Rocking the pump handle in the dark tunnel of the tarpaulin had an almost hypnotic quality. The steady rhythm of the pump, the dark wet tunnel, and aching tiredness combined to produce a sense of detachment from one's surroundings. The feeling was heightened by the incongruously pretty little flashes of phosphorescence which slid aboard with every second or third wave crest, and dripped brilliantly down the inside of the leather skin of the boat in random patterns that confused one's weary eyes and created illusions of depth and motion. The motion of arm and torso, rocking back and forth relentlessly at the pump handle, was matched visually by a strange phosphorescent glow in the translucent bilge pipes. This strange glow varied in intensity with each wave, sometimes soaring to bright sparks of luminescence, but usually a somber green pulse like a ghostly heartbeat. Under the dark tarpaulin, eyes tricked, shoulders aching, head drooping down onto the thwart with exhaustion, it was desperately tempting to drop off to sleep while still mechanically rocking back and forth. Only to be jerked awake by the rattling crash of yet another wave breaking onto the tarpaulin just above one's head.

At 6:00 A.M. dawn came, and I looked at the crew. They were haggard with exhaustion, but no one had the slightest thought of giving up. In the night watch I had surreptitiously stolen five minutes to lever up the stern floorboards and check the aft section of the bilge to try to find the mysterious leak. It was a job that really should have been left until morning, but I could not restrain my curiosity. When I told George what I had done, he confessed that he had made exactly the same investigation in his forward berth and already examined the bow section without finding the leak. It seemed there was no holding back *Brendan*'s crew.

"Well, here's the battle plan," I explained. "Each man has a cup of coffee and a bite to eat. Then Trondur and Boots work on both pumps amidships to get the water level as low as possible, and keep it there. This will allow George and me to work down the length of the boat, shifting the cargo area by area, and checking the bilge for leaks. We already know that the leak must be somewhere in the main central section of the hull."

The others looked very tough and confident, and utterly unperturbed. We had just eight hours, I reminded myself, to find and repair the leak before I should be in touch with the Canadian Coast Guard.

Three of us had coffee and then I went forward to relieve George at the bilge pump.

As I sat by the pump, waiting for George to drink his coffee so that we could begin our search, I wondered where we should commence our hunt—aft, under the shelter? But this meant shifting all our personal gear. By the foremast? But this was where we had put the heavy stores like the anchors and water cans. Then, quite unconnected, a thought occurred to me. Last night, while pumping in the dark, the flashes of phosphorescence over the gunwale had been repeated almost simultaneously *inside* the boat and in the bilge pump tube. I knew nothing of the physical properties of phosphorescence, but imagined some sort of electrical connection was required. If so, then the phosphorescence had traveled directly from outside the hull to inside the hull, apparently by a direct link—the leak.

With a faint stir of interest I abandoned pumping and traced the line of the bilge pipe to its intake amidships on the port side. At that point I peeled back the tarpaulin and hung head first over the gunwale. There, just on the water line, was the most encouraging sight of the day—a sizeable dent in the leather hull. The dent was about the area and shape of a large grapefruit, an abrupt pockmark in the curve of the leather. With growing excitement I scrambled back inside the hull and began shifting away the food packs which had been stored there. As soon as I had uncovered the

[241]

hull, I saw the grapefruit-shaped pocket and the cause of our trouble: Under tremendous pressure from outside, the leather had buckled inward into the gap between two wooden ribs, and opened a tear about four inches long. The force of the pressure had been so great that it had literally split the leather. The skin had not been cut or gashed. Despite a tensile strength of two tons per square inch, the leather had simply burst. Now, whenever *Brendan* wallowed, a great gush of sea water spurted through the tear and into the bilge. Jubilant, I poked my head up over the tarpaulin and called "Great news! I found the leak. And it's in a place where we can mend it." The others glanced up. There was relief on all their faces. "Finish your breakfast," I went on, "while I check that there are no other leaks." Then I went round the boat, hanging over the gunwale to see if there was any more damage. In fact, apart from that single puncture the leather was still in excellent condition. Indeed it was scarcely scratched by the ice. The other floes had simply glanced off the curve of the hull or skidded on the wool grease.

Except that one puncture. There, a combination of the curve of the hull, the wider gap between the ribs at that point, and the nipping between the two floes had driven a knob or sharp corner of ice through *Brendan*'s hull. By the same token, however, we also had room to wield a needle between the ribs and could sew a spare patch of leather over the gash. George and Trondur came forward. "The patch had better go on from the outside," I told them, "where the water pressure will help squeeze it against the hull. First we'll make a pattern, then cut the patch, and stitch it in place."

"We must cut away some wood," suggested Trondur, examining the ash ribs.

"Yes, whatever's needed to get at the work properly."

"I'm going to put on an immersion suit," George announced. "This is going to be a cold job."

He was right. George and Trondur in their immersion suits now had three hours of bone-chilling work. First they cut a patch of spare leather to size, then George hung down over the gunwale, his face of few inches above the water, and held the patch into position. Trondur poked an awl through the hull and the patch, followed by a long nine-inch needle and flax thread. George reached for the needle with a pair of pliers, gripped, tugged and

[242]

pulled, and eventually hauled it through. Then he took over the awl, stabbed from the outside of the hull, groped around until he could poke in the tip of the needle, and Trondur gathered it up from the inside.

It was a miserable chore. The top row of stitching was difficult enough, because it lay just above water level, so that each time the boat rolled on a wave, George was lucky if he went into the water only up to his elbows. With the heaviest waves, his head went right under, and he emerged spluttering and gasping. Each large wave then went on to break against the hull, and drenched Trondur who was crouching in the bilge, stitching on the inside. All this was done in a sea temperature of about zero degrees Centigrade, with occasional ice floes and icebergs in the immediate vicinity, and after nearly two days without proper rest. Inch by inch the stitching progressed, and a pancake of wool grease and fiber was stuffed between the hull and the patch to serve as a seal. Then the last row of stitches went in. This last row was completely under water, and George had to use the handle of a hammer to press in the needle.

Finally it was done. The two men straightened up, shivering with cold. George wiped the last of his protective wool grease from his hands and they had a well-earned tot of whiskey in their coffee. Even Trondur was so exhausted that he went off to curl up in his sleeping bag. Arthur pumped the bilge dry, and scarcely a trickle was coming in through the mend. I inspected the patch. "It's almost as neat and tidy as if you had put it on in Crosshaven Boatyard and not in the Labrador Sea—John O'Connell would be proud of you," I congratulated George.

"Well, that's a job I would not like to have to do again," he replied with quiet understatement.

That afternoon I reported our success to the Coast Guard radio station at St. Anthony's. The operator's voice revealed his delight. "Well done," he said. "I'll pass on the information to Rescue Coordination. I believe they want to move a Coast Guard ship into your area as a precaution, anyhow. Good luck with the rest of your voyage." I switched off the set and reflected that the Canadian Coast Guard were worthy colleagues for our friends in the Icelandic Coast Guard Service. Then for the first and only time in

[243]

the entire voyage we let *Brendan* look after herself. We dropped all sail, lashed the helm, and all four of us retreated to our sleeping bags and took a few hours of well-earned rest. My last thoughts before dropping off to sleep was that we had been able to repair *Brendan* because she was made of leather. If her hull had been made of brittle fiberglass or metal, or perhaps even of wood, she may well have been crushed by the ice and foundered.

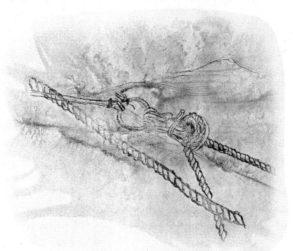

13

Land in the West

Neatly patched and safely clear of the pack ice, *Brendan* began the last lap of her voyage toward Newfoundland. Every day, we still saw icebergs drifting athwart our track. But after our recent escapade we were content to admire them at a distance, and at night keep a sharp look-out for their tell-tale ghostly shapes in the gloom. By now our chief feeling was the growing anticipation of finishing the voyage. We had been at sea for six weeks and were feeling worn. The constant strain of keeping alert for bad weather, the perpetual confines of our tiny boat, and the monotony of our daily seagoing routine had imposed its own form of mental strait jacket that became daily more constricting. It was more than just good seamanship that made us scan the horizon for signs of land: we were eager for our landfall. We knew that the icebergs meant that the New World could not be far away, because the bergs were drifting south in the Labrador current which runs close to the Canadian coast. We began to see other evidence of land—logs floating in the water, occasional patches of weed, and an increase in bird-life. But *Brendan* seemed to be dragging herself forward with deliberate sloth. She stalled in the calm weather and light airs, and drifted aimlessly in the current.

There was plenty of time to reflect that *Brendan* was not the first Irish leather boat to have reached the fringes of the Arctic sea ice. The monk Dicuil at Charlemagne's court had said that Irish priests had sailed to the edge of the frozen sea, a day's journey beyond the land where the sun scarcely sank below the horizon. And the *Navigatio* itself spoke of a "coagulated sea" which Saint Brendan reached during his voyage, a place where the sea was uncannily so still and flat that it seemed coagulated. Perhaps he had reached an area of frazil ice, one of the first stages of pack-ice development, where spillicules of ice hang in the water in total calm and then coalesce into lumps which resemble the curds floating on the surface of coagulating milk.

But there is a more spectacular description of sea ice in the *Navigatio*. One chapter seems to tell how Saint Brendan and his crew sighted a great iceberg drifting along at sea, surrounded by its halo of broken ice. They sailed over to investigate this marvel, rowed around it and even coaxed their curragh into the natural caverns and arches of the drift ice which surrounded the iceberg.

"One day after they had celebrated Mass," the *Navigatio* says of this episode, "there appeared to them a column in the sea which did not seem to be far away. And yet it took them three days to get near it. When the Man of God had come near, he looked for the top, but could see very little because it was so high. It was higher than the sky. Moreover it was surrounded by an open-meshed net. The openings were so large that the boat was able to pass through the gaps. They did not know what the net was made of. It was silver in color, but it seemed to be harder than marble. The column itself was of clearest crystal." Stripped of the storyteller's imagery, the incident is not difficult to interpret: Icebergs are visible from very far off because of their size and color, and the fact that they stand up from the horizon in clear weather. Apparently the crew of Saint Brendan's curragh were deluded by this, and they underestimated the distance to the iceberg when they began to row after it. More important, they failed to realize that the iceberg itself would be moving along with the current, perhaps at one or two knots, and this would greatly extend the time it took them to catch up. When they did reach the berg, they then seem to have run into the ring of broken ice which often surrounds a major iceberg recently released from the pack, and they were puzzled that this "net" was made of a different substance than the main "crystal" of the berg. Probably the outer floes were of opaque sea ice in contrast to the pure-white glacier ice of the main berg.

The *Navigatio* continues: "Then said Brendan to his brothers,

[246]

40.

39 (*preceding page*).   Trondur nets another
fulmar for dinner. At times the log line drifted at
a 30-degree angle to our course because of
Brendan's leeway. **40.**   Dangerous pack ice slips
by to port. A short time later *Brendan* was
sandwiched between two floes and her side was
punctured. The dark line at the top of the picture
was caused by a camera shutter jammed by
exposure to the cold and sea water. **41.**   Looking
astern of *Brendan*, the crew could see danger
safely passed. Then, with a shudder from the top
of her mast to the skid under her, *Brendan* ran
her bow into a great lump of sea ice. **42.**   It was
sew or sink. With the heaviest waves George's
head went right under. "That's a job I would not
like to have to do again," he said with quiet
understatement when he finished. But the patch
held and *Brendan* was water-tight again.

◄41.   42.►   43.►

▲44. ▼45.

3 (*preceding page*). *Brendan* touched the New World at 8 P.M. on June 26, 1977, at Peckford Island, Newfoundland.
4. Approaching landfall and the lighthouse n Peckford Island. 45. We made it! A eather boat that some had feared would disintegrate in the first gale had successfully crossed the Atlantic. There was no longer any practical objection to the idea that Irish monks might have sailed leather boats to North America before the Norsemen, and ong before Columbus. 46. The fishermen of Musgrave Harbor welcome *Brendan* and her rew. Would we attend a little celebration? 7. What *Brendan* looked like at journey's nd. Dinner still hung on the stern. 48 (*next age*). Aerial view as *Brendan* approaches er Promised Land.

'pull in your oars and unship the mast and sail, and some of you hold on to the meshes of the net.' There was a large space of about a mile between the net and the column, and similarly extending into the deep. When they had done this, the Man of God said to them 'Push the boat through a gap, that we may inspect the wonders of our Creator.'

"When they had gone in and looked here and there, the sea appeared to them to be as clear as glass, so that they could see everything down below. For they could see the base of the pillar and the fringe of the net lying on the sea floor. The sunlight was no less below the water than above.

"Then Saint Brendan measured a gap between four sides of the opening, which was four cubits in all parts. They then sailed all day along one side of the column and through its shadow could still feel the heat of the sun. They stayed there until three o'clock. All the time the Man of God kept measuring the one side. Seven hundred yards was the measurement of one of the four sides of that column. The venerable father was busy for four days in this way between the four angles of the pillar.

"On the fourth day they found a chalice in the same material as the net, and a plate of the color of the pillar, lying in a window in the southern face of the column. Saint Brendan at once took hold of these vessels, saying 'Our Lord Jesus Christ has shown us the miracle, and given me these two gifts in order to be shown to be many that they may believe.' Then the Man of God ordered his brothers to perform divine novice and afterwards refresh their bodies, because they had not had any free time to eat or drink since they had seen the pillar.

"When the night was over, the brothers began to row toward the north. When they had passed through an opening in the net, they set up the mast and raised the sail, and some held on to the net, while all was made ready on the boat. When the sail had been spread, a fair wind began to blow from astern so that there was no work to sailing, but they had only to hold the sheets and rudder."

So ended the episode with the iceberg, an encounter which obviously made a profound impression on the travelers of the *Navigatio*. The "chalice and plate" they found in a niche in the berg were probably no more than curious-shaped pieces of broken ice which resembled church ornaments to the devout minds of the crew, overawed by the huge "crystal pillar," and it is interesting how Saint Brendan is credited nevertheless with the intellectual discipline to set about taking measurements of the iceberg to satisfy a more scholarly outlook. From the geographer's point of view, the iceberg is very important to the *Navigatio*, because it emphasizes that the main events of the voyage were taking place along a northerly trans-Atlantic route and not, as has been suggested, along the easier southern route using the trade winds to the West Indies. There was no possibility of seeing an iceberg at sea along the southern route. Rather, the "crystal column" is geographically consistent with the other episodes of the northern route, particularly with the volcanic Island of Smiths as Iceland, the Island of Sheep as Faroes, and the simple practical fact, so clearly demonstrated by *Brendan*, that leather boats survive longer in the colder waters of the North.

Light airs and calms off Newfoundland also meant fog and mists. *Brendan* was now in one of the foggiest areas of the North Atlantic. Even in the summer months the visibility is notoriously bad off the east coast of Newfoundland. The naval handbooks advise that visibility is less than five miles between forty and fifty percent of the time during May, June, and July, and that it drops to under half a mile in fog for between thirty and forty percent of recorded observations. Once again, the *Navigatio* bore out the facts with similar information about approaching the Promised Land. According to the text, Saint Brendan went back to the Island of Sheep after his seven years of fruitless voyaging and took on board sufficient stores for forty days and—very important—a pilot. This pilot was the "Steward" who lived on the Island of Sheep, and he told the travelers that without his help they would not be able to find the Promised Land. The Steward then led the way and after forty days the boat came into a thick fog which enveloped her. "Do you know what this fog is?" asked the Steward. "What?" replied Saint Brendan. "This fog," the Steward replied, "encircles the island for which you have been searching for seven years."

Literary scholars have pointed out, correctly, that the notion of a dark cloud hiding the goal of a search is a well-rubbed device of medieval storytellers, and so the fog which surrounds Saint Brendan's Promised Land should be treated with some caution.

[248]

Nevertheless it is a fascinating coincidence on the long path that matches the geography of the North Atlantic from Ireland to the foggy coast of northeast America with the episodes of the *Navigatio*.

Three days of mist and low cloud had hidden the sun from *Brendan*, too, when on June 23 we picked up a radio message to say that the Canadian Coast Guard ship *John Cabot* was hoping to rendezvous with *Brendan* that day. Our little boat was being swept south by the Labrador current, and without an accurate sunsight my dead reckoning for position was thirty miles wrong.

So *John Cabot* found us quite by chance. Her skipper Captain Les Eavis had altered course to investigate a large iceberg when his lookout called down from the crow's nest to say that he could see a small shape in the water. It was *Brendan*, and we were about 120 miles off the Newfoundland coast.

"Actually we were lucky to run into you," said Captain Eavis as he came aboard *Brendan* from a rubber dinghy to see what life was like aboard a medieval vessel.

"You know, we were heading a little more to the eastward, and we were looking at that iceberg, and then the look-out called down and said there's something fine on the port bow. I was looking and said 'Jesus! He's supposed to be thirty-eight miles away. Can't be him. It's awfully small! But after the second or third look we realized it had to be you. We could see the cross on your sails. The red cross."

Captain Eavis was an old sailing-ship man himself, and intrigued with *Brendan*'s rig. "Well, you didn't need any help, and you've shown that the old boats can make it," he said after he had taken a look around and shared a tot of whiskey. "You can imagine it's a bit different aboard my vessel. So it's nice to see that such things can still be done. I'm taking *John Cabot* back to port in the next thirty-six hours, and I'll make sure that there's a welcoming committee for you. Just let me know if there's anything we can let you have."

Before she steamed off, *John Cabot* left us with more fresh food, extra kerosene for the cooker, spare batteries for our torches, and five pairs of dry socks from the first mate's wardrobe. Her visit had finally broken our sense of isolation, and in conse-

[249]

Humpback whale

quence the impressions of those last days became a blur, smudged under the growing anticipation of a landfall, and the realization that we were nearly at journey's end.

The weather held mild with light winds which were so fickle, switching to all points of the compass, though mostly from the west, that *Brendan* closed erratically with the coast of Newfoundland. Now we were heading toward St. Johns, now swinging so far north that it seemed we might almost be making back toward Labrador. But we were taking no chances. A single gale from the wrong direction could blow *Brendan* back out to sea for another week, and so we disciplined ourselves not even to speculate about the place and day of our landfall. The weather would bring *Brendan* to land when and where it chose, and our single-minded purpose was to see that the boat was given her best chance.

To our delight the number of whales actually increased as we approached Newfoundland. It was as if the companions of our odyssey were coming to see *Brendan* complete her mission. We were passed by several schools of pilot whales, some traveling in scattered groups so that the sea for a mile in either direction was dotted with the regular rise and fall of their bodies as they swam leisurely past, and one bright afternoon a pair of dolphin put on a superb display of acrobatics, leaping for sheer joy in head-to-head double arcs as if they were entertainers in an aquarium. On the

[250]

final days we were inspected by large numbers of white-bellied humpback whales from a great whale colony which spends the summer in Sir Charles Hamilton Sound on the Newfoundland coast. We followed the surging movements of the humpbacks on all sides of *Brendan*, surfacing and blowing, diving with the unmistakable slow arching of their backs which gives them their name, followed by the graceful skyward wave of the tail before the animal slips below the surface. Then we could trace the huge white patch beneath the water as the whale swam over toward *Brendan* and passed close beneath the hull to inspect it. In the distance other whales were leaping clear out of the water and toppling back with great splashes, or sometimes thrusting their tails from the water and repeatedly slapping down their flukes on the sea with mighty bursts of spray as if in farewell.

During the night of June 25 we were able to distinguish faint pinpricks of shore lights to the south of us; and when a dull grey morning broke, we began to make out the indistinct line of land ahead. Our noses confirmed the sighting. Across the water came the definite smell of pine trees wafted by a gentle off-shore breeze from the great forests of Newfoundland. I set *Brendan*'s course toward Hamilton Sound because I wanted to be sure that there was land on three sides of us and no contrary wind could drive us clear. At last, and gradually, we began to accept the fact that we were certain to make landfall. The coast drew closer. It was low and featureless, and protected by a string of small islands. The radio began to chatter with messages from Coast Guard radio stations. A helicopter loaded with photographers clattered out and circled around us, its pilot careful not to capsize *Brendan* with the downdraught from his rotor blades. Another, larger helicopter appeared from the airport at Gander. It too was loaded with cameras, wielded by servicemen from the airbase. Suddenly, from behind one of the islands a pair of small Coast Guard boats came skimming over the water toward us. "There's a small fishing port three miles or so up the coast called Musgrave Harbor," shouted one of the coxwains as he roared up. "We can tow you in there if you like."

"No. Thank you. First we want to land by ourselves," I called back, and checked the chart once again. Downwind of *Brendan* lay the small island chain of the Outer Wadham Group, uninhabited

[251]

except for lighthouse-keepers. The islands were an ideal spot for a quiet landfall. The nearest was called Peckford Island. "There's nowhere to land on that island. It's all rocks on the beach," warned a voice from the Coast Guard boat as *Brendan* changed course. But it did not matter. There had been no port in Saint Brendan's day either, and I reckoned that if *Brendan* had come through the Labrador ice, she was tough enough to stand a final landing on a rocky beach.

"Trondur, stand by to drop over an anchor. Boots, pull out an oar and get ready. We're going to make our touchdown."

George went forward to lower and stow *Brendan*'s little foresail for the last time. Under mainsail alone, she crept toward the rock-ribbed shore. The swell heaved and sucked on ledges of bare, grey rock. Boulders dotted the shore, and grass and scrub covered the inner dunes. "Let go the anchor!" There was a splash as Trondur dropped the anchor overboard, paid out line, and gave a great tug to make sure that it had set firmly. We would need the anchor to pull *Brendan* off the rocks once a man had been put ashore.

"George, can you take a line onto land?" He looked doubtfully at the slippery rock ledges and the foam of the undertow. "Yes, if I don't break a leg," he muttered. "There's no point in getting wet at this stage." Pulling on his immersion suit, he climbed out on the bow with his legs dangling on each side.

Brendan eased forward. Not with style or speed, but in the same matter-of-fact manner that she had crossed three and a half thousand miles of sea. The red ring cross on her mainsail began to sag as I eased the halliard a few feet to slow the boat even more. Trondur took up the slack on the anchor rope and handed it gently over the gunwale. Arthur made a couple of dips at the water with his blade to keep the boat straight. *Brendan* nosed quietly onto the rocks. George leaped. His feet splashed, and touched ground . . . and I thought, "We've made it!"

Brendan touched the New World at 8:00 P.M. on June 26 on the shore of Peckford Island in the Outer Wadham Group some 150 miles northwest of St. Johns, Newfoundland. She had been at sea for fifty days. The exact spot of her landfall has no particular significance to the story of the early Irish voyages into the Atlantic.

[252]

It was merely the place where the wind and current had brought a twentieth-century replica of the original Irish skin vessels. Earlier navigators could have made their landfalls almost anywhere along the coast of hundreds of miles in either direction. What mattered was that *Brendan* had demonstrated without a shadow of a doubt that the voyage could be done.

A leather boat that some had feared would disintegrate in the first gale off the Irish coast had successfully crossed the Atlantic.

When *Brendan* nuzzled her bow onto Peckford Island, she may have looked more like a floating bird's nest than an ocean-going vessel, an untidy muddle of ropes and flax, leather and wood. But she was strong and sound; and the four of us who sailed her knew that she was still seaworthy to our highest expectations. She had brought us safely through gales and pack ice and through two seasons across some of the most unforgiving waters in the Atlantic. We had put our trust in her, and she had repaid that confidence. She was a true ocean-going vessel, and there was no longer any practical objection to the idea that Irish monks might have sailed their leather boats to North America before the Norsemen, and long before Columbus.

Brendan had demonstrated that the voyage *could* be done with medieval material and medieval technology. But in the final analysis the only conclusive proof that it *had* been done will be if an authentic relic from an early Irish visit is found one day on North American soil. Perhaps it will be a rock scratched with an early Irish inscription, or the foundation of an Irish beehive hut that can be dated accurately to the days of the extraordinary Irish voyages. Admittedly the chances of such a discovery are slim. Irish relics have not yet been found in Iceland, where it is known the Irish hermits settled for some time; and if the early Christian Irish did touch on North America, they would have left only the lightest fingerprint. It would be singularly fortunate if such a faint trace is located on a very long coastline which is either desolate and little known, or in well-favored areas covered over by more recent development.

This being so, it was all the more vital that *Brendan*'s successful voyage should have rescued the early Irish seafaring achievement from the category of speculation and doubt, and returned it to its proper arena of serious historical debate. At best, land archaeologists should now be encouraged to search for Irish traces in the New World, and at very least, it is difficult any longer to bury the early Christian Irish sailors into a footnote in the history books of exploration on the excuse that too little is known about them and their claims are physically impossible.

Brendan's success also went a long way to vindicate the *Navigatio* itself. Episodes in that remarkable narrative, which had seemed so fanciful, now appeared in a new light. In fact it was remarkable to review the number of times where it had formerly been necessary to conjure up imaginative, learned parallels to explain the puzzles of the *Navigatio* when simpler and more practical explanations would have fitted the facts better. For example, it is easier to explain the episodes of the Island of Smiths and the Island of the Fiery Mountain as first-hand descriptions of volcanic Iceland seen from a visiting curragh than to ransack the classics for similar Latin descriptions of submarine and land volcanos. And it is more logical to place the Island of Sheep in the Faroes, in company with the Island of Birds, when we know that the Irish could easily have sailed there and seen the very scenes that the *Navigatio* touches on than to dismiss such places as fantasies.

Then *Brendan* had also produced some unexpected solutions to the *Navigatio*'s riddles. Surely the famous story of Jasconius, the friendly "great fish" who returned again and again to Saint Brendan's leather curragh, is rooted in the actual reaction of the great whales when they meet leather boats at sea and come back time after time to inspect the stranger at close quarters. Such leviathan behavior must have made a deep impression on the minds of the medieval monks, perhaps seeing these huge creatures for the first time in their lives and astonished by their massive bulk swirling alongside an open boat far smaller than the animal. And the great Pillar of Crystal with its surrounding net of "marble" fragments is sufficiently like an iceberg, newly freed from the pack ice and still surrounded by its patch of broken field ice, that it would be impossible for the storyteller to imagine the details without first-hand knowledge at his disposal. Even today it is difficult for the scholar to understand the allusion unless he too has seen the northern icebergs.

Brendan helped to redress the balance. She demonstrated that the *Navigatio* is more than a splendid medieval romance. It is really a story hung upon a framework of facts and observation which mingles geography and literature, and the challenge is how to separate one from the other. This mixture is hardly surprising. Scholars of epic literature know from experience that many of the truly durable legends, from the *Iliad* to the *Romance of Alexander*, are founded upon real events and real people which the later storytellers have clothed in imaginitive detail.

Where, then, was the Land Promised to the Saints which Saint Brendan is said to have found beyond the swirling fog? There is no reason to suppose that the Promised Land was any more fictional than the Island of Smiths, the Paradise of Birds, the Island of Sheep, the island monastery, or any other locality in the *Navigatio*. The text gives a few clues to its identity. When Saint Brendan's boat reached the shore of the Promised Land, it says, "they climbed out of the boat and saw a spacious land full of laden fruit trees as if in autumn. But when they had made a circuit of that land, night had still not come upon them. They took as much fruit as they wanted and drank from the springs, and for forty days explored the whole land without finding an end to it. But one day they came to a great river flowing through the middle of the island. Then Saint Brendan said to his brothers: 'We cannot cross this river and we do not know how big this land is.' When they were considering this to themselves, behold a young man arrived, embraced them with great joy, and calling each one by his name, said 'Blessed are they who dwell in your house. From generation to generation they will praise you.'

"When he had said this, he said to Saint Brendan 'Behold this land which you sought for so much time. You could not find it immediately, because God wanted to show you his diverse secrets in the great ocean. Return, then, to your native land carrying with you the fruits of this land and as many jewels as your little boat can hold. The final day of your wanderings draws nigh so that you may sleep with your fathers. After many ages have past, this land will be made known to your successors, at a time when Christians are undergoing persecution. This river which you see divides this island. Just as it appears to you laden with fruit, so the land will remain for ever without the shadow of night. For its light is Christ.'"

[255]

What facts can be extracted—with caution—from this rapturous medieval description of the Promised Land? There is the great extent of the land; the abundance of the natural fruit; and the great river dividing it. They are all general features which could apply to many places on the North American coast. But what is immediately striking is how these features resemble the descriptions which later visitors first remarked when they reached North America, whether the Norsemen who wrote of its woods and wild grapes, or later settlers who praised the favorable climate for crops. The overlap might well be another simple coincidence, but it could equally well be a hazy description passed down by word of mouth of the great land which lay at the far rim of the great western ocean and at the end of the Stepping Stone Route which the *Navigatio* so consistently seems to follow and identify. Even the obvious exaggerations, such as the claim that the land provided precious stones, are no hindrance to treating the *Navigatio* as a possible description of North America. Christopher Columbus was to make very much the same claim for the West Indies when he returned to Spain, and it is hardly surprising that the goal of Saint Brendan's long search, when he finally reaches it in the pages of the *Navigatio*, should be credited with fantastic wealth by the storyteller. Our modern error would be to dismiss the statements of the *Navigatio* themselves as no more than imaginary.

To bring home the tale of his voyage, Saint Brendan had of course to return to Ireland from the Promised Land and make the journey complete. The *Navigatio* treats of the return voyage briskly: "Then, when they had taken from the fruits of the land and all kinds of its gems, and dismissed the steward and the young man with a blessing, Saint Brendan and his brothers returned to their curragh and set sail through the middle of the fog. When they had passed through it they came to an island called the Island of Delights. There they received hospitality for three days and then, after being blessed, Saint Brendan returned home by the direct route." Once more there is a sound and straightforward explanation of this passage. Having sailed out from the fog, the Saint's curragh picked up the Gulf Stream and the steady winds of the great slant of westerlies and southwesterlies which blow across the Atlantic, and they headed directly back to Ireland. This is the logical eastbound route, the path which is still sailed by small yachts and has been taken by open rowing boats smaller than a leather ocean-going curragh. It is the downwind route, and it is perhaps worth noting that the rowing boats, though they started hundred of miles apart on the North American coast, made their landfall directly on to Ireland's west coast, precisely where the *Navigatio* returns Saint Brendan.

Arriving at his own monastery, concludes the *Navigatio*, Saint Brendan was greeted joyfully and "he told of everything he remembered happening on the voyage and the great and splendid wonders that God had deigned to show him." Then he reminded his followers of the prophecy that he would soon die, set his affairs in order, and very shortly afterward, fortified with the Sacraments of

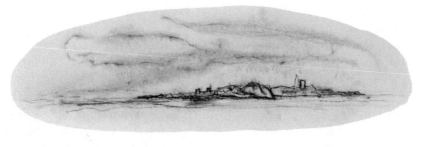

Peckford Island

the Church, lay back "in the hands of his disciples and gave up his spirit to the Lord." So died peacefully the most famous sailor-monk of the Celtic Church in Ireland. But did the Irish voyages end with his death? Once more the answer lies in the *Navigatio*. Nowhere does it claim that Saint Brendan was the first to reach the Promised Land. On the contrary, it states unequivocally that he was told about the Promised Land by another Irish monk, Saint Barrind, who had already visited it in company with an Irish abbot of the west coast by the name of Mernoc, who was a regular visitor there. And when Saint Brendan still had not reached the Promised

Land after seven sailing seasons, it is the "Steward" from the Island of Sheep who acts as his pilot, guides him there, and tells him what to expect.

In the Promised Land too, the newcomers meet a young man who is living there already, knows the Saint's name, and can speak with him in his own tongue. In short, the picture that the *Navigatio* provides is the same picture that is found in the writings of Dicuil, in the Norse sagas, and in other contemporary sources: the idea that the Promised Land is the ultimate point in a number of scattered North Atlantic localities which have been settled by tiny groups of Irish monks who passed from place to place in small and seaworthy boats. In this context the voyage of Saint Brendan is less a voyage of primary exploration than a tremendous pastoral tour by a leading churchman who is visiting the farthest outposts of his devout countrymen and, in so doing, ventures to the limits of the ocean and their known world.

Here, then, lies another crucial fact about the *Navigatio*. The text stresses that Saint Brendan did not make a single, long, voyage to the Promised Land. Instead he made a whole series of trips, season by season of his seven-year search, before he is guided to his eventual destination in the Promised Land. In the gap between the Saint's death and the date the *Navigatio* was composed in the form we now have it, it would have been natural to include into Saint Brendan's own voyage the experiences and adventures of other Irish monks in their small boats in the North Atlantic and place them as episodes during the seven years of Saint Brendan's voyage. This is the normal process of building an epic—the central hero is credited with the experiences of lesser figures until his single endeavor embodies the feats of many. Nor does this process detract from Saint Brendan's own achievement. Rather, it enhances his journey because clearly it was the symbol for the rest, and an example for the monk-navigators who followed him. Also it has stood through the succeeding centuries as a monument to the achievements of the other Christian monks who took to the sea from Ireland. Without the *Navigatio* the least glimmer of their endeavors would be all that is left to us. The collective experiences within the *Navigatio* is not likely to be the story of one boat's crew who set out on a single voyage to search for the Promised Land. It is the main surviving record of a Christian seagoing culture which sent boat after boat into the North Atlantic on regular voyages of communication and exploration.

If so, then the Irish voyages into the Atlantic stand in very special relationship to the entire history of man's exploration of his world. Usually the first scouts have been forgotten. Their efforts are not recorded or, if they were written down, few people read them. Outside Scandinavia, for example, the Norse visits to Greenland and North America were little heard of. By contrast the Irish voyages, represented in the *Navigatio* of Saint Brendan, won great attention. The *Navigatio*'s religious flavor ensured that Saint Brendan's travels achieved intellectual respectability throughout Europe for five hundred years. Thus strengthened, it helped to demolish the mentality of a closed world, encouraged men of learning to think of a great western land. It prompted map-makers to mark islands in the western sea. And the truly fascinating possibility is that the medieval scholars who read and believed Saint Brendan had reached a western land were right: that the Irish really had sailed their skin boats to Greenland and North America as we now know they could have done. If so, then Europe from the tenth century onward was already perceiving the New World in the manner of the time.

What sort of men, then, were these monks who deliberately launched out into the Atlantic in small open boats? Many must never have returned, but perished at sea. Aboard *Brendan* we had the advantages of being in touch with the outside world by radio, and we knew that if they could reach us fast enough, the Coast Guard or the deep-sea fishermen of the North Atlantic would have tried to rescue us in an emergency. But the Irish monks and their curraghs had none of these advantages. A dozen or more men would have been packed into a boat the size of *Brendan* and would have endured far greater discomfort. They would have been colder, wetter, and—in one sense—more isolated than we were aboard *Brendan*. Such men must have been special people, even by the exacting standards of their own day. They were directed by a sense of dedication which had to have been the single most important factor in their success. Out of this dedication came much of their suitability as open-boat sailors on long northern voyages. As monks they were inured to hardship. Life in a medieval monastery with its meager food, seasonal shortages, stone cells, abstinence, long hours of tedium, obedience, self-mortification and discipline, was an ideal training for a long journey in an open boat. Equally, their mental preparation must have matched their physical readiness. The outlook of their leaders, if not of the rank and file, was a bold combination of intellectual curiosity and a fearless trust in God. This trust encouraged them to launch their voyages and, once at sea, to sustain their efforts through adversity. The journey itself was regarded as important in its proper execution as reaching a landfall. To venture out in a boat was by its very nature an act of faith in a God whose divine providence would show them wondrous sights and, if He so wished, bring them safely to journey's end. Should adverse winds or currents beat them back, that too was His will. If their craft foundered underneath them and the crew perished, then they reached their divine reward doubly blessed because they had died in God's service.

God's service on these voyages did not have its modern sense of an overseas mission to go to convert heathen lands. On the contrary, the territories that the Irish monks sought were the unknown and uninhabited lands beyond the horizon, the special places, the wondrous lands to be revealed by God. In the apt phrase of the time, they were the Promised Lands. To reach these farthest territories was a heavenly gift; to be able to live in them, isolated from the evils of the world, was an even greater prize. There can seldom have been a stronger drive to probe the unknown in the entire story of human exploration. It was the quintessential motive for exploration at almost any price, and there is no reason why it should not have brought them across the Atlantic.

Brendan had also shown us that the quality of medieval boat equipment was easily equal to the task of promoting the ocean-going ambitions of the sailor-monks. Indeed, it was an interesting fact that the medieval equipment on *Brendan* was often a match for its modern equivalent, and occasionally superior to it when used in the grindingly harsh conditions of an open boat in the North Atlantic. Timber, leather, and flax proved to be more durable in many instances than metal, plastic, and nylon; and certainly the former were much easier to work with and could be adapted for day-to-day requirements. This was vitally important when, aboard our small craft, we were only able to carry a few hand tools and a very limited stock of spares. The modern equipment worked better, until it broke, but then the traditional gear, clumsy and inefficient though it was, managed to survive the adverse conditions—and this is what mattered. Perhaps historians do not realize just how well the medieval seafarers were equipped for their endeavors with bronze fittings, handpicked timbers, leather, and flax cordage; and the modern seafarer forgets the tremendous advantages of flexibility and durability in the traditional materials which are all-important when the crises occur, as they always do at sea.

Similarly, there is little that the medieval sailor would want to borrow from the modern sailor to improve his personal comfort and sustenance. Apart from modern waterproof outer clothing, the medieval sailor was better clad in his woollen trousers, shirt, and cloak than in garments of synthetic fibers. And when he embarked on a cold, wet voyage in an open boat, his diet of dried meats and fish, oats, fruit, and nuts was unsurpassed. It was more nutritious and palatable, and lasted better, than the dehydrated packaged foods of today. His supply of drinking water could be carried in leather flasks, and replenished in emergency by the ample rainfall of northern waters collected in upturned sheets of leather, or topped up by landings on the islands of the Stepping Stone Route. For extra food the medieval sailor could fish or take seabirds from the wealth of the sea around him. Saint Brendan and his monks were lucky to salvage a dead whale, which gave them enough meat for three months, but it is equally clear that they were accustomed to picking up fresh provisions at every inhabited island they visited, and they were using what amounted to a chain of supply places along the Stepping Stone Route to ease their logistical problems.

Perhaps one reason why the medieval Irish voyages have been so little appreciated for what they were is because they have been described by storytellers whose tales of distant lands and fantastic monsters seem naïve to the modern critic. Such yarns appear overblown, simple-minded, incredible. But the real fault lies not with the medieval author for his writing, but in the modern perception of the older experience. It is easy to dismiss such tales as worthless and childish when they are viewed from the commanding heights of twentieth-century knowledge. But *Brendan* taught us to look at them otherwise. *Brendan* helped us to

[261]

understand them by placing us back in situations similar to the original. Time and again we too found ourselves deeply impressed, and sometimes awed, by what we encountered at sea. Some episodes were unforgettable because their visual splendor was combined with the excitement of physical danger. For example, the breath-taking advance of *Brendan* toward the stark and looming cliffs of the Faroes in mist and tide race; or the long engagement among the ice floes of Labrador, incredibly beautiful in their shades of color, will stay long in our minds.

Other memories were more—perhaps the beauty of the slow northern sunsets, or the damp half world of the Greenland fog banks when one's vision focuses on the tiny, near objects like the glistening droplets forming on a woollen sweater. Or there were the moments of total surprise like the first wondrous rush of a school of pilot whales surfacing around our leather boat in a puffing and wallowing mass, surrounding us with glimpse upon glimpse of our ocean companions. One may have read in advance of such scenes, half imagined them, or even seen excellent photographs of them. But the reality was far greater than the expectation, and stirred us even with our twentieth-century attitudes. How much more impressive these same scenes must have been to medieval sailors who were eager and expectant to see God's marvels. In a sense even their vivid prose fails to capture the splendor of the occasion, and it is scarcely surprising that they should have come back and reported so extravagantly and with such wonder.

This appreciation of their medieval outlook was one of *Brendan*'s most valid lessons to us, a balance to the more scientific data of laboratory reports on flax and oak-bark leather, the rowing and towing tests to try to fix the boat's theoretical performance, the daily records of winds and sea states, leeway and miles made good, as we assessed the ocean-going behavior of our leather boat for nautical archaeologists. And running parallel to the medieval aura was a modern lesson: from the moment we first sailed from Brandon Creek to the day when we put ashore in Newfoundland, we had a privileged contact with the seafaring communities around the North Atlantic as they still exist today. When we moved *Brendan* from her landfall at Peckford Island across to the little fishing port of Musgrave Harbor on the mainland, the local fishing boats returning from their day's work escorted us home. As we drew near the harbor entrance, we saw the pier was thronged with spectators. They had come down to the harbor from the neighboring fishing hamlets and from the scattered line of wooden frame houses which curved around the bay. Now they stood and waved, and cheered, and greeted *Brendan* with the same generous enthusiasm which had met us all along the route the leather boat had sailed.

Among the first to scramble aboard as we tied alongside the fishing boats was a deputy from the community. Would we attend a little celebration? Of course we would. All next day the fishermen's wives cleaned and prepared the food that their menfolk brought in from the sea and donated—piles of lobsters, heaps of crabs' legs, and the local delicacy of cod tongues fried in batter.

That evening I found myself gazing down the long table piled with food and reflecting to myself how lucky we on *Brendan* had been with all the people we had met on our long path to the New World. With their encouragement we had achieved what we had set out to do, and we had very many happy memories of our landfalls around the North Atlantic.

Then the band, three men who themselves worked by day as fishermen, began to play the local songs of the Newfoundland coast, many of their tunes based on traditional Irish airs that were brought to Newfoundland by the Irish immigrants who came there in the last century. The dancing began. Listening to the swirl of the music and watching the spontaneous gaiety of the dancers, I thought of what lay ahead for us. George would be returning home to England with his wife Judith and looking to start a new job very different from his role as *Brendan*'s sailing master. Trondur had his ticket back to the Faroes, where he would be working up the sketches that he had made aboard and taking up his sculpture once more; and Arthur, as easy-going as ever, planned to tour the United States and Canada. I had the reports and results of the entire project to correlate and develop back at my desk and in the libraries where the preliminary work had been done so very many months ago.

It seemed a good time to ask myself the question that I knew we would be asked many times in the future: Would we go on the

Brendan Voyage again, knowing the discomfort and difficulties that faced us? For my own part I was sure of my answer: If the venture would help our understanding, if it would increase our appreciation of the past, and if there was the same enthusiasm and help—and good luck—available from the beginnings of the project to its journeys end, the answer was—yes.

Musgrave harbor

Appendix I
The Navigatio

So many manuscripts of the *Navigatio Sancti Brendani Abbatis* have survived that it took an American scholar nearly thirty years to track them down—and even then he admitted that he had not found them all. Nevertheless a great debt is owed to this scholar, Carl Selmer, for his painstaking labors in compiling a much-needed comprehensive edition of the *Navigatio* in its Latin version. He used eighteen of about 120 *Navigatio* manuscripts to produce his edition, which was printed by the University of Notre Dame Press as Number IV in their Publications in Medieval Studies (1959).

Until Selmer's work there was no good composite edition generally available to scholars of the *Navigatio*'s Latin test. Since then, both Penguin Books in *Lives of the Saints* (1965) and Professor John J. O'Meara of University College Dublin, with his *The Voyage of Saint Brendan* (1976), have produced English translations. Their translations, particularly the latter, catch the flavor of the original narrative with all its important religious, scholarly, and maritime overtones. The following synopsis is only intended as a paraphrase. It is the bare bones of the *Navigatio*, rendered down into the factual narrative of a remarkable venture by sea:

The Text

Chapter 1. Saint Brendan was living at Clonfert as the head of a community of 3000 monks when he was visited by a monk named Barrind. Barrind told Brendan how he had visited Saint Mernoc, a former disciple who had gone to live as an anchorite and was now the abbot of a monastery on an offshore island. Saint Mernoc had invited Barrind to go with him by boat to the Promised Land of the Saints. Setting out westward, they passed through a thick fog and reached a wide land, rich in fruit and flowers. For fifteen days they walked around the land, until they reached a river flowing from east to west. There they were met by a man who told them that they should go no farther, but return home. He told them that the island had been there since the beginning of the world, and that they had actually been ashore for a year, though they had not needed food or drink. This man accompanied the travelers back to their boat and they re-embarked. Then he vanished, and the travelers sailed home through the fog back to Saint Mernoc's monastery. There the monks told Barrind that Saint Mernoc often sailed away to the same Promised Land and stayed away a long time.

Chapter 2. After Barrind had left him to return to his own cell, Brendan picked fourteen monks from his own community, and told them that he dearly wanted to visit this Promised Land of the Saints. Promptly they volunteered to accompany him.

Chapter 3. After fasting, the Saint and his companions paid a three-day visit to the island of Saint Enda (Inishmore, Aran Islands) for his blessing.

Chapter 4. Then Brendan and his monks pitched tent on a narrow creek under a mountain called Brendan's Seat. There they built a wood-framed boat, covered in oak-bark-tanned oxhides, and smeared the joints of the hides with fat to seal them. In the boat they put a mast and sail, steering gear, supplies for forty days, spare hides and fat for dressing leather.

Chapter 5. Just as they were about to set sail, three monks came down to the beach, and begged to be taken aboard. Brendan agreed, but he warned that two of them would meet a hideous fate, and the third also would not return from the voyage.

Chapter 6. Sailing westward for fifteen days, they lost their bearings after a calm and were blown to a tall rocky island, with streams falling down the cliffs. With difficulty they found a tiny harbor like a cleft. Here they landed and were met by a stray dog who led them to a settlement, where they entered a hall and found food set out for them, which they ate. For three days they stayed, seeing no one but always finding food ready set out.

Chapter 7. Toward the end of their visit, one of the latecoming monks tried to steal a silver bridle he had found, but Brendan rebuked him. At that, a small devil jumped out of the monk's bosom, and the man died.

Chapter 8. Just as they were re-embarking in their boat, a young man came up with a basket of bread and jar of water which he gave them for their voyage, which he warned would be a long one.

Chapter 9. Their next landfall was an island with many large streams, full of fish. It was called the Island of Sheep, because flocks of splendid white sheep ran wild all year round. Here the travelers stayed from Maundy Thursday to Holy Saturday. An islander brought them food, and prophesied they would visit a nearby island for Easter Day and then land on a third island not far to the west called the Paradise of Birds, where they would remain until the eighth day of Pentecost.

Chapter 10. This nearest island was stony and without grass. Beaching their boat on it, the monks hauled it up with ropes and lit a fire to cook some of the meat from the Island of Sheep. But as the pot began to boil, the island started to shake and move, and the monks scrambled back into their boat in panic. They watched the "island" move off to sea, the fire still burning on it, and Brendan told them that the "island" was the biggest fish in the ocean, called Jasconius.

Chapter 11. Now the monks sailed to the Paradise of Birds, lying across a narrow channel to the west of the Island of Sheep. They hauled their boat for almost a mile up a narrow stream to its source, where they found a vast tree covered with a multitude of white birds. One bird was very tame and flew down to land on the boat and spoke to Saint Brendan to explain that the birds were men's spirits, and that Saint Brendan would search seven years before he reached the Promised Land. At vespers and other times of prayer the birds sang hymns and chanted verses. The travelers spent some time on the Paradise of Birds, eating supplies brought over by the Procurator or "Steward," the same man who had supplied them on the Island of Sheep. He also brought them fresh water, warning them not to drink direct from the island spring, water from which would send them to sleep.

Chapter 12. Continuing on their voyage for three months with only sea and sky around them, the travelers were so exhausted when they next sighted land that they could scarcely row there against the unfavorable wind. But they managed to reach a small landing place and fill their water-vessels at two wells, one clear and one muddy. Here they were met by a grave and white-haired elder who led them to a monastery two hundred yards from the landing place. Eleven silent monks greeted them at the entrance with reliquaries, crosses, and hymns. They embraced the travelers, and the abbot of the monastery washed their feet. Then they sat down to a meal of sweet roots and white bread, sitting down with the monks. The abbot now broke his rule of silence to explain to Brendan that the loaves were brought miraculously to their larder and that the lights in their chapel never burned away. No cooked food was eaten at the monastery and the monks, of whom there were twenty-four in all, never seemed to grow any older.

After the meal Brendan was shown their church with its circle of twenty-four seats and church vessels of square-cut crystal. The church itself was also square. After compline, the visiting monks were taken away and given accommodation in the cells of the monks, but the abbot and Brendan stayed behind to witness the miraculous lighting of the lamps. As they waited, the abbot explained that they had been on the island eighty years, hearing no human voice, and communicating only by gestures, and no one had ever been sick or afflicted by worldly spirits. Abruptly a fiery arrow sped in through a window, touched and lit the lamps, and then suddenly sped out again.

Chapter 13. Brendan and his monks spent Christmas with the Community of Saint Ailbe, and on the eighth day after Epiphany set out again by sea, rowing and sailing until Lent. Their food and drink ran out and they were very distressed, but three days later they came upon another island. On it they found a clear well of water, surrounded by plants and roots, and fish swimming along the river bed toward the sea. They gathered the plants and roots to eat, but the well water caused some of them to fall into a deep sleep, some for three days, others for two days, some for a day. Saint Brendan prayed for them and, when they recovered, told them they must quit the island. Loading only a little water and taking fish from the river, they set out again in their boat and sailed north.

Chapter 14. Three days later the wind dropped and the sea was so smooth it seemed to be coagulated. Brendan ordered his crew to ship their oars and let God direct the boat. For twenty days they drifted aimlessly until a westerly wind sped them eastward.

Chapter 15. The wind brought them back to the Island of Sheep where, at the same landing place as the previous year, the Steward greeted them joyfully, pitched a tent, made ready a bath, and provided them with fresh clothes. Then after they had celebrated Holy Saturday and eaten supper, he told them to go again to the whale to celebrate Resurrection Sunday and afterward to proceed to the Paradise of Birds. He himself would ferry across bread and drink while they stayed there.

This they did—landing on the whale, then sailing on to the Paradise of Birds and listening to the birds. The Steward told Brendan that for seven years he would repeat the cycle, spending Maunday Thursday on the Island of Sheep, Easter on the whale; from Easter to Pentecost on the Paradise of Birds; and Christmas with the Community of Saint Ailbe.

So it turned out, and the Steward brought them their food until it was time to set out again in the curragh with provisions from the Island of Sheep.

Chapter 16.   After sailing in the ocean for forty days, they saw a beast of huge size following the boat. He spouted foam from his nostrils and came ploughing toward them at great speed as if to devour them. The monks were very frightened and called upon the Lord, but Brendan comforted them. Then the huge beast came even closer, pushing great waves before him right up to the boat, and the monks were even more terrified. At that moment another mighty beast appeared from the opposite direction, the west. Passing near the boat, he attacked the first monster, breathing fire. Before the monks' eyes, he cut the first great beast into three pieces, then swam back the way he had come.

Another day, the travelers saw a very large wooded island. Landing on it, they came across the tail portion of the dead sea beast. Brendan told them they would be able to eat it. Setting up a tent, they cut off as much flesh as they could carry, and in the south part of the island found a clear well and many plants and roots which they gathered. In the night, unseen beasts stripped the carcass, leaving nothing but bones next morning.

Storms, strong winds, hail, and rain kept the monks on the island for three months. One day a dead fish was washed ashore and the monks ate part of it, and Saint Brendan told them to preserve the rest in salt, for the weather would improve, and the swell and waves would diminish, and allow them to leave.

Loading the boat with water and food and collecting supplies of plants and roots, the monks launched and, raising sail, headed north.

Chapter 17.   One day they came to an extraordinary flat island, barely above sea level. It had no trees, but was covered with purple-and-white fruit. Around the island moved three choirs, one of boys in white, one of youths in blue, and one of elders in purple. As they moved, they sang hymns. Brendan's curragh landed at ten in the morning, and at midday and 3:00 P.M. the choirs chanted appropriate psalms, as well as for vespers. When they finished, a bright cloud rolled over the island and hid the singers from view. Next morning dawned cloudless, and the choirs sang again and celebrated communion, after which two members of the choir of youths brought a basket of purple-and-white fruit to the boat. They also asked the second of the latecoming monks to join them. Brendan gave his permission, and this man stayed behind with the choir of youths when the curragh set to sea again. At three o'clock the travelers ate one of the purple-and-white fruit which had been given them. The fruit were all the same, the size of a large ball and full of juice. Saint Brendan squeezed a pound of juice from one fruit, which he divided between his men. Each fruit fed a man for twelve days and tasted of honey.

Chapter 18.   Some days later a great bird flew over the boat, carrying the branch of an unknown tree. The bird dropped the branch into Saint Brendan's lap. At the tip of the branch was a cluster of bright red grapes the size of apples. The monks ate the grapes, and lived on them for eight days. Then, after three days without food they came in sight of an island covered with trees bearing the same fruit. The air smelled of pomegranates. For forty days they stayed, pitching a tent on the island, gathering the fruit and also plants and roots of all kinds which grew near the springs.

Chapter 19.   Sailing on at random with a store of fruit, their boat was attacked by a flying Gryphon. But just as the Gryphon was about to strike its talons, the same bird which had brought the grapes reappeared and drove off the Gryphon, tearing out its eyes, so that the Gryphon flew higher and higher and was finally killed, falling into the sea in view of the monks. Then the savior-bird flew away.

Chapter 20.   Soon afterward the travelers regained Saint Ailbe's Community, and again spent Christmas with them. Then they sailed in the ocean for a long time, only calling at the Sheep Island and Bird Paradise as before from Maundy Thursday to Pentecost.

Chapter 21.   Once on these travels, on the Feast of Saint Peter, they found themselves sailing in sea water so clear that they could see the different kinds of fish lying on the sand, like herds at pasture. They lay in rings, head to tail, and when Saint Brendan sang, they swam up to the curragh and swam in a great shoal around it as far as the monks could see. When Mass ended, the fish swam away as if fleeing. It took eight days at full sail to cross the area of clear sea.

Chapter 22.   Another day they saw a pillar in the sea. It seemed close by, but they took three days to come up to it. It was so high that Brendan could not see the top of it, and a wide-meshed net was wrapped around it.

The boat could pass through an opening in the mesh which was the color of silver but harder than marble, while the column itself was of bright crystal. Taking down the mast and sail and shipping the oars, the monks pulled their boat through the mesh, which they could see extending down into the clear water, as did the foundations of the pillar. The water was as clear as glass and the sunlight was as bright below as above.

Saint Brendan measured the mesh as six to seven feet each side. Then they sailed along one side of the pillar, which was square, and Saint Brendan measured each side at seven hundred yards. In its shadow they could still feel the heat of the sun. On the fourth day they found a chalice and paten of the crystal, lying in a window in the side of the pillar.

After taking his measurements, Saint Brendan told his monks to eat. Then they took hold of the mesh and worked their boat out of it, raised the mast and sail, and sailed to the north for eight days.

Chapter 23.   On the eighth day they came to a rocky, rough island, full of slag and forges, without grass and trees. Brendan was worried, but the wind blew them straight toward it, and they heard the sound of bellows and thud of hammer and anvil. An islander came out of a forge, caught sight of the curragh, and went back indoors. Brendan told his men to row and sail as fast as they could to try to clear the place. But even as he spoke, the islander reappeared and hurled a great lump of slag at them. It flew two hundred yards over their heads, and where it fell, the sea boiled and smoke rose up as from a furnace. When the curragh had gone about a mile clear, more islanders rushed down to the shore, and began hurling lumps of slag at the monks. It looked as if the whole island was on fire. The sea boiled; the air was filled with howling; and even when they could no longer see the island, there was a great stench. Brendan said they had reached the edges of Hell.

Chapter 24.   On another day they saw through the clouds to the north a high smoky mountain. The wind drove them fast toward it, and they ran aground a short way from land. Before them was a coal-black cliff like a wall, so high they could not see the top of it. The third of the latecoming monks jumped from the boat and began to walk toward the base of the cliff, crying out that he was powerless to come back. The monks saw demons carrying him off and set him on fire. Then a favorable wind blew them clear, and looking back they saw that the smoke of the mountain had been replaced by flames which shot up and sucked back, so that the whole mountain glowed like a pyre.

Chapter 25.   Sailing south for seven days, they saw the strange sight of a man sitting on a rock with his cloak suspended on an iron apparatus in front of him. The rock was being battered by the waves which sometimes broke over the man's head, while the wind flailed his cloak into his eyes and forehead. Brendan asked who he was, and he replied he was Judas, and that the Lord spared him to sit on the rock on holy days free from the torment of Hell in the fiery mountain. At the evening hour, innumerable demons covered the sea, circling the rock and shrieking at Brendan to go away. Brendan argued with them, and the demons followed the boat as it left, then they turned back and lifted Judas up with great force and howling.

Chapter 26. Three days to the south Saint Brendan and his companions came upon another small island. This one was circular—about two hundred yards in circumference, with sheer cliffs and no landing place. The flintlike rock was bare. Eventually they found a landing, a ledge so narrow it could just take the prow of the curragh. Brendan went ashore by himself and climbed to the top of the island, where he found two cave entrances facing one another on the east side of the island. At one cave entrance was a tiny spring of fresh water. In this cave dwelt an ancient anchorite, entirely clothed in his long white hair and beard. He told Saint Brendan that he had once been a monk at Saint Patrick's monastery, and when the Saint died, Patrick's ghost had told him to set out on the sea in a boat. Of its own accord the boat had brought the anchorite to the island, where for thirty years he had lived on fish brought every third day by an otter, who also brought him firewood. Then he had found the twin caves and the spring, and lived there for sixty more years. The anchorite said he was now 140 years old, and he told Saint Brendan to stock up with water from the spring because he had a forty-day journey before him, back to the Island of Sheep and the Paradise of Birds. After that, he would have a forty-day voyage to the Promised Land of the Saints, a forty-day stay there, and then God would bring Brendan safely back to Ireland.

Chapter 27. Saint Brendan and his crew received the old anchorite's blessing and began to sail south. They were carried hither and thither, living only on the fresh water from the island. Eventually, on Holy Saturday, they came again to the Island of Sheep. There the Steward met them at the landing place, helped each man out of the boat, and gave them supper. Then he came aboard with them, and they beached on the whale Jasconius, who took them on his back across to the Paradise of Birds. The Steward told them to fill their water vessels, because this time he would sail on with them and be their guide. Without him, he said, they would not reach the Promised Land of the Saints.

Chapter 28. Saint Brendan, the Steward, and the crew now crossed back to the Island of Sheep to stock up with supplies for the forty-day trip. Then they sailed forty days to the east. The Steward went up into the bow of the boat to show them the way. One evening after forty days a great fog swallowed them, so they could scarcely see one another. The steward told Brendan that the fog perpetually encircled the land which Brendan had been seeking for seven years. An hour later a great light shone, and the boat came to shore. The monks disembarked in a wide land full of autumnal fruit-bearing trees. When they had gone in a circle around the land, it was still light. They ate fruit and drank water, and in forty days' exploring did not come to the end of the land. But one day they came upon a great river, which Brendan said they could not cross, nor did they know how big the land was. Here they were met by a young man who embraced them, called them all by name, and told Saint Brendan that God had delayed them in their quest to get there in order to show them his secrets in the great ocean. He instructed them to gather fruit and precious stones, and to return home as Brendan's last days were near. The land, the young man said, would be made known to Saint Brendan's successors when the Christians were being persecuted, and the river divided the island.

Brendan gathered samples of fruits and gems, took his leave of the Steward, and sailed out through the fog. Then they came to the Island of Delights, where they stayed three days with the abbot, and then Brendan went home to his own community.

Chapter 29. His monastery received Brendan joyfully, and he told them of everything he remembered happening on his journey. Finally he told them of his approaching death, according to the young man in the Promised Land. The prophecy was correct. Shortly after Brendan had made his proper arrangements and taken the sacraments, he died among his disciples and went to the Lord. Amen.

Appendix II
The *Navigatio* and *Brendan*

The Brendan Voyage was in some ways a detective story. One might imagine the medieval text of the *Navigatio* as the list of clues which aroused the first suspicion that a felony has been committed. The "felony" was, of course, the discovery of North America several centuries before the date that is generally accepted; and the suspects are the seafaring monks of early Christian Ireland. Cast in this classic detective format, the building of a replica skin boat to follow the trail of clues around the North Atlantic to see where they led is the well-tried technique of reconstructing the suspect's movements to see if they were physically possible, and what light may be shed on the suspect's motives and methods.

The best detectives, in fiction anyway, begin by trying to establish the exact time of the crime, and here the historical detective dealing with Saint Brendan's voyage must start out cautiously. The earliest date at which such a voyage, or voyages, would have taken place if they were made by the Christian Irish, as seems likely by the consistently Christian tone and style of the *Navigatio*, is after the conversion of Ireland to Christianity in the early fifth century A.D. Very probably the voyage(s) would not have taken place before Saint Brendan's own lifetime, c. 489-c. 570 or 583. At the other end of the scale, the *latest* time for the voyage(s) is obviously the date that the *Navigatio* was composed. But when was that? Scholars who have tackled the problem disagree by a very wide margin. The most conservative estimate is that at least three of the surviving manuscripts of the *Navigatio* are from the tenth century. But this is only the date of the writing down of the manuscripts themselves; the actual composition of the tale is clearly much older. One view maintains that the *Navigatio* was actually composed in the ninth century, but Professor James Carney of the Dublin Institute of Advanced Studies, certainly one of the most eminent Celticists to have looked closely at the problem, would go much further back. He argues that the *Navigatio*, much as we know it, was produced in Latin around A.D. 800, and that a primitive version of the story probably existed within Saint Brendan's lifetime. He has even found reference to the fact that Saint Brendan himself was recognized as a composer of poems.

These literary scholars are the forensic experts called in to assist the historical detective, and it is clear that even their disagreements on the date of the *Navigatio* do not detract materially from the importance of the case: Even by the most conservative dating, the "Promised Land" described in the *Navigatio* is earlier than any known Norse reference to the New World. And it is therefore worthwhile investigating whether the Irish had reached North America before Leif Eriksson.

Traditionally, the detective's next step is to try to weigh up the value of the list of clues as a whole. With the *Navigatio* this means deciding whether the text is sufficiently reliable to warrant a full-scale investigation of Saint Brendan's alleged voyage. Here the first point to remark is how consistent the different manuscripts of the *Navigatio* are, one to another, in the areas that concern the investigation. Considering that there are some 120 surviving manuscripts in Latin, not counting other languages, it is remarkable how little they vary. Put another way, the witness tells the same story over and over again, and cannot be shaken. Even so, the detective has again to be cautious. Used as geographical or historical evidence, the contents of a medieval manuscript can be notoriously tricky. Usually the texts are vague on details, or, when the details exist, they are contradictory and erratic. The truth of the matter is that a medieval text like the *Navigatio* was not intended to be read as a practical handbook or an Admiralty Pilot. So the historical detective must simultaneously strain out all the religious, allegorical, and mystical matter in the text, while still remaining alert to the chance of finding a useful nugget of practical information.

Nowhere is this better illustrated than in the *Navigatio*'s use of numbers and points of the compass. The *Navigatio* is full of numbers when compared to most contemporary texts. It gives the number of days sailed in different legs of the Saint's voyage, the number of crewmen at different times, the dates of some departures and landfalls, even the number of yards an island monstery lies from the boat harbor. But the numbers quoted in any early text are unreliable. Numbers are the first items to be misquoted or misread in transmission from one storyteller or copyist to the next. Then, too, the medieval author was often tempted to use his numbers symbolically—perhaps three to reflect the Trinity, twelve the apostles, and of course that vague favorite of "forty days" to represent "a long time" which is used regularly in the *Navigatio*. Consequently the skeptical investigator must look for numbers that have no such symbolism, and even then place little trust in the figures unless they make some sort of sense in context.

Exactly the same is true of the *Navigatio*'s compass bearings. It is gratifying how often the *Navigatio* gives the direction in which the Irish monks are sailing here and there in their leather boat. But once again it would have been very easy for a copyist to have made a slip, changing *north* to *south* or a similar careless error. As before, the basic check is to make sure compass bearings agree in context, and even then to be a little hesitant about accepting them. Thus, one criticism of the *Navigatio* is that when Saint Brendan sets out on his final and successful run to the Promised Land, he is said to sail from an Atlantic island and head toward "the eastern beach"—i.e., eastward. This, the complaint maintains, shows that the monks were not sailing west across the Atlantic at all, but in the opposite direction. But this criticism is misplaced. The whole notion of the Promised Land throughout the text is that it lay far away in the West across the ocean. This is where it is stated to be in Chapter 1 of the *Navigatio*; then, to try to get there, Saint Brendan sets out in a specially built curragh westward "toward the summer solstice" and when he actually finds the Promised Land and comes home, he makes a direct course by sea and lands on Ireland's west coast, presumably having come from the West. In fine, the whole context and trend of the story is that the Promised Land lay to the west, and this must be the deciding factor in trying to interpret a medieval text into a modern idiom.

It is here that the exercise of practical reconstruction like the Brendan Voyage can help. If all goes well, a field experiment of this type can put the details of a text like the *Navigatio* into a perspective which is obtainable in no other way. Thus the Brendan Voyage in 1976 and 1977 not only established the basic fact that it is entirely possible to sail from one side of the North Atlantic to the other in a skin boat built to medieval specifications, and by a rugged northerly route; but it also established criteria against which to measure the original voyage tale. The results are interesting.

In the first place, the flavor of the medieval text now seems wholly authentic when judged against our experiences aboard *Brendan*. The author of the *Navigatio* obviously knew—as we now know—what it was like to be in an ocean-going curragh. He knew that it is impossible to row upwind in a boat which sits so high in the water that a foul wind blows you down on a hostile shore, however much you want to get clear. And when the *Navigatio* describes how a big curragh beaches, or how Saint Brendan's crew pulled their craft up a shallow stream using tow ropes, we now understand what was involved and that this was feasible. Even the spectacular incident with the iceberg—the floating "pillar of crystal" in the *Navigatio*—found its parallel with the twentieth-century skin boat. Certainly we were not expecting to have to seize onto ice floes when coaxing *Brendan* through open pack ice off Labrador; but when we had to do this, it was very like the *Navigatio*'s description of Saint Brendan's crew manhandling their craft through a "net" made of "marble" to get a closer look at an iceberg. In this case the exercise of reconstruction did not merely check on a detail which was previously untested; it brought to light an item which was previously unrecognized. The same could be said of the *Navigatio*'s information that Saint Brendan carried spare oxhides and grease on board. We expected to have to regrease *Brendan*, as we eventually did in Iceland, but without the spare oxhides to rig as a wave defector off East Greenland, we could well have been swamped and foundered. Perhaps the moral of the tale is that every detail on practical matters in a medieval text ought to be noted, however trivial it might appear.

On a more scientific level, a project like the Brendan Voyage can also be productive. *Brendan* has made some advance in our ideas about medieval seafaring. With a crew of only four or five, *Brendan* was chronically undermanned. Saint Brendan's fourteen-man crew (a figure, incidentally, that has no apparent symbolism and is a sensible one) would presumably have been able to do better under oars. Even so the *Navigatio* makes it clear, just as we found, that long ocean passages in northern waters are best made under sail and not by rowing. The medieval crewman may have been more disciplined and patient, especially if he was a monk, but he was not so dull that he would not prefer to sail his way when out of sight of land rather than row in broken water. Equally, we can hazard an estimate that an ocean-going curragh—and perhaps other unwieldy early ships too—would have been content with a daily average log of forty or sixty miles a day during a long passage. Exceptionally, perhaps, a light boat in the hands of an experienced crew might have covered 150 miles in the ideal conditions of a following gale. But claims for 200 miles, day after day, are over-optimistic; and if *Brendan*'s performance is anything to go by, one should increase passage distances by 40 percent over the great circle route to allow for wander.

Conversely, *Brendan* amply supported those theorists who claim that early boats were capable of making new discoveries by being blown off course by heavy weather. In July 1976, while trying to sail from the Faroes to Iceland, we experienced a spell of such persistent and strong east winds that we would have been blown clear across to Greenland, if we had not made special efforts to heave-to and keep our original landfall in Iceland where we needed to resupply.

As for the geography of the *Navigatio*, the Brendan Voyage succeeded in linking together the different locations which have been suggested as the places mentioned in the medieval text: the Faroes as the Island of Sheep; Mykines or perhaps Vagar, also in Faroes, as the Paradise of Birds; southern Iceland as the region of the Fiery Mountain and the slag-throwing Island of Smiths; and the identifications of iceberg and curious whales with the "Column of Crystal" and the Great Fish Jasconius. More original, perhaps, is the fact that *Brendan* showed how these landfalls could be made in a logical progression around the North Atlantic using the wind patterns of the summer sailing season, and that in every case local folklore, as well as current archaeological research, is firmly based on the tradition of the Irish visits. Again, the significant factor is the overall agreement between the modern Voyage and the original tale. A single identification between one of Saint Brendan's landfalls and a present-day location would be overly subjective, but an entire progression of such identifications seems to be more than mere coincidence.

At the same time the Brendan Voyage did not expect nor try to explain every locality mentioned in the *Navigatio*. Some of the places are too vaguely defined by the text to be identified; others lay off our route. Indeed, if the *Navigatio* is an amalgam of several voyages carried out by other monks besides Saint Brendan, as seems likely, there is no reason that some of these places should not lie in other directions. The general trend of the *Navigatio*, however, is north and west, and as *Brendan* demonstrated, this is also the route to take a skin boat to America.

Another question which *Brendan* has left in her wake concerns the Norsemen themselves. There are three references in the sagas to an Irish connection, however faint, with the New World. Erik's Saga has a report from two American "Skraelings," or natives, that they knew of men near their tribe who wore white clothes and marched in procession bearing poles before them to which cloths were fixed, and yelling loudly. At the time, the Norsemen thought the reports referred to Irishmen. Then secondly, the Icelandic *Landnamabok* talks about a country "which some call Ireland the Great. It lies west in the sea near Vinland the Good." A Norseman who was driven there by bad weather, it says, was unable to escape and was baptized by the inhabitants. Finally there is a report from an Icelandic trader named Gudleifr Gunnlaugsson, who was gale-driven across the sea from the west coast of Ireland, and made land on an unknown shore where he thought he recognized the natives using Irish words in their language. As usual the details are casual and, by themselves, light-weight. Taken together they gain a little more substance, and after the successful Atlantic crossing of *Brendan* it may be worth considering the whole attitude of the Norsemen toward North America. It is interesting how the saga writers readily accepted the idea of Ireland the

Great in the far West. After all, when the Norsemen arrived first in the Hebrides, in the Faroes, and in Iceland they found that Irish seamen had been there before them, and that Irishmen had settled these islands. And if the Norsemen resembled any other explorer-navigators in history, they would have gone to great lengths to obtain local seafaring knowledge and to employ pilots who had sailed the unknown waters before them. Thus even the choice of the land scouts the Norse employed is interesting. Erik's Saga says that when Thorfinn Karlsefni reached the western land he set on shore two Scoti (i.e., Irish) who were very fleet of foot and could explore the new land effectively. Under the circumstances one wonders if the Norsemen did not also carry Irishmen on their exploring ships for pilots as well as scouts.

But this must remain speculation, even for the most imaginative detective hoping to solve the riddle of the *Navigatio*. A more tantalizing clue is being examined on the coast of Newfoundland. There, overlooking the entrance to Saint Lunaire Bay, archaeologists were investigating some lines incised on a boulder and trying to decipher their meaning even while *Brendan* was sailing across the Atlantic. The lines on the rock appear to be man-made and to have been cut with a fine pointed tool, possibly of metal. Some of the lines are obscured beneath an encrustation of lichens which covers most of the rock surface. But one criss-cross pattern seems to have been rubbed clean for inspection at some time in the past, and what looks like a fresh lichen growth has begun to grow again on top of it. By chance this fresh lichen includes a variety that grows at a measurable rate, and it has been calculated that even this growth is at least 150 to 200 years old, which is longer than the present habitation of the area. The lichens covering the other lines may be far older, and some observers have been quick to claim that the criss-cross lines are ogham, the early Irish form of writing, particular on stone, favored by the Christian monks. Scholars of ogham are doubtful, and certainly the inscriptions are very cryptic, if not completely undecipherable. Work on them is continuing, including an attempt to date the more heavily encrusted markings and to ascertain if the lines really were incised with metal. But there are other candidates for their authorship: Saint Lunaire lies not far from the presumed Norse settlement at L'Anse au Meadow and the marks could have been cut by a straggler from that camp; and there is the wreck of a cannon-bearing vessel in the waters of Saint Lunaire entrance, right under the lookout where the mysterious rock is set in the hillside. Perhaps a survivor swam ashore and cut the marks with a knife. Whatever the answer, there is plenty of room for speculation and further investigation, particularly now that *Brendan* has shown that one group of suspects could certainly have reached the scene of the "crime" at the time alleged. Clearly the file on North American's discovery by Europeans is far from closed.

[279]

Appendix III
Brendan

Design

Brendan's design was based on three sources—ethnographic, literary, and archaeological. The ethnographic data were the most fruitful and included the design and construction details of the Irish curraghs of the Dingle pattern as described by James Hornell in "Curraghs of Ireland," *Mariner's Mirror,* January 1938. Hornell's data was compared with the present-day Dingle curraghs, which range up to 21'4" in length for the "four-hand" size, and augmented with information from John Goodwin, curragh-builder of Castlegregory, County Kerry. The literary evidence for the historic use of leather boats in western Europe is widely scattered throughout many early texts, and the majority of references have been collected together by G. J. Marcus in his "Factors in Early Celtic Navigation," *Etudes Celtiques,* Volume 6, 1952. Leather boats, for instance, are mentioned by Caesar, Pliny, and Solinus. But the most relevant details for *Brendan* were found in Adomnan's *Life of Columba* and, of course, the *Navigatio Sancti Brendani Abbatis* itself. Early Christian artifacts in the Irish National Museum, Dublin, show how wood, leather, and metal were worked in Ireland, and this information decided the actual construction techniques of *Brendan*. With particular reference to leather-working techniques, John J. Waterer's study, "Irish Book Satchels or Budgets" in *Medieval Archeology,* Volume 12, 1968, was invaluable. Pictures of early boats are rare, but fortunately an outline of an open Irish boat can be seen carved on the vertical shaft of an Irish stone cross, still in situ near Bantry, County Cork. This carving has been dated to the eighth century A.D., and is described by Paul Johnson in *Antiquity,* Volume 38.

In designing the boat, Colin Mudie was concerned with keeping the hull weight as low as possible to allow for a heavy load of stores and the intended use of the craft on long open-water passages, beaching, and propulsion by sail and by oar with a crew of only four or five. Also for stability, the sections were made rather firmer than those of some current smaller curraghs. His design was for a boat 36' overall and with a beam of 8'. The estimated weight was 2400 pounds for bare hull, plus 1284 pounds for sails and rowing equipment. With stores, water, crew, and sea-water uptake into the leather, *Brendan*'s final cruising displacement was close to five tons. Her sail area was 140 square feet on the mainsail and 60 square feet on the foresail. Both sails were made in flax by Arthur Taylor and Son of Maldon, and could be extended by the addition of a bonnet, 3 feet deep on the main and 2 feet deep on the fore, at the foot of the sails. The addition of side panels was found to be effective only in a wind from dead astern. Steering was by a large-bladed paddle on the starboard quarter, though twin steering paddles and a steering sweep were tested in sea trials and found to be ineffective or unnecessary. Oars of different lengths were also tested, and the most suitable length was found to be 12 feet. Oars worked on thole pins and "bulls"—triangular pieces of wood pegged to the oarshaft—and the oar blades were of the traditional curragh pattern, being extremely slim.

Materials Research

Perhaps the most fascinating and rewarding phase of the Voyage preparations was the research into the performance of the medieval materials. The aim was to try to determine if the medieval materials had any chance of standing up to a trans-Atlantic voyage. Some of the tests were very simple—for example, samples of leather were hung on frames in sea water to see if they would decompose or pick up barnacles. Other tests were conducted in the laboratory, thanks to the enthusiastic cooperation of the British Leather Manufacturers' Research Association at Milton Park led by Dr. Robert Sykes, and the associated work by the tannery of W. & J. Richardson of Derby, and by Harold Birkin's team at the tannery of Joseph Clayton and Son in Chesterfield. There was plenty of room for error, because although leather is a remarkable and rewarding material to work with, it must be handled absolutely correctly or it will be ruined. In preparing the leather for *Brendan*'s hull, the tanners and scientists had to be concerned with such matters as surface crack, the tightness of the grain in the leather, the lower surface tension of salt water, and a host of other considerations, including the dimensional stability of damp leather. To general satisfaction, the lesson was learned

[281]

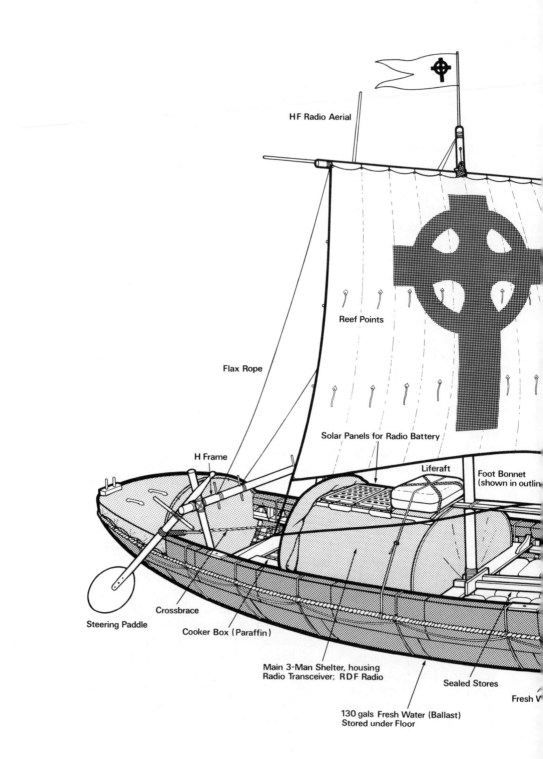

HF Radio Aerial

Reef Points

Flax Rope

Solar Panels for Radio Battery

H Frame

Liferaft

Foot Bonnet
(shown in outlin

Crossbrace

Steering Paddle

Cooker Box (Paraffin)

Main 3-Man Shelter, housing
Radio Transceiver; RDF Radio

Sealed Stores

Fresh V

130 gals Fresh Water (Ballast)
Stored under Floor

Schematic diagram of Brendan

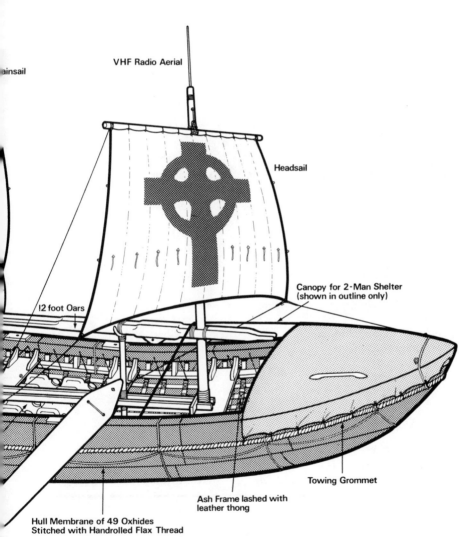

ainsail

VHF Radio Aerial

Headsail

Canopy for 2-Man Shelter
(shown in outline only)

!2 foot Oars

Hull Membrane of 49 Oxhides
Stitched with Handrolled Flax Thread

Ash Frame lashed with
leather thong

Towing Grommet

ard

that the medieval materials, if prepared correctly, were exceptionally suited to the task of crossing the Atlantic.

1. *Hull leather.* The *Navigatio* states that Saint Brendan's monks covered the wooden frame of their boat with "oxhides tanned with the bark of oak" and carried similar oxhides on board as spares, and to make two smaller skin boats presumably as tenders to the larger vessel. Dr. Sykes' researchers tested samples of oak-bark leather supplied by Josiah Croggon and Sons of Grampound, Cornwall, and compared their performance to other types of leather tannages under similar conditions. The properties that were sought were resistance to water; dimensional stability, particularly after immersion in salt water; and tensile strength. The following table, supplied by the B.L.M.R.A., indicates the remarkable stability of the dressed oak-bark leather throughout various testing procedures:

TABLE I

1. (a)

	(a) Dressed oak-bark leather	(b) vs Dressed oak-bark leather churned in saline for 3 days, dried, rewetted for 24 hours, and tested
Ultimate tensile strength kg/mm²	2.5–3.0	2.8–3.2
Elongation at break	20–25%	35–37%

2. Testing under dynamic conditions on permeometer

	(a) Dressed oak-bark leather without pre-treatment	(b) vs Dressed oak-bark leather, churned in saline for 3 days, dried, and tested
Apparent weight increase after 24 hrs.	0.4%	3.3%
Increase in area	0.7–1.8%	2.1%
Transmission rate after 24 hours kg/m²/hr	Not detectable	Not detectable

In effect, the tests showed that traditional oak-bark leather was very strong even when wet; that this strength did not diminish; and—from earlier data available at the Research Association—that the comparatively open-fiber structure of oak-bark leather rendered it particularly suitable for "stuffing" with a waterproof grease or dressing. Croggon's of Grampound eventually supplied 57 "butts," oxhides trimmed of their upper shoulder and leg skin, for the boat. These butts were oiled with cod oil, rolled, and rough-dried.

2. *Dressing.* The dressing of the 57 butts with grease was undertaken by Joseph Clayton and Sons under the supervision of Harold Birkin, whose own laboratory had been testing samples of greased leather in conjunction with the B.L.M.R.A. The *Navigatio* stated that the monks used "fat for preparing hides to cover the boat" and "smeared all the joints of the hides on the outside with fat," so only fats and greases which were known from early medieval times were tested—tallow, beeswax, fish oil, and wool grease, singly and in mixture. The correct dressing was vital to the durability of the leather hull. The problem was not merely to

TABLE II
TRANS-ATLANTIC PERFORMANCE OF *BRENDAN* LEATHER

	(a) Leather as supplied for boatyard	vs.	(b) Leather after Atlantic crossing
% DCM extractibles (largely grease and fats)	34		27
Water uptake after 72 hrs. churning in saline (w/w)	+14%		+10.5%
Change in area after 24 hrs. flexing	Less than 1%		+2.7%
Water uptake after 24 hrs. flexing	0.4%		+2%
Penetration time on permeometer	No detectable penetration after 2,000 hrs.; test discontinued		No detectable penetration after 750 hrs.; test discontinued

grease the leather well enough so that it kept out the water, but to grease it without damaging the quality of the leather. If too much soft grease was put into the leather fibers, the leather became too limp; too little grease, and the leather was not water-tight. After very many experiments, it was found that the most suitable dressing was raw wool grease. This wool grease was given through the generosity of W. & J. Whitehead (Laister-dyke) Ltd., Top makers and Worsted Spinners of Bradford; and was put into the leather by dipping the oxhides in a bath of wool grease at 50° C. for up to twelve hours and then leaving the hides stacked for weeks, with grease between the layers to ensure complete penetration of the grease into the leather. This produced a 30- 37-percent uptake of grease. The monks might have achieved the same result much more slowly by hand, applying successive dressings of wool grease to damp oxhides, or by pouring on hot grease and rubbing it in by hand. The success of the collaboration between Joseph Clayton and the B.L.M.R.A. in producing *Brendan*'s hull leather can be judged from the comparison between the leather first supplied to *Brendan* (Column a) and the same leather after it had crossed the Atlantic (Column b). In sum, there was no major change in the composition or performance of the leather from the beginning to the end of the voyage.

3. *Thongs.* W. & J. Richardson of Derby provided the two miles of leather thong which were used to lash *Brendan*'s frame together, also the thongs employed on board in place of short lengths of rope. Initially five different types of thong were sent to the research laboratories for testing and their values were shown as follows:

TABLE III
THONG TESTING PROGRAM

	TYPE				
	Alum Undressed	*Alum Dressed*	*Alum Stuffed*	*Sulphur*	*Rawhide*
% water absorbed after soaking 20 mins.	82	77	74	12	29
% water absorbed after soaking overnight	76	78	71	23	101
Tensile strength kg/mm² before soaking	1.25	3.76	0.81	5.22	10.58
After 20 mins. soaking	1.31	2.90	0.81	3.70	4.59
After soaking overnight	1.44	3.32	0.54	1.99	2.44

TABLE IV
Flax Thread Tests

	Thread as Received
(a) Breaking load in kg/f	
No treatment	6.37
After seawater immersion for 2 weeks	6.30
After seawater immersion for 2 weeks in oak-bark leather	8.69
(b) Breaking extension percentage	
No treatment	3.75
After seawater immersion for 2 weeks	4.30
After seawater immersion for 2 weeks in oak-bark leather	5.75

Alum-dressed thong—a system known at least in Roman times—was selected as the most suitable, and the thongs were treated with a tallow and fish-oil dressing before they were sent to *Brendan*.

4. *Thread*. Henry Campbell and Company of Belfast made the 23 miles of flax thread which stitched *Brendan*'s oxhides together, and also made up the improved flax ropes for her rigging with the help of Belfast Rope Works. At the suggestion of James Henshall, the director concerned, samples of Campbell's flax thread were tested (in conjunction with *Brendan* oak-bark leather) by the Shoe and Allied Trades Research Association. The following table shows how well the flax thread performed in these tests, growing stronger when wetted and stronger again when sandwiched in oak-bark leather. It can also be assumed that the thread became more rot-proof when the tan from the leather migrated into the thread and discouraged bacterial decomposition.

Construction

The scantlings in Colin Mudie's design for *Brendan* were of the order of 1″ × 6″ oak for the gunwales, 2″ × ⁵/₈″ ash for frames, 2¹/₂″ × ⁵/₈″ ash for stringers. The fore- and mainmasts, 12 and 19 feet long respectively, were initially cut as single ash saplings, but these developed splits during trials, and were replaced by single lengths cut from close-grained ash under the personal supervision of Paddy Glennon of Glennon Brothers, County

[287]

Longford, who also provided all ash used for frames, stringers, and oars. The masts were set in socketed mast-steps of oak which rested directly on the keelson.

Pat Lake and Michael Murphy of Crosshaven Boatyard faired up the hull frame, which was then fastened with alum thong lashings. Each thong was pre-stretched by hand to reduce its initial elasticity, soaked, and then hand-lashed in place while still wet. The fastened hull frame was then liberally coated with wool grease to preserve the timber. Subsequent inspection showed that the wool grease had penetrated deeply into the wood grain.

Forty-nine oxhide butts were needed to cover the boat. The hides averaged about one-quarter inch in thickness, and measured on average 45" × 47".

The thread to stitch the hides was "fourteen cord," i.e., handrolled from 14 single threads. It was then waxed with a combination of wool grease, beeswax, and resin so that it filled the awl holes when drawn through. John O'Connell, harnessmaker, and Eddie Hinton, master saddler from the Walsall saddlery firm of Eldonian Brookes, decided the most suitable method of stitching. This was back-stitch for the hides along the center line of the boat, and double-handed stitching for the remainder of the work. The double-handed stitching had to be done by pairs of stitchers stationed opposite one another on each side of the leather. Stitch length was approximately two to the inch, and double lines of stitches were put in, approximately 1 inch apart. Every joint was a plain overlap of about 2 inches width. At the prow and the leading ridge of the keel, where collision and grounding were anticipated, John O'Connell overlapped four thicknesses of hide for extra strength. And at the stern an extra fillet of leather was applied at the keel to protect against stern beaching.

The keel-skid of oak was fastened through the leather with $1/2$" copper rivets. Riveting was a very highly developed technique in early Christian Ireland. The leather skin was not otherwise fastened directly to the hull frame but tensioned over it, pulled over the upper gunwale, and lashed down to the lower gunwale with hair-on round leather belting. Harold Birkin suggested this unusual use for hair-on belting, which was supplied by the Lion Leather Company.

Performance

1. *Rowing.* Five weeks after landfall at Musgrave Harbor, *Brendan* was in a very different setting to the wild Newfoundland coast. In sight of the skyscrapers of Boston on the lower Charles River she was rowed by ten volunteer oarsmen from the Union Boat Club. The purpose of the

experiment was to try to find out just how many oarsmen, albeit inexperienced in rowing leather boats, were needed to row *Brendan* effectively under different states. Table V illustrates what we had also learned from the voyage itself: namely that *Brendan* was severely undermanned with a crew of only four. But it also shows that a crew of ten oarsmen could make headway in all but very adverse conditions; and that under more favorable conditions a rowing crew of six or eight men could edge a cruising curragh upwind. It should be stressed, however, that the tests, our own ocean experience, and the medieval texts indicate that long-distance voyages in Irish leather boats would have been made under sail. Oars would normally have been used in emergencies, when coasting, or when in sight of a landfall.

TABLE V
Rowing Tests

Average of up- and downstream runs over 510-meter course, lower Charles River, in westerly wind Force 3 with a current of c. 1.3 knots.

	mph
10-man crew— racing rate with coasting load	5.03
—cruising rate with coasting load	3.78
—cruising rate with full ocean load	3.80
6-man crew—cruising rate with coasting load	3.19
—cruising rate with full ocean load	3.00
4-man crew—cruising rate with coasting load	3.98 (downstream only; unable to row upstream)

Note: A coasting load was calculated as the stores and equipment needed for a curragh making day passages within sight of land. A full ocean load was calculated as the weight on board of water, food, and gear needed for a 3-week ocean passage for 10 men.

---

2. *Sail.* The lack of suitable instruments made it difficult to measure accurately *Brendan*'s performance under sail. Obviously it was impractical to fit a "through hull" log impellor in an oxhide, and the only feasible instrument was a trailing log. A Walker Knotmaster was used, and the manufacturers warned that their instrument was ineffective at speeds below two knots. However, on a cruising basis, the following observations were made:

a. The maximum distance achieved in a 24-hour period was 115 miles.

[289]

The minimum day's run was, of course, nil in a flat calm, and on bad days *Brendan* was actually set back on her course by adverse winds. The average day's run under sail was 40 miles, and a cruising speed of 2 to 3 knots was considered satisfactory. This required a wind F 3–4 where the boat was fully laden. In ideal conditions of a following wind of F 5–6 the log would register sustained periods of 5 to 7 knots. The maximum reading on the log scale was 12 knots and this speed was achieved comparatively frequently in heavy weather and high seas, though in Mykins Sound in the Faroes a prolonged burst of 12+ knots was achieved due to the funneling effect of the surrounding cliffs.

b. Leeway had to be judged by eye, taking the angle between the wake and the trailing safety line. Against a headwind *Brendan* would point about 50° to 60° off the wind, but leeway of 30° meant that she made an effective 90° to the wind. At F 6 and above, it became dangerous in most sea states to continue to reach across the wind, and it was safer to run downwind. The use of leeboards may have been anachronistic, as there is no evidence for or against the use of leeboards in the early Middle Ages. But we did not use leeboards above F 5 to 6 because they tended to scoop too much water into the boat, and at lesser wind strengths they were not as effective as lee-side rowing would have been with a larger crew. Several leeboard positions were tried, and a position 16 feet from the bow was found to be most effective. The addition of a second leeboard, aft by the helmsman, was found to be detrimental as it actually increased leeway. In sum, the use of a leeboard reduced leeway by up to 10° when sailing, but did not enable *Brendan* to point higher. Lee-side rowing by a larger crew would have been more effective.

c. *Sea keeping.* The most impressive aspect of *Brendan*'s performance was her sea-keeping ability even in severe weather. She successfully negotiated prolonged periods of heavy seas and strong winds. The normal tactic was to reduce sail by one reef in the mainsail at F 5–6, and at F 6+ to lower and stow the mainsail, and then turn downwind under headsail alone, which was later reefed. It was the designer's opinion that *Brendan* was undercanvased, but this was a deliberate safety factor. In heavy seas both main warps were streamed in loops from the stern and played a vital part in keeping the boat straight to the sea. Oil was also spread from a half-gallon canvas bag and was a help. However it was necessary, and often difficult, to stay directly downwind of the oil slick. Extra oil bags on a spreader bar would have made this easier. Fish oil is considered to be better than mineral oil for this task, and whale oil, which we used, the best. A sea anchor was streamed from the bow and proved effective in moderate seas, but it was considered too dangerous to try using the sea anchor in very heavy seas. It was feared that the boat would be held up into the force of the waves, and the protective tarpaulins would be split by the weight of water.

Brendan's stability was a vital factor in her success. This stability was due in large part to Colin Mudie's design, and enhanced by ballasting with 1600 pounds of fresh drinking water, over half of it stowed beneath the floorboards. Without doubt, the chief danger was capsize at sea. Deliberate capsize during sea trials proved to be extraordinarily difficult, even when the boat was unballasted. After being capsized with a shoreline to the mast, *Brendan* could be turned right way up by a 5-man crew and it took 12 minutes bailing with buckets to empty her. In the event of total swamp, buoyancy blocks of polyurethane foam were placed at bow and stern, and under three thwarts.

Safety

In view of the hazardous nature of her voyage, close attention was paid to the crew's safety. *Brendan* was equipped with an 8-man life raft specially prepared by Beaufort (Airsea) Equipment Ltd., and through the kind permission of the Commanding Officer, *Brendan*'s crew attended a short course at the Royal Naval Safety Equipment and Survival School at Seafield Park. There we were instructed in the use of life raft and flares and in general survival procedures. In the waters *Brendan* sailed, the danger from cold if a man went overboard was much more real than the risk of drowning. So each member of the crew wore, and used, a clip-on lifeline supplied as an integral part of his Helly Hansen sailing suit. In very foul weather this same lifeline was transferred to the Beaufort immersion suits (helicopter passenger suits; general purpose coveralls), which were provided to *Brendan*'s crew through the generosity of the Irish Leather Federation, and made a great difference in the worst spells of weather. The use of lifelines was encouraged by the knowledge that if a man fell overboard while *Brendan* was underway, it would have been impossible to turn round to pick him up.

To report our daily position a crystal-controlled SSB Raytheon 1209C transceiver was used, operating on the 2-,4-, and 8-megacycle bands. The aerial was a 15-foot whip, and gave a range of between 150 and 250 miles depending on latitude and radio traffic density. The Raytheon gave sterling service, and its power was successfully supplied by two Lucas solar panels lashed to the shelter roof (with thongs) which trickle-charged a pair of Lucas Pacemaker car batteries. Despite initial fears, the Lucas solar panels provided enough power for 5 minutes' transmission daily, and their great advantage was that they required no maintenance. *Brendan*, of course, carried no form of engine, either to pump her out or to charge batteries. VHF links, wherever possible, were achieved ship-to-ship with a Seavoice portable transceiver in its waterproof Portaphone mode; and ship-to-air communication was with a transceiver, loaned by Park Air Electronics. The success of *Brendan*'s radio communications depended to a large degree on the patience and skill of the radio operators concerned at the shore stations of Valentia, Malin Head, Stornoway, Torshaven, Vestmanna, Reykjavik, Prins Christianssund, Cartwright, St. Anthony, and St. Johns, Newfoundland. Special thanks are also due to the radio operators aboard the Icelandic Fishery Research Vessel, *Arni Fridriksson*, and to the air crews of many translantic airlines—especially Loftleidir/Icelandic Airways, who listened out for *Brendan*'s often weak signals as she crept across the Atlantic. Burndept Electronics of Erith, Kent, were kind enough to loan a BE 369 Flotation Beacon in case a search-and-rescue operation had to be mounted. During the 1976 season when *Brendan* was close to land, weather forecasts as well as radio direction bearings were obtained with a Brookes and Gatehouse Homer/Heron which survived even the drenching of heavy weather off Greenland, which was also when *Brendan*'s bilge pumps by Munster Simms were put to vital use, and again when the vessel was holed by ice. The medieval monks, of course, would have used wooden bailing scoops or buckets of wood or leather.

braunin... r̄ue dm̄. ⁊ ita uolo hoc anno de mde p̄s
se ad in̄ula cuiū appinquabr̄. aūt ad portū deb̄mari
ipi Aule om̄s aues cantabant q̄ una uoce dn̄ces.
Salus dō n̄o sedentī sup̄ chn̄ ⁊ agn̄o. Et itiū dn̄s
de ill̄uit nob. Soltūit diem sollem̄e ī coder̄use us
q̄ ad cornu altaris tam uocib̄ q̄m alis resdnabr̄
dm quasi dimediū hore uscp du sōs pac̄ cū sua sc̄a
familia ⁊ omib̄ q̄i erant ⁊ nā q̄si sc̄o fuisset.
⁊ resedisset ī tentorio suo. Q̄ūq̄ ibi cū suis famulis
celebrasset festa paschalia p̄ces nam̄q̄ peurator
uenit ad illas statim p̄dicat. in die dn̄co octabas
pasche. porrexit sc̄u om̄ia q̄ ad uic̄tu uite p̄tine
nent. Cū aūt resedisset ad un̄stā Ecce p̄ca aūs
resedit m̄ prora nauicule excelsis alis strepuit fa
ciēs sic sonūd organū maxm̄. ⁊ aīt iur. dr̄ Agnouit
quia noluit sibi m̄dicare aliqd. Sic nā q̄ eade̅ aūs
de p̄oluit uob quatuor loca. p nn̄. tempra usq̄ dn̄
funeus. uj. Am̄ per̄naco̅s uir̄ 1. Incertā dm̄ ann
uī̄o peuratore q̄i p̄sens est om̄ī anno. In dorso be
lue pascha celebrabat̄ ⁊nob̄sc̄ festa paschalia us
q̄ m̄ octabas penthecostes. Apud familia Adelber nati
iurare dm̄ celebrabat̄. Uit. uj. n̄o annos q̄ioc̄de
tb̄ magnis Ac diuisis p̄dicacōnib̄ memetus cr̄a re
preulsionus sc̄or̄ q̄m q̄iras ⁊ ibi h̄icabr̄us ul. dieb̄ Et
porbea reducet uos deus in cr̄a natiuicatē ur̄e. ⁊aūs
pat̄ ur̄ Audiuit. prostAuit se Ad cr̄a cū frib̄ Auis. ⁊cetra